From the Mines to the Streets

THE WILLIAM & BETTYE NOWLIN SERIES
in Art, History, and Culture of the Western Hemisphere

From the Mines to the Streets

A Bolivian Activist's Life

Benjamin Kohl and Linda C. Farthing,
with Félix Muruchi

University of Texas Press ⟨⟩ Austin

Requests for permission to reproduce material from this work should be sent to:
Permissions
University of Texas Press
P.O. Box 7819
Austin, TX 78713-7819
www.utexas.edu/utpress/about/bpermission.html

♾ The paper used in this book meets the minimum requirements of ANSI/NISO
Z39.48-1992 (R1997) (Permanence of Paper).

Library of Congress Cataloging-in-Publication Data

Muruchi Poma, Feliciano Félix, 1946–
    From the mines to the streets : a Bolivian activist's life / Benjamin Kohl and Linda
Farthing ; with Félix Muruchi. — 1st ed.
        p.   cm. — (The William and Bettye Nowlin series in art, history, and culture of
the Western Hemisphere)
    Includes bibliographical references and index.
    ISBN 978-0-292-74392-2

    1. Muruchi Poma, Feliciano Félix, 1946–   2. Political activists—Bolivia—
Biography.   3. Labor leaders—Bolivia—Biography.   4. Miners—Bolivia—
Biography.   5. Bolivia—Politics and government—1952–1982.   6. Bolivia—Politics and
government—1982–2006.   7. Bolivia—Social conditions—1952–1982.   8. Bolivia—
Social conditions—1982–   9. Indigenous people—Bolivia—Social conditions—20th
century.   I. Kohl, Benjamin H.   II. Farthing, Linda.   III. Title.
    F3326.M88A3 2011
    984.052092—dc22
    [B]

                                                                                    2010043512

To my former Siglo XX mining comrades, who provided me with the political foundation that shapes my life; to my brothers and sisters from Wila Apacheta, who are my ongoing guides; to my family, who were able to endure the suffering of my persecution and captivity; and to my friends for the solidarity they have shown.

—FÉLIX

To Bolivia's indigenous and working-class people, who, for twenty-five years, have inspired us with their struggle for a more just world; to Elayne Zorn, who shared our love of the Andes; and to Gavriel Cutipa-Zorn, who will carry on.

—BENJAMIN AND LINDA

Contents

List of Acronyms

ADN	National Democratic Action (Acción Democrática Nacional)
CEBEMO	Central Mission Commission (Centraal Missie Commissariaat)
CEPB	Confederation of Bolivian Private Businessmen (Confederación de Empresarios Privados de Bolivia)
COB	Bolivian Workers Central (Central Obrera Boliviana)
COMIBOL	Bolivian Mining Corporation (Corporación Minera de Bolivia)
COMSUR	Southern Mining Company (Compañía Minera del Sur S.A.)
COMTECO	Cochabamba Telecommunications and Services Cooperative (Cooperativa de Telecomunicaciones y Servicios Cochabamba)
CONDEPA	Patriotic Conscience (Conciencia de Patria)
COR	Regional Workers Central (Central Obrera Regional)
CSUTCB	Confederation of Campesino Workers' Unions of Bolivia (Confederación Sindical Única de Trabajadores Campesinos de Bolivia)
DOP	Department of Political Operations (Departamento de Operaciones Políticas)
ELN	National Liberation Army (Ejército de Liberación Nacional)
EMUSA	Consolidated Mining Company (Empresa Minera Unificada S.A.)
FEJUVE	Federation of Neighborhood Organizations (Federación de Juntas Vecinales)
FIS	Social Investment Fund (Fondo de Inversión Social)

FODENPO	Support for Popular Nutritional Development (Fomento al Desarrollo y Nutrición Popular)
FRI	Left Revolutionary Front (Frente Revolucionario de la Izquierda)
FSB	Bolivian Socialist Falange (Falange Socialista Boliviana)
FSE	Social Emergency Fund (Fondo Social de Emergencia)
FSTMB	Federation of Bolivian Miners' Unions (Federación Sindical de Trabajadores Mineros de Bolivia)
FUL	Local University Federation (Federación Universitaria Local)
IMF	International Monetary Fund
INE	National Institute of Statistics (Instituto Nacional de Estadística)
INEDER	Popular Education Institute for Development (Instituto de Educación Popular para el Desarrollo)
INRA	National Institute of Agrarian Reform (Instituto Nacional de la Reforma Agraria)
LPP	Law of Popular Participation (Ley de Participación Popular)
MAS	Movement towards Socialism (Movimiento al Socialismo)
MBL	Free Bolivia Movement (Movimiento Bolivia Libre)
MIR	Left Revolutionary Movement (Movimiento de Izquierda Revolucionaria)
MNR	National Revolutionary Movement (Movimiento Nacional Revolucionario)
NEP	New Economic Policy (Nueva Política Económica)
NGO	Nongovernmental Organization (Organización nogubernamental)
OPDECH	Office for the Promotion of Development in Chiloé (Oficina Promotora del Desarrollo Chilote)
PCB	Bolivian Communist Party (Partido Comunista de Bolivia)
PCML	Marxist-Leninist Communist Party (Partido Comunista Marxista-Leninista)
PIR	Party of the Revolutionary Left (Partido de la Izquierda Revolucionaria)
POR	Revolutionary Workers' Party (Partido Obrero Revolucionario)
POR-Lora	Revolutionary Workers' Party–Lora (faction of the POR) (Partido Obrero Revolucionario–Lora)

PRIN	Revolutionary Party of the Nationalist Left (Partido Revolucionario de la Izquierda Nacional)
SIT	School for International Training
SOA	School of the Americas
UDP	Democratic and Popular Unity (Unidad Democrática y Popular)
UMSA	San Andrés University (Universidad Mayor de San Andrés)
UNHCR	United Nations High Commissioner for Refugees
UPEA	Public University of El Alto (Universidad Pública de El Alto)
UTO	Oruro Technical University (Universidad Técnica de Oruro)

Preface and Acknowledgments

Books by researchers and academics typically are the culmination of years of thinking about a specific problem. They often grow organically as an author works through a series of theoretical, conceptual, and methodological issues. That was not the case with this book: its origins lie in a series of coincidences and (fortunate) mistakes in judgment.

In June 2005 Linda and Ben were in La Paz finishing *Impasse in Bolivia: Neoliberal Hegemony and Popular Resistance* (2006) when a desperate e-mail arrived from Puno, Peru. Two young U.S. activists, Jason Tockman and Gretchen Gordon, were stuck in Puno, frantically trying to get into Bolivia to report on the political crisis that would provoke the resignation of the country's second president in less than two years. The roads to La Paz—and for that matter almost every road in the country—were blockaded by growing social protests, and absolutely nothing was moving. Should they take local transport to the border and then walk across the altiplano? No, we said, campesinos are angry, and the sight of two beleaguered gringos swearing they supported their struggle did not presage a happy ending.

Our friend Dick Beckett happened to drop by that morning and offered the sensible suggestion that they fly, as a local airline had begun ferrying out tourists anxious to escape Bolivia's political chaos. He guessed, correctly, they would have no problems finding a seat on the flight back to La Paz. They arrived shortly thereafter, the only two passengers on the plane.

Jason expressed an immediate interest in learning more about El Alto. We sent him off to visit our longtime friend Félix Muruchi Poma, who not only had an interesting analysis of events in Bolivia, but also, because he had spent time in exile, was able to interpret that experience for northerners. Linda knew that Jason and Dana Brown, then coordinator of Cornell's Community on U.S.–Latin American Relations (CUSLAR), had been discussing a U.S. tour for a Bolivian activist, but was too busy to give it much thought. Jason came back glowing from his meeting with Félix.

"He's the one, he's the one," he told us over lunch. Jason was convinced that a U.S. tour with Félix would be terrific.

We agreed, pleased that we might have the chance to show Félix our home after so many years in his. We had met Félix in 1987, shortly after we arrived in La Paz as volunteers for the Canadian volunteer organization CUSO. Linda first knew Emilse Escobar, then Félix's wife, in 1984 on her first contract as a CUSO volunteer in the mining center of Llallagua. We quickly recognized in Félix a very special person—someone who came from a poor and disadvantaged background but who had gained a broad understanding of the world and was willing to share his story with outsiders.

Over the years we became good friends and had even vacationed together *en famille*, traveling in 1991 from Arica to Mejillones in Chile with four adults and four kids under the age of ten crammed into a 1975 Ford Bronco, and to Santa Cruz (although in a bigger jeep) a year or two later. (He and his family also hosted our School for International Training, or SIT, students for years.) We figured the challenges of a U.S. speaking tour were trivial when compared to the task of juggling the demands of a multifamily road trip through the Andes.

By the time Félix was committed to the tour, Jason had started a master's degree at Simon Fraser University in Vancouver, and Dana was swamped with CUSLAR responsibilities. So the organization fell to Linda, and, with the generous assistance of myriad people in the eastern United States, in March 2006, Félix arrived in Philadelphia on the first stop of his multicity solidarity visit. With Ben, Félix began refining the two very different presentations that he had prepared with Juan Arbona, our mutual friend and colleague, then in La Paz on a Fulbright. The first talk was on urban social movements, and the second, "From the Mines to the Prisons to the Streets," was his life story.

After Félix's first talk at Temple, Art Schmidt, a history professor and editor of the Voices of Latin American Life series, approached Ben about doing a book with Félix and gave him two books from the series. Ben started the first, the *Drug Dealer's Woman*, but it disappeared before he could finish it. Our son Minka, at that time a sophomore in college, had made off with it, reading it in a couple of sittings before passing it on to his sister Maya, who had just graduated high school. She went through it quickly as well and lent it to a friend, at which point we lost track of it. Ben became convinced he wanted to write the type of book that our kids might read.

As well, in our first book (*Impasse in Bolivia: Neoliberal Hegemony and Popular Resistance*), Linda had wanted to ground a somewhat structuralist analysis in the everyday lives of actors through including series of vignettes that showed how larger political and economic events affect people's lives, but the publisher rejected the idea. We realized that the project suggested by Schmidt provided the opportunity to develop a more accessible account of recent Bolivian history from the perspective of an active participant.

We approached Félix, who embraced the idea, and we agreed to write somewhat different versions in English and Spanish, given the differing audiences. After his return home, Félix started to record his story on tape, with some assistance from his daughter Khantuta. We arranged for our goddaughter, Marlen Magne, and Khantuta to transcribe the tapes, which were of varying quality. Marlen, who had done transcriptions for anthropologists, provided a literal transcription with no attempt to sully the narrative with punctuation or other grammatical encumbrances. Linda then distilled about 50,000 words from the initial 165,000-word transcript, working the text into a coherent story. As is typically the case with oral histories, Félix did not produce a linear narrative but often doubled back as memories surfaced through the story's telling. We kept the original tapes and transcripts and sent the edited narrative to Félix with comments and requests for clarification.

Two important issues arose in the initial draft: First, the language was flat. Second, Félix did a better job of telling the broader story of Bolivian history than he did of positioning himself as an agent within those processes. Our northern readers wanted to understand more about how Félix felt when things happened, and they observed that he responded more emotionally to the political than the personal. We viewed this, in part, as a reflection of the tendency of northern readers to privilege the individual actor, while an indigenous narrator was more likely to emphasize the collective.

By June 2007 we had a basic manuscript, and Ben spent a month working with Félix in Cochabamba going through the text line by line, clarifying, ordering, deepening the story and probing for more emotional content, constantly requesting stories to give an idea of what it was like to work as a miner, as an activist, as well as belaboring him with the constant refrain, "How did that make you feel?" This was an intense, often difficult process as he sifted for material and walked the tightrope between reaching the emotional depths that we needed for a compelling story while simultaneously respecting Félix's unwillingness to relive certain events. As we progressed, Félix also began to reveal anecdotes that to him appeared secondary, but which he slowly grasped would interest our readers. He was learning the form of the Western narrative and willingly adapted his story if that's what it took to win an audience.

In our initial proposal we suggested a "collaborative," rather than a "mediated," narrative. As Félix is university-educated, and revised and reviewed the text with us, we thought we might address some of the criticisms commonly voiced in postcolonial critiques and reviews of oral and testimonial literature regarding the appropriation of voice and the imposition of "Western" (or modern or colonial) sensibilities that are the warp and weft of the narrative fabric. But in reality, through the editing and reediting of the text, we moved from a *testimonio* closer to a biography (although written in first person) that was increasingly structured for a modern, literate, urban, largely non-Bolivian audience. Félix read and approved the text in Spanish but not in English, which departs from the former not only because of the normal issues that arise during translation, but also because we varied the language of the English text to make it more readable without changing the fundamental meaning. We alone are responsible for the complementary text.

Through the winter of 2008 we translated the text to English in turns, and we found that we took increasing liberties as we introduced elements into the narrative that we had talked about with Félix but that somehow had not made it into the Spanish original. Even so, when we first sent the English manuscript to friends for review, it bombed. Our readers wanted yet more emotional detail, more material that would give the reader cause to engage with Félix, and we went through a second round of changes in Bolivia in June and July 2008, writing introductions, finding photos, and arranging for Bolivian publication. The final text, for better or worse, is a hybrid—a Western narrative grafted onto testimonial roots.

While Félix was comfortable with the final draft, the manuscript, as our friend Vicky Aillón reminded us, still had a hagiographic quality common in testimonial literature. These narratives follow a format, beginning with the birth to an impoverished family, following the subject through a life of struggle and advancement against enormous odds. Typically, like hagiographies, which portray the lives of saints, testimonials only show the character in a positive light: a portrait that has been airbrushed of the blemishes, inevitable contradictions, and weaknesses that make us human. Unlike a biography, these narratives are not vehicles for criticism. We decided that we were willing to accept that as a part of the package.

There is another characteristic of the genre that we were less willing to accept. Rigoberta Menchú's famous testimonial reflects a collective, rather than personal, experience. In this work, while Félix's memory and interpretation of events may differ from those who shared his various journeys, they are the experiences of a single life, not a compilation. From the beginning we planned to publish a version of the book in Spanish in

Bolivia, where there are a considerable number of people who are familiar with the events he describes.

The political and social analysis throughout the narrative is Félix's, not ours. As a political activist Félix became steeped in Marxian theory and discourse, so while to the reader it may seem strange to read a "peasant" or a miner reflecting on social relations of production or the historical division of labor, this type of language and analysis is common among activists of Félix's generation. Visitors to Bolivia are often surprised when a taxi driver, for example, launches into an analysis of global capitalism often as sophisticated as one would hear in a graduate seminar in North America.

As we were finishing the text, Félix's family requested we minimize their presence in the story (especially that of Emilse, a powerful figure in her own right). We were surprised at their response, as women are often absent from these narratives even as they play critical roles in social and political struggles. There is no question that Félix's wife, who was politically active and involved in local development organizations, played a critical role in his life, especially after their return to Bolivia. We felt that including information about her would have enriched an understanding both of Félix and his times. However, we could only respect the family's wish for privacy.

In constructing the text we were faced with the challenge of making the book accessible and interesting while also providing a gateway to understanding Bolivia. We decided to include text boxes to provide contextual material that could guide readers whose curiosity was piqued by the story. In an attempt to minimize disruption to the flow of the narrative, we have not included in the text footnotes to additional sources, but have provided the material in a bibliographic essay included as an appendix. We decided to keep the bibliography brief, using only references in English, as we realized that scholars could easily access the ever-increasing literature both in English and Spanish.

We hope we have created a book that can help readers understand the events that led us to a deep sympathy with the people of Bolivia, and countries like it, in their struggles for social and economic justice. We hope too that Félix's story achieves what June Nash wrote in her review of our manuscript: the "book demonstrates precisely how personal experience . . . enriches the analysis of social processes."

This book, like any, is more than the work of the authors. We want to thank Art Schmidt for pushing us to take on the project, along with four anonymous reviewers who provided critical observations and enthusiastic support. We also want to thank our children, Minka and Maya, for challenging us to write something they might read. Félix's daughters Valeria and Khantuta Muruchi Escobar reviewed the text, and Khantuta also did some of the interviews with her father. Both daughters suggested edits. Seena and Martha Kohl (Ben's mother and sister, respectively) shared their experiences transforming oral histories into text. Susanna Rance provided not only a home away from home in La Paz, but also critical comments on both the politics and theory of oral histories. Vicky Aillón read and commented on the manuscript in Spanish. Cristian Vera Ossino edited the Spanish text, and Amaru Villanueva Rance helped translate the introduction into Spanish. Elayne Zorn helped with the glossary. Once we put the manuscript together, William P. Mitchell and June Nash provided excellent and often detailed suggestions in their reviews. We would also like to thank Charlie Hale, who suggested UT Press might be interested in the manuscript, Theresa May, who shepherded it through to publication, and Paul Spragens, who provided expert copyediting guidance.

Temple University provided multiple grants for research and publication of a version of the book in Spanish, in support of its increasing international mission. Thanks as well to the people at Plural Editors in La Paz who helped us make this story available in Bolivia.

BENJAMIN KOHL AND LINDA FARTHING

When I returned from exile the second time in 1987 and settled in El Alto, I spent time thinking about my life and considered whether I should continue fighting for the liberation of the Bolivian people or whether I should pay more attention to my private life and family. I decided to change the type of work that I did, but I also thought it important to share my experiences with both my family and a broader public, as I believed that by doing so I could provide a story to help consolidate the memory of a generation of struggle.

Over time it became clear I needed support to tell this story, given the demands of daily life, and I let the project sleep. In 2005, Linda, whom I had met shortly after my return to Bolivia, asked me if I would be interested in doing a solidarity tour in the United States, which included speaking at a number of universities. I enthusiastically accepted, and my first stop was in Philadelphia, where Ben had arranged an invitation at Temple University. Arthur Schmidt was in the audience, and apparently my story interested him enough that he invited me to present my *testimonio* for inclusion in the series he edits for the university press. I accepted the invitation, as it provided me the chance to achieve my goal of sharing my story.

Some readers may note that I minimize the role of my family in this account. I have done so, not because they are unimportant to me—to the contrary—but because they requested I do so to protect their privacy.

I want to thank the University of Texas Press and my friends Linda and Ben for the support and work that have made this book possible.

Félix Muruchi Poma
La Paz, July 2009

Introduction

TIWANAKU, JANUARY 21, 2006

Félix Muruchi Poma

The indigenous people—who are the majority of the Bolivian population . . . historically we have been marginalized, humiliated, hated, insulted, and condemned to extinction. This is our history: our people were never even recognized as human beings. . . .

This early morning, I am very happy to see our brothers and sisters singing in the historic Murillo plaza: the Plaza Murillo, like the Plaza San Francisco, where, 40 or 50 years ago, we did not have the right to enter. . . . This is our history, our experience.

And, above all, I want to say to our indigenous brothers and sisters who have gathered here in Bolivia: the campaign of 500 years of indigenous-black-popular resistance has not been in vain.

EVO MORALES AYMA, INAUGURAL ADDRESS

I remember January 21, 2006, a day that brought a close to one phase of the political work to which I have dedicated a great deal of my life. This was the day that Evo Morales, a peasant, a coca-producer of Aymara origin, a person indigenous to the altiplano like me, received the *bastón de mando*, the symbol of indigenous authority in the Andes. This act marked the beginning of a new epoch in Bolivian politics: for the first time since the founding of the Republic in 1826, a First Nations person became president.

Along with hundreds of thousands of people who had arrived from both around the country and all over the world, I traveled to Tiwanaku to witness the symbolic possession of office. The joy and emotion I felt were reinforced by the wonderful music played by different indigenous groups scattered about the ancient archaeological site where the ceremony unfolded. Throughout the dusty fields that surrounded the ruins of Tiwanaku, the center of an empire that endured six hundred years, I saw people dressed in all kinds of indigenous clothes: men in *chullos*, the characteristic Andean hats with flaps over the ears, and red ponchos, women in traditional wide skirts and bowler hats that had actually been introduced by the Spanish. Everyone there had on something that could be identified as indigenous dress.

The thunder of drums and fireworks filled the air along with a powerful feeling of brother- and sisterhood that spread through the crowd like wildfire: coca, bread, bananas, and tea were freely distributed, and people shared whatever they had. Many people had traveled through the night along bumpy dirt roads in dilapidated buses or open trucks, but their hunger and exhaustion were forgotten in the contagion of enthusiasm and the joy of the moment. The hope was palpable that an indigenous leader—one of our own—as president would improve the lives of our people far more than the criollos, descendants of the Spanish conquerors, had ever done. I was among the multitude that danced to the rhythm of the music that pulsated and echoed throughout the valley.

Amidst the revelry, the *pututus*—large horns that serve to announce meetings, assemblies, and, during the times of the Inka, the arrival of the *chaskis*, the empire's messengers—boomed, focusing everyone's attention. The rite that marked the transfer of authority was about to commence. People began to applaud, and the cry "¡*Jallalla* Evo!" (long live Evo!) bounced off the hills surrounding the meadow. Evo gradually approached the stage that had been set up at the Door of the Sun. While I was quite far away, between the loudspeakers and the radios that people tuned to the event, we listened in a hushed silence to the symbolic transmission of office. A momentous change, and it was over in only a few minutes. Around me people cried and embraced, as through our tears we shared the dream that Evo's taking office meant for all of us.

When I was born in 1946, some sixty years earlier, indigenous people in Bolivia lacked almost all basic rights. Our decades of struggle led us to this day: for the first time, the majority of the Bolivian people truly felt represented as Evo Morales assumed his position as President of the Republic. In the following pages, I offer my personal story as a participant in these social and political struggles, marked as much by incremental defeats as by victories, to offer one partial vision of what brought us to this day.

Introduction to Bolivia

In the geographical heart of South America, landlocked and often isolated Bolivia has for centuries intrigued fortune-seekers, adventurers, and travelers alike. One of the most culturally, physically, and ecologically diverse places on the planet, Bolivia soars over two Andean mountain ranges and the high, cold plateau between them known as the altiplano, before dropping eastward through high, dry valleys and then plunging into the dense humidity of the Amazon basin in the north and the arid, dusty Chaco plain to the south.

Although two-thirds of its territory is lowland, most outsiders only know its western mountainous region, home to the majority of its 9 million people. Roughly 65 percent of Bolivians consider themselves indigenous, the highest proportion in the Americas. Most are Aymara or Quechua speakers in the western altiplano and high valleys. The peoples commonly known as "the Quechua" are in fact a conglomeration of different ethnicities forced by the fifteenth-century Inka conquerors to adopt their language, religion, and culture. The Aymara in the northern highlands, who only developed a sense of separate ethnic identity in the eighteenth century, have successfully clung to their own language despite repeated efforts by the Inka, Spanish, and Bolivian elites to exterminate it (Rivera 1987). The Guaraní, about 150,000 in all, are the third-largest group, living in the southeastern lowlands, where they form the northern extension of the much larger Guaraní population in Paraguay. As many as thirty-five other, smaller groups, among them Chiquitanos, Ayoreos, Chimanes, and Moxeños, totaling another 150,000, live scattered throughout the eastern lowlands.

About 25 percent of the population identify themselves as mestizos: strictly speaking, those of mixed European and indigenous heritage. But given the fluidity of indigenous identity, in practice, mestizos are usually urbanized people of indigenous heritage who largely reject their culture of

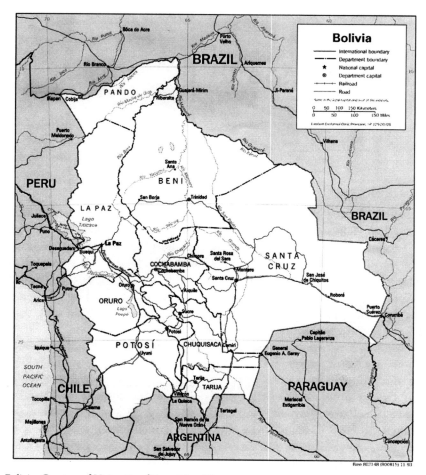

Bolivia. Courtesy of University of Texas Map Library.

origin's customs. Though smallest in number, the most powerful economic and political group, comprising less than 10 percent of the population, is an elite claiming pure European heritage, known as criollos.

Since the sixteenth-century Spanish Conquest, Bolivia has almost invariably served the needs of foreigners and the national criollo elite. The dominant economic pattern, no matter what the economic and political model, has been based on the export of Bolivia's vast natural resources. Shaped by resource boom-and-bust cycles centered on silver, tin, quinine, rubber, coca, and, most recently, natural gas (Morales 2010), Bolivia's economic foundation closely resembles that of other countries that supply primary materials to international markets. Even though it gained independence from Spain in 1825, the legacy left by colonialism and a rapacious extractive economy has persisted, profoundly damaging the physical environment and creating one of the most extreme cases of economic dependency in Latin America (Farthing 2009; Malloy and Gamarra 1988). It has also highly skewed Bolivia's income distribution: according to the United Nations Development Programme (HDR 2009), the country was second only to Haiti as the most unequal in the world's most unequal region, with 10 percent of the population controlling 40 percent of all income and an even greater share of land and other wealth.

Resistance by the indigenous majority to this domination has been a constant (Thomson 2002). Until the 1952 revolution brought the first promise of citizenship, indigenous people had few rights and little place other than as a source of labor and tax revenues. The revolution successfully overthrew the country's mining oligarchy thanks to a coalition drawn from the tiny middle class, a burgeoning labor movement based in the mines, and the indigenous majority. Latin America's second revolution (after Mexico's) wrought profound changes in a dependent and virtually feudal country, granting the vote to indigenous people and women, nationalizing the mines, breaking up the large estates (haciendas) in the western part of the country, and redistributing land to indigenous people.

The middle-class-dominated government that grew out of the 1952 revolution was generally moderate, following other Latin American countries along the path of import-substitution industrialization. This aimed to protect local industries by forging a strongly centralized state administration that controlled natural resources and shifted 70 percent of the economy into government hands.

In 1952, the labor movement formed the Bolivian Workers Central (Central Obrera Boliviana, or COB), which cogoverned with the new administration during the 1950s, pushing it to institute its most radical changes, such as nationalization of the mines and partial land reform. In the late 1970s the COB, which served for almost forty years as Bolivia's primary force for social and economic justice, brought down the military dictatorships that plagued the country between 1964 and 1982, and played a crucial role in the country's often halting return to democracy (Dunkerley 1984).

While the 1952 revolution certainly improved life for the majority, the criollo minority maintained much of Bolivia's exclusionary society intact and blocked indigenous peoples from fully integrating socially, economically, and politically. This created a deeply fractured country where social unrest and conflict have been the norm. Despite the Agrarian

Reform in 1953, about 12 percent of landowners still control 90 percent of the farmland (Weisbrot and Sandoval 2008). In a country where almost half the population lives in the countryside, over 80 percent of people there are poor, giving Bolivia one of the region's highest rural poverty rates (Pica-Ciamarra 2009).

In 1985, Bolivia experienced one of the earliest and most radical neoliberal restructuring programs, under the aegis of the three major international financial institutions (the World Bank and the International Monetary Fund). The rapid control of hyperinflation by the "New Economic Policy" appeared almost miraculous, turning the country into a global poster child for neoliberalism's successes. But the cost to workers was enormous: over fifty thousand lost their jobs, and the labor union movement was virtually destroyed. By 1988, almost 70 percent of the urban workforce worked in the informal economy (Farthing 1995).

International development assistance was a central element of economic stability, growth, and development. Aid per capita was estimated as high as US $75 per year, three times the average for the world's least developed countries, and more than twice the average for countries receiving debt relief assistance. Until the election of Evo Morales' government (2006–) and his party Movement towards Socialism (Movimiento al Socialismo, or MAS), aid was particularly crucial to government functioning and estimated to make up between 7 and 9 percent of annual gross domestic product (GDP) (Weisbrot and Sandoval 2006).

Despite efforts to create a modern state and expand private investment, both domestic and international, neoliberalism ultimately failed to solve Bolivia's recurring difficulties: attracting broad-based investment, improving living standards, addressing indigenous demands for basic rights and resources, and balancing demands from the regions for more local control (Kohl and Farthing 2006).

By the end of the 1990s, growth had stagnated, and neoliberalism's failure to deliver on its promises led to a resurgence of social protest. In 2000, Bolivia gained a global spotlight as a symbol of resistance to neoliberal globalization. From the 2000 Cochabamba "water war," which successfully overturned the privatization of the city's water supply, to the 2003 and 2005 "gas wars," which ousted two presidents, social movements have demonstrated the ability of poor people in a small, marginal country to successfully challenge powerful companies, governments, and institutions (Hylton and Thomson 2007). In a significant victory in December 2005, participants succeeded in finally electing one of their own as president: the indigenous, left-wing leader of the Chapare coca growers, Evo Morales.

Despite being thwarted by weak administrative capacity in many government ministries, sometimes violent opposition from the right-wing oligarchy, particularly in the eastern lowlands, and Bolivia's historically fractious left, the Morales administration accomplished a great deal during its first term in office. The resounding mandate Morales won in 2005 allowed him to convene a Constituent Assembly, enact a partial recovery of hydrocarbon resource rents, and increase the participation of historically marginalized groups in the state (Kohl 2010).

From the Mines to the Streets

PART ONE

Growing Up in the Fields and the Mines

Chapter 1

Rural Life

On April 30, 1946, I was born the fourth of thirteen children to an indigenous mining family in Maraq'a, the community of my mother, Lucia Poma, located in the Karacha *ayllu*, in the department of Potosí. Normally my family lived in Wila Apacheta, my father's village, part of Bombo *ayllu*, in the department of Oruro. At that time my father worked at the mine and made the half day's walk home to visit us once a month.

Just before my birth, my mother walked ten hours to visit my father at the mine. When she went into labor, she hurried off to her parents' home in Maraq'a, three hours by foot, far closer than Wila Apacheta, but she still barely arrived in time for my birth. A few days later, she carried me home, a twelve-hour walk.

At that time about fifty families lived in Wila Apacheta, each with an average of five children, so in all about 350 people were scattered over the *ayllu*'s territory. We lived so dispersed because we dedicated as much time to raising llamas, which we used as pack animals as well as for their meat and skins, and alpacas, which we used for their fine wool, as we did to tending our crops.

When I was born most of Bolivia's people lived under a dictatorial political regime. "Democracy" was limited to an oligarchic minority because workers, indigenous people, and women did not have the right to vote. As well, the system of *pongueaje*—a kind of slavery—dominated on the haciendas, the large estates controlled by criollo families of Spanish descent. Even though *pongueaje* was officially abolished in May 1945, semifeudal social relations and debt peonage existed throughout the country until the 1952 revolution. Unfortunately, these relations still persist in some of the more remote parts of Bolivia today. When I was born, *pongos* did not have the right to leave the hacienda, indigenous people were not allowed to walk freely in the plazas of the cities nor contract their labor independently, and workers were prevented from organizing freely. Many people, however, escaped either to the mines or distant rural areas. Wila Apacheta was one of those isolated free communities.

Life in the mines was a little better, although it was hard and short. Many miners employed in Siglo XX and Catavi mines, for example, lived in giant sheds, more like a military barracks than family homes. These flimsy sheds, although they were 12,500 feet above sea level, where temperatures dropped below freezing every night of the year, were equipped with neither heat nor basic services. And even as poor as those conditions were, not all miners had the opportunity to live there; some slept in caverns in the surrounding hills. A small group of privileged workers had houses with their families, but even these houses were only thirteen by thirteen feet, with a tiny separate kitchen. Miners earned very little, and, as well, the foreman beat them if they fell off the pace. It was common that a miner, who began working at sixteen, died at thirty-five or forty years of age from *mal de mina*—literally, the "disease of the mine," black lung (silicosis)—often found in combination with tuberculosis.

My father worked in Uncía, one of the mines owned by Simón Patiño, then the third-richest man in the world, who had mansions in Oruro, Cochabamba, Paris, and New York. My dad was lucky, because instead of laboring in a hard rock mine interior, he worked in an open pit at the top of a hill known as Juan del Valle during colonial times and, before that, Intijalanta, a word that means west wind. He lived in the Miraflores mining camp in a small house that had four families crammed into it.

PRE-HISPANIC ANDEAN PEOPLES

Sophisticated Andean civilizations flourished centuries before the Spaniards invaded the area that would become Bolivia and Peru in the sixteenth century. As long as 21,000 years ago humans settled in the region, and archaeologists consider Andean civilizations among the ancient world's most important (Mann 2005; Renfrew and Bahn 2008).

The Tiwanaku civilization, centered on the altiplano south of Lake Titicaca, dominated the south central Andes between CE 400 and 1000. Its remarkable and complex hydrological systems permitted agricultural success and expansion in a very cold, dry climate, but after a seventy-year drought in the eleventh century, it collapsed. In a process so far unclear to archaeologists, what remained coalesced into twelve Aymara-speaking kingdoms that stretched from central Peru into Bolivia and farther south (Kolata 1993).

A hundred years before the Spaniards invaded, the Inkas, headquartered farther north in Cuzco, rapidly expanded their empire through either negotiation or conquest, subsuming indigenous groups to both their north and south. When the Spaniards arrived in 1532, the Inka ruled over 10 million people from southern Colombia to northern Chile.

To ensure their control, the Inka sometimes moved entire communities from one part of the Andes to another, forcing people to speak Quechua, their language, and practice their religion and culture. The exception was Aymara speakers, who fiercely resisted the Inka takeover. Their relative success defying both the Inka and Spaniards has bequeathed today's Aymara a deep sense of identity, even when they live in urban areas (Luykx 1999).

Highland Andean society was organized around the *ayllu*, which merged kinship and territorial affiliations into a coherent political, social, and economic unit. *Ayllus* were characterized by mandatory participation in rotational leadership, consensual decision-making practices, and mechanisms to ensure a relatively equitable distribution of resources (Platt 1982). The *ayllu* structure effectively integrated agricultural production and exchange across sharply different ecological zones, as it controlled territory from the tropical lowlands to the cold highlands. Despite the enormous disruption associated with the Spanish invasion, *ayllu*s still survive in some areas, notably the north of Potosí, where Félix is from, but the ties with valley and tropical regions were effectively broken by the Spanish (Murra 1980).

The community of Wila Apacheta, 2006. From the private collection of Félix Muruchi.

The house in which Félix lived before the family moved to Siglo XX, 2006. From the private collection of Félix Muruchi.

Wila Apacheta

My father, Manuel Muruchi Quispe, came from an indigenous Aymara community in the department of Oruro, close to the border of Potosí. His family was possibly descended from the Urus, considered the original inhabitants of this part of the Andes. Wila Apacheta was first settled during the second half of the nineteenth century when campesinos—my great-grandparents among them—migrated from Sora Sora, on the pampa—a plain—near Oruro. They fled in 1868 when President Melgarejo decreed the Law of Separation, which allowed for the takeover of traditional indigenous homelands and the expulsion of people from their homes. The law resulted in the wholesale slaughter of indigenous people and the burning of their houses in many parts of Bolivia.

When my great-grandparents narrowly escaped a massacre in Sora Sora, they found a safe spot about 13,500 to 13,900 feet above sea level. It was a cold, dry, and isolated place with such limited productive and commercial capacity that it was of no interest to the criollos who had robbed the more productive land in the relatively low altitude (12,300 feet above sea level) pampa. This community was completely composed of indigenous people whose lands had been stolen thanks to Melgarejo.

My father started working in the mines when he was thirty-five years old—only three years before I was born. But in July 1947, when I was a year old, hundreds of miners, my father among them, were fired in Uncía during what they called a "white massacre." They lost their jobs for two reasons: after World War II the demand for tin on the international market plummeted. In addition, the miners had organized the Federation of Bolivian Miners' Unions (FSTMB), which increasingly demanded better wages and improved living conditions. As a result of the white massacre, my parents had no choice but to return to their place of origin, which in our culture is the man's community and in our case meant Wila Apacheta.

At the time I had three siblings: two sisters, Cristina and Cursina, and a brother, Apolinar, who died when I was a baby. Two years after I was born, another baby boy died just after birth, and two years later my brother Germán was born, followed by Carmen, then a girl who died quickly at three months. Two years later Margarita was born, then Máximo. The next child was another girl who died a month after birth and who was followed by Wilfredo. The last time my mother gave birth was to another girl who also died shortly after birth.

Two generations after being settled, Wila Apacheta was a well-consolidated high Andean community. Most families had two small houses, one in the village center and another, the main house, on community land. A typical house was constructed of adobe and consisted of a single room of ten by sixteen feet, with a straw roof whose rafters served to store food. The kitchen was a separate round building, about thirteen feet in diameter with a conical roof, similar to houses built by the Chipayas in southwestern Oruro department. The kitchen also served as a dining room and bedroom, as we took advantage of the heat put out by the cooking fire to keep warm in the altiplano cold. We had a small shed to store tools and fuel, primarily *taquia*, which was the dried dung of our llamas. As the area was treeless, we formed doors from cactus that we cut when wet and relatively soft into planks and then dried. The houses had no windows because we couldn't afford glass and it was too cold outside to simply have an uncovered opening.

Most of the year people lived in houses away from the village center so that they could pasture their animals more easily. In my family, we used about 2,400 acres of communal land for pasture, and most of the land was over 13,900 feet above sea level. Although we didn't own the land independently, we had usufruct rights, as did other members of the community. The land included hills, creeks, and some small *bofedales*, wetlands at the foot of hills where mountain springs were found. Most of the land, however, was low-quality pasture—*paja brava*—covered by a tough, dry grass. In the dry season, from May to August, which was also the coldest time of the year, we traveled far from the center of the community to pasture the animals and build shacks, which we called *jhantas*, and small corrals. During the rainy season, between December and March, we brought the animals back closer to the community because once again pasture bloomed in the lowlands.

The community also built its own church, although no priest ever turned up to perform a Mass. Neither the Catholic Church nor the Protestants had much influence over us.

My older brother, Apolinar, had died as a baby of diarrhea, so I was the oldest boy, and my parents spoiled me, creating resentment in my sisters. They were forbidden to make me cry, and, while my parents worked, they had the task of carrying me when they pastured sheep. Often, while they moved the flock about, they set me down in a certain spot. I remember one day when I was left alone, I saw a red dog, similar to one of ours that had died, playing with one of the sheep, embracing her first from one side and then the other. The sheep just stood still quietly. After a few minutes it appeared as if the sheep had a red kerchief around her neck. At that moment my sister ran up screaming at me, "Why are you letting that fox eat the sheep?"

I answered, "Camisani [the name of our dog that had died] is playing with it."

She told me, "Camisani has been dead for a while. That is a fox."

Fortunately, the sheep didn't die, although she always had a red stain around her neck. That was how I came to know what a fox is.

ANDEAN INDIGENOUS HISTORY

When the Spaniards invaded, the highly centralized and fragile Inka Empire perched on the brink of civil war, disintegrating rapidly even though the Spanish force comprised fewer than two hundred men. As they explored the country, the Spaniards stumbled upon vast silver deposits at Potosí in 1545 in what is now southern Bolivia, and their greed accelerated a reorganization of Andean society to facilitate their frenzied extraction of the prized mineral (Klein 2003).

A late-1500s Spanish resettlement program, called Reducciones, concentrated dispersed indigenous households into villages, effectively decimating the *ayllu* in much of the Andes. The impact was devastating: for example, in one region, nine hundred communities were herded into only forty-four towns, so that they would be easier to tax and control. The Spaniards adapted the Inkan labor levy system, the *mita*, to coerce one of every ten adult men to labor in Potosí's mines. The rest were forced, through the encomienda, a land grant system that the Spanish crown used to reward loyal colonial subjects, to pay tribute on what evolved into large semifeudal estates known as haciendas. These gradually spread throughout the highlands and absorbed about a third of the population (Thomson 2002).

To avoid almost certain death deep in the suffocating and dangerous mines, some indigenous people successfully escaped to become *forasteros* (outsiders) and live in free communities on marginal lands beyond Spanish control. While the death toll in the mines was staggering, the diseases the Europeans brought with them wrought even greater damage. Within forty years of the conquest, 75 percent of the population had been exterminated (Mann 2005).

Right on the heels of the conquerors came the priests, anxious to save heathen souls for the Roman Catholic Church. While they often moderated the worst abuses of the Spaniards against the indigenous population, they committed their own in the course of serving as important transmitters of new values and religion. However, in many ways, Catholicism in Bolivia remains only skin-deep. Older religious beliefs incorporated those imposed by the Spaniards to create a deeply etched and complex religious syncretism (Orta 2004). The Catholic tradition of naming godparents, for example, has merged with the indigenous rite of an infant's first haircutting (*rutusqa*), carried out when the child is between eighteen and twenty-four months old and the highest risk of infant mortality has passed.

In the eighteenth century, silver production dropped, and as the importance of Bolivia (then called Alto Peru) to the empire flagged, Spanish control steadily eroded. From 1742 to 1782, indigenous people repeatedly rebelled, with the failed six-month siege of La Paz by the Aymara under the leadership of Tupaj Katari and Bartolina Sisa marking the culmination of the "age of rebellion."

At the beginning of the nineteenth century, indigenous participation became critical in the long and ultimately successful republican struggle against Spanish control. In 1825 the Republic of Bolivia was founded. Despite promises to the indigenous people to gain their support, the criollo elites had little intention of relinquishing their well-entrenched privileges, and not much changed for the indigenous majority (Larson 2004).

Some indigenous people, however, had beaten the odds to retain control over their lands and survive at the margins of the hacienda system. In the late nineteenth century, Bolivian (rather than Spanish) elites went after these lands as well. Even though indigenous resistance was fierce, between 1880 and 1930 communally held rural lands fell by 40 percent (Klein 2003). Communities located farther from potential markets with less productive land, such as those in the north of Potosí where Félix is from, were more successful in protecting their holdings as well as their *ayllu*s through, for example, resistance to government surveying, seen as the first step to appropriating land (Platt 1987).

At the end of the nineteenth century, economic power shifted from the silver-producing regions centered in the administrative hub for Potosí's mines, the southern colonial city of Sucre, to tin production managed from the northern city of La Paz. Sharp political division between (southern) Conservatives and (northern) Liberals coalesced around Liberal demands to shift the country's capital to La Paz to provide them more direct access to government resources. The Liberals seized the government in 1899, arming indigenous people to secure their victory over the Conservatives. But once in power, they moved to halt what was perceived as an ultimately far greater threat—the growing indigenous rebellion under the leadership of Zarate Willka. Although he was defeated, Zarate Willka emerged as an important hero of indigenous resistance.

The next key moment for indigenous peoples came with the 1930s Chaco War, which transformed Bolivia when men from all over the country were trucked to the southeastern lowlands to confront Paraguayan troops. For the first time, indigenous people developed a sense of Bolivian nationhood and an awareness of the citizenship rights that they were denied (Morales 2010).

Miners and urban workers mobilized into unions, inspiring indigenous peoples, particularly in the Cochabamba valleys, to organize. By the 1940s, the left-leaning military government of Major Gualberto Villarroel permitted the first national indigenous congress in La Paz, which drew over one thousand highland and valley, community and *ayllu*, leaders. Villarroel promised to establish schools in free communities and abolish bonded labor (*pongueaje* for men and *mitanaje* for women) on the large agricultural estates, but he was overthrown and killed, and his body hung in La Paz's main square, in July 1946. The proposed reforms had to wait until the 1952 revolution.

The most moderate and middle class of the revolutionary parties, the National Revolutionary Movement (Movimiento Nacional Revolucionario, or MNR), seized power in a 1952 popular insurrection that united indigenous peoples, miners, and other workers, backed by the urban middle class. The MNR leadership was resolutely anticommunist, implementing the most radical changes only in the face of sustained pressure from left-wing union and rural indigenous movements. Pressure on the MNR from indigenous people and middle-class women extended suffrage to all Bolivians over twenty-one, enlarging the voting population in one fell swoop from 200,000 to 1 million people, although the new government failed to incorporate either women or indigenous people in any meaningful way (Nash 1993).

Under sustained pressure from the grass roots, Víctor Paz Estenssoro, the MNR's leader, established national education and health-care systems. But as government revenues were insufficient to build rural schools, in many communities, campesinos built their own classrooms and then applied for government-paid teachers.

The MNR was not a radical government, however, and was pushed to implement some of its most important reforms. The 1953 Agrarian Reform was written into law only after indigenous people drove landowners off their haciendas in Cochabamba and La Paz, making de jure the de facto land takings of a mobilized peasantry. While this law undercut the power of the 6 percent of landowners who owned 92 percent of cultivated land, the MNR did not implement the reform throughout the country (Dunkerley 1984). In the eastern lowland departments of Beni, Pando, Tarija, and Santa Cruz, where campesinos never took up arms, land ownership remains highly concentrated.

With a strong commitment to Westernization, MNR government discourse transformed *indios* (a pejorative term for noncitizen indigenous people) into citizen campesinos. This creation of campesinos—literally, people who live in the countryside—as a social category after the 1952 revolution reflected a modernist discourse that sought to overcome the "backwardness" of the indigenous small farmers, who made up the majority of Bolivia's rural people, in order to create a mestizo, or mixed-race, nation.

In the highland and valley areas, campesinos received small landholdings from the breakup of the haciendas, eroding in most areas what remained of pre-Columbian communal organization by transforming farmers into small property owners. The MNR never channeled technical and credit resources to the newly freed peasants to facilitate increases in productive capacity (Klein 2003). Campesinos faced (and continue to face) daunting climatic conditions (short growing season in the highlands and a lack of water in both the highlands and valleys) and an inadequate transportation system. As a consequence, many farmers utilize highly labor-intensive methods to produce primarily for their own consumption. Reflecting deeply entrenched practices oriented to avoiding uncertainty, they often emphasize productive strategies aimed at minimizing risks rather than maximizing yields. Bonds of mutual obligation ensure both community and family survival.

Given the discrimination they routinely face in cities, an often limited command of Spanish, and lack of direct market access, many farmers sell their produce to middlemen for low prices. As is common in low-income countries, government policies have consistently depressed prices for agricultural produce to contain urban protest, and smallholders have limited access to the credit and technology that are an integral part of global agroindustrial systems. Until ten years ago, rural infrastructure was virtually nonexistent. Taken together, these circumstances have ensured profound and widespread rural impoverishment. Through the end of the 1980s, campesinos grew as much as 70 percent of the country's food supply, but this percentage has steadily eroded as cheaper imports flooded the market under trade liberalization, and large-scale agricultural production has burgeoned in the eastern lowlands (Rance 1991).

With each generation since the 1952 revolution, the highland and valley plots of land have been divided, usually among sons. This fragmentation has created a patchwork of *minifundios* (smallholdings), where agricultural families lack sufficient land to even minimally support themselves. In some cases *minifundios* are the size of suburban lots in North America or Europe. People survive by increasing both temporary and permanent migration to agricultural colonization zones in eastern Bolivia (including coca-growing regions), urban areas, or abroad. Cities have mushroomed since the 1960s, with more than half the population now living there. As well, an estimated 1.5 million Bolivians had moved to Argentina by 1999, many to Buenos Aires, and smaller, but significant, numbers have gone to Brazil, Chile, the United States, and Europe, especially Spain (Kohl and Farthing 2006).

The coca leaf is fundamental to the rhythm of our lives in the countryside and is omnipresent. While the leaf is also the agricultural precursor to cocaine, we use it in its natural state and consider it magic: one of the blessings of the gods. It lessens hunger and fatigue, provides vitamins, cures headaches and cramps, and is even thought to lessen the toxic effects of the putrid air in the mines.

At home, after we finished breakfast, when people were preparing to go to work with animals or in agriculture, everyone took a short pause to chew some coca leaf, what we call *pijcheo*. Sometimes if you were in a real hurry, you stuck a wad in your cheek as you hurried along the path. Later, after lunch, you chewed again. Consuming coca is something that is done with great care. People remove the leaf itself from the stem in a series of maneuvers that make it look like an art. Normally children didn't start chewing coca until they were at least twelve years old. I always understood that coca was an adult thing, and something to be taken seriously and responsibly. I actually never began to chew until I started to work in the mines.

Sharing coca is an integral part of any project where people work together. In fact, the best way to ensure people will help with a project is to send them some coca along with the invitation. If they accept the coca, then they are obligated to help. Coca inspires seriousness, responsibility, and the fulfillment of promises.

Coca is also used to predict the future, cure illnesses, and determine the weather. This is usually done by the community healers called *yatiris*. It also plays a key role in festivals and parties. For example, young couples hook up in several ways. Sometimes the boy takes the girl home, which obliges his parents to go to her parents' house with a gift of coca in order to initiate discussion about the relationship. Whenever there is a serious conversation to be had, coca is used to break the ice. At community meetings, it is essential to *pijchear* before beginning any discussion. Coca is present at every moment of Andean life from birth to death, and in every possible event and activity both personal and communal.

Coca

The sacred coca leaf, consumed in the Andes for millennia, is central to indigenous culture and values. When rural people meet, they usually sit and chew coca together as a sign of mutual respect before any business is conducted. Coca use is widespread in cities as well, and every restaurant in the country serves mate de coca (coca leaf tea).

Grown on the eastern slopes of the Andes, traditionally Bolivian coca has been cultivated in the semitropical Yungas region east of La Paz, and this is where the best leaf for chewing comes from. The Spaniards recognized that coca's ability to suppress hunger, alleviate altitude-induced discomfort, and increase energy could increase mine productivity, and they arranged for vast quantities to be shipped to Potosí to hasten silver extraction. It has continued as an important part of Bolivian and Peruvian mining culture and miners' survival underground ever since (Nash 1992).

Coca produces four crops a year, is plague-resistant, requires little attention, and, light in weight, is easy to transport, making it an ideal crop for peasant farmers far from roads. These characteristics made it an obvious choice for farmers in the lowlands east of Cochabamba, who flocked to the area called the Chapare when the 1980s cocaine boom in the United States brought demand for the leaf to new heights. The subsequent repression and efforts to replace the crop have failed to permanently destroy production, which responds to ebbs and flows in northern demand, and the level of suppression in Peru and Colombia, the world's other sources for coca. With Bolivia's president being a former Chapare coca grower himself, a new law has been passed that attempts to limit production, repress drug trafficking, and actively seek legal international markets for the leaf in the form of shampoos, toothpaste, teas, and so on.

In rural areas children are born at home, and every community has a midwife, although many times she was only called for the most difficult births. Generally a midwife transferred her skills on to her daughter so that a community could always count on having a birth assistant.

I particularly remember the birth of my brother Germán, when I was four. It was a hard birth, and my mother needed assistance, so my older sister ran for the midwife, who first diagnosed the problem by reading coca leaves. The leaves told her that the baby was upside down and needed to be turned around. She asked for a blanket, which she spread on the floor, and had my mother lie on it. Then the midwife held one side and my father grabbed the other. First the midwife raised her side, making my mother roll over towards my father, and then my father did the same, forcing her to roll back. I think they did this three times. Once again the midwife consulted the coca leaves and determined that the birth would now be normal. That afternoon my baby brother was born without any more difficulties. That was the only time I remember that my mother had trouble during childbirth.

Normally we ate potatoes, wheat, and freeze-dried potatoes we call *chuño*, combined with a little bit of meat and cheese. The meat was mostly llama jerky, or *charqui*, and the cheese was from our sheep. Everything we ate we produced on our land. Sometimes my parents and older sisters raced off in the morning for the fields and pastures without leaving me any prepared food. So from the time I was four or five years old I often had to fend for myself. They left me cooked whole-grain or corn, but I had to grind it using heavy stones, as the whole grain is inedible. To a small child the grinding mortars seemed huge, as they were almost as big as I was, and it was a challenge to handle them.

My mother was responsible for taking care of all the food and stored both the cheese and the dried meat in the rafters of the house, out of the reach of both mice and children. One day when we were alone, my sister Cursina proposed, "I'll give you a small piece of cheese"—a special food—"if you don't tell Mom."

I readily agreed, and when my mother came back, I said hello and excitedly told her, "Mom, Cursina and I ate cheese."

When confronted, Cursina, of course, denied everything. My mother checked closely and no cheese appeared missing. But a few days later, she found a cheese that, while intact on the outside, had its inside eaten away, and she scolded my sister.

In campesino families, no matter how small children are, they have to share in the work. One of the most critical jobs during the agricultural cycle was to harvest potatoes. The entire family headed to the fields where we dug potatoes and stacked them together in piles. Because I was the smallest, and still couldn't dig, it was my job to collect the ones that rolled away from the mounds. I'm not sure if it was because my sisters were jealous of me or simply wanted me to work harder, but it seemed that they intentionally threw potatoes far away and sometimes just pitched them directly at me to make me cry.

When I reached six or seven my parents began to send me alone to pasture the sheep. I always left the house in the morning with food, my slingshot, a poncho, and a musical instrument, as it was customary for boys to learn to play music. Each instrument had its season and its function in relation to some natural phenomenon. Instruments to call down the rain— this was a very dry place and without rain we couldn't grow anything— were those constructed of wood that had a special, sharp sound. We played these—the *pinquillos* and the *taraq'as*—during the rainy season, between November and March, to encourage the rain to fall. But when the rainy season was over and the harvest began, we played instruments made of bamboo like the *quena*, the *quena-quenas*, the *sicus*, and the *zapoñas* because, like the wind, they were supposed to blow the rain away.

When I left the house in the morning, I immediately began to play, and practiced for most of the day. When I came home in the evening I played with great enthusiasm to show my family what I had learned. Music filled a central part of everyday life.

When I first began pasturing animals, even though I was told explicitly what to do and how to do it, I made mistakes. Besides the fox, the condor was the biggest danger, because if a lamb wandered near the top of a hill, the big bird could swoop down and grab it. One day when I wasn't paying enough attention, I inadvertently allowed the sheep to graze on the hilltop. All of a sudden a giant condor was circling overhead, looking even bigger than the airplanes I sometimes saw. With each pass it closed in on the sheep.

I began to scream and cry because I was sure it would nab one of the lambs, and the sheepdog seemed completely oblivious to what was going on. I shot rocks at the huge bird with my slingshot, but it had no effect as the condor whirled menacingly closer and closer. Fortunately, my neighbor's dog suddenly appeared out of nowhere running and barking, which brought my dog to life. Between the two of them they drove the sheep away from the point of the hill, and the condor soared off. I never made that mistake again. Often we need to experience something personally to learn life's most important lessons.

We always carried food when we pastured the sheep. One time one of our cousins had wrapped her food in an *aguayo*, the hand-woven shawl that we carry things in, to keep it warm. When she came back from making the rounds of the animals she found a snake sleeping on top of the *aguayo;* it was surely attracted by the heat and smell of the food. She was frightened and let out a scream that woke the snake, scaring it away. When a person sees a snake—because of the cold weather we don't see too many of them—it means that someone is going to die. The snake represents the intestines of that person. The news of the sighting spread quickly through the entire community, and we all started talking about the old people or people who were sick. A few days later an aunt died.

For the funeral, first we had a wake where my aunt's body was laid out on the floor of the food storage room. The body was covered with an *aguayo* with coca leaves scattered on top. Everyone chewed coca, drank alcohol, and smoked cigarettes. Funeral rituals were accompanied by a llama sacrifice, but first the rope attached to the llama was placed in the dead person's hand. Sometimes a dog was sacrificed too and tied to the body. And the dead really held on to the rope; I saw it with my own eyes. The belief is that the llama and dog will guide the soul to a paradise where flowers grow in abundance.

Everyone goes to this paradise, whether they lived good or bad lives, but there can be difficulties on the route. The road isn't straight, and if you have not behaved well during your life, obstacles pop up everywhere. You have to carry everything for the next life with you, like utensils to eat with, food, pots, and pans. The llama is loaded with these things before it is slaughtered. On the path to paradise, you have to scale large rocks, so you have to bring a ladder with you as well.

When conducting these rites, it is critical to ensure that the soul can complete its journey. Otherwise it will return to harass the living and can even cause deaths in its endless quest for company.

Often the llama is killed, and its meat is distributed to the two pallbearers who transport the body to the cemetery on an improvised ladder, running all the way there. Then the body is interred directly into the ground without any sort of casket.

Later, on the first of November, known as Todos Santos (All Saints' Day) and one of the year's most important holidays, or fiestas, we prepare a special reception for the visiting souls of the person or people who had died in the nine months between the last Todos Santos and August. We only receive visits from these souls, because they are considered fresh or new. This custom has its origins before the Spanish Conquest, when nobles died and were mummified before being placed in a *chullpa*, or mausoleum. In any case, bodies that had not yet been mummified were considered to present a health risk. Even though mummification has disappeared, this tradition carries on, and so souls who have died within the last three months are not part of this holiday.

Preparing for Todos Santos takes a lot of time. First, starting in mid-October, the family, normally the women helped by the children, makes *chicha* (corn beer) and then prepares dough and bakes breads, called *tantawayas*, in the shape of people or other figures. Then the family cooks the food that the dead person particularly liked. When everything is ready, an altar is erected where everything is spread out in time for the souls, who arrive at midday on November 1. The timing is critical because it is believed that the soul does not show up alone but with other dead family members and friends. Usually some kind of unexpected movement—like the lid of a pot falling over by itself—occurs when you are eating lunch or placing offerings on the table. That's when everyone knows the souls have arrived.

The *tantawayas* are shaped into figures from everyday life, like a llama, the sun and the moon, and the person who has died. Later this offering is given to those who helped with the burial, as well as preparing the table and the public prayers for the soul. The altar stays decorated until about two in the morning, when the families return from the cemetery to dispatch the soul or souls. In the cemetery, everyone prays alongside the tomb, and sometimes they erect another table or altar there. To avoid having the souls linger past the allotted time, somebody hits the walls with a *chicote* (a small whip), telling them it's time to depart. Because if they don't leave, you run the risk that they will carry off some other living person with them.

Todos Santos also marks the beginning of the planting season, when we begin to sow beans and potatoes and other foodstuffs. It is also the time that young couples court, renewing life after the period of honoring and mourning the dead.

After the 1952 Revolution

The 1952 revolution was a turning point in Bolivia's history because it brought the epoch of semifeudal rule to an end. I was six years old at the time. All the men left the community, and planes buzzed overhead, back and forth, all day and night. I asked my oldest sister why there were so many planes, and she said that my father had gone off to war. A little while later the men returned, loaded with sugar, rice, and wheat in hundred-pound sacks, which they began to sell at very low prices. The maximum authority in the community—the *jilakata*—took charge of the sale. People saw these new goods as one of the revolution's positive results, and for me, at six years old, bags bulging with wheat and sugar were more tangible than the citizenship rights that we, as indigenous people, had won. For my parents, however, for the first time ever, it was possible to travel fairly easily to the mines and cities. Before the revolution they always faced the risk that someone would simply appropriate their things, which was one of the ways that indigenous people were commonly abused, as we had no laws to protect us.

Through the revolution we won universal public education. In Wila Apacheta, community members built a school that they supported themselves, which was common in rural Bolivia at the time because the government provided very few schools even in the cities, much less in indigenous communities. The school was a single room constructed of adobe, about thirteen by twenty-six feet, with a straw roof, two glass windows, and a door. Not a single piece of furniture was made of wood. Instead adobe benches served the students and a black linoleum sheet attached to the wall worked as a blackboard. The teacher's desk was also adobe, with the desktop a piece of black stone. The school lasted two years because the teacher, a man from the community, had only finished second grade and we had no chance of getting a government-funded teacher.

Only about sixteen or eighteen children in Wila Apacheta attended school each year, even though the community had many more boys and girls. If a family had five children, it only sent two or three of the smaller ones—the ones least able to do any useful work. The labor of the others was needed to care for the sheep and llamas, to plant, tend the crops, and harvest. If they allowed all the children to study, the only agricultural labor available would be that of the parents, which would not guarantee enough food for the entire family, as everything was done by hand. The school was a few miles from our house. Early in the morning I walked there for about an hour with some of my neighbors.

I remember more of the toys we each had than what we actually did in the classroom, as a pretty strict form of social control ruled our few belongings. One day two boys got into a fight because one had made off with the other's toys, something that was very unusual in our community. The teacher called us together and said, "Today we're going to identify your toys so this never happens again. Make a list of everything you have, which you will present to the class. That way you will never lose anything, nor will anybody be able to take something of yours."

We did as we were told, and when it was my turn, I headed to the front and said, "I have ten marbles: three red ones, four green ones, and three white ones; twenty beans: ten black ones and ten red ones; a metal top and its string." All morning each student stood up and described very similar toys.

I studied there for one year. Mostly I learned to draw and a little bit of the Spanish alphabet. The next year they had to close the school because we couldn't find a teacher willing to live in the community for the small salary we could afford. The following year they still couldn't find a teacher, so many families considered taking their children to the mines or to the cities to attend school.

Outside of school, the other boys and I arranged to play *t'inku* when we were moving our animals to pasture. This game served as a way to practice one of the most important rituals in the life of the *ayllu*. The *t'inku* literally means "encounter," but in practice, it is a yearly ritual battle between members of differing *ayllus*, where blood is spilled to fertilize the Pachamama, the mother earth.

To play, preparation was essential. We needed gloves to protect our hands, a helmet, and a scarf, but even more important we had to bring the *jula julas*, wind instruments made of bamboo. Sometimes we borrowed them from our parents; other times we just snuck them out of the house. A *jula jula* is a type of pan pipe, with only four notes. Each one has its own scale, but it was really difficult to learn how to play it correctly because each instrument only had half the tones. Two of them must be played together to get the range of notes necessary for a tune, which meant that either we needed our friends to play or we had to practice both parts alone.

As music is so important, every year a community member, usually someone with special skills, writes a new song that is played as the community dances into the area where the *ayllus* hold the *t'inku*. An *ayllu* that shows up playing the same tune as the year before is considered incapable of defending its territory. When we played at the *t'inku* as children, while we didn't write new songs for each encounter, learning to play correctly was important. Sometimes four boys—two in each group—arranged to meet, but often only two or three of us showed up, in which case the person who came alone had to play both parts of the song alone as we tried hard to replicate the *t'inkus* we had witnessed.

The group that arrived at the *t'inku* first stood around practicing their *jula julas*. The second group approached the *t'inku* playing music and dancing, weaving back and forth, dancing in the figure of a snake. At some point one dancer bumped into a member of the other group. And the two boys dropped their instruments, put their gloves on, and began to fight, wailing away at each other using primitive boxing techniques. Even as boys we fought until someone had a bloody nose or was in tears. Sometimes during the fights someone would step or fall on an instrument, breaking it. Then we tried to sneak the instrument back into our houses without getting caught and punished.

ALTIPLANO INDIGENOUS COMMUNITIES

The majority of Bolivia's rural population is concentrated on the altiplano, the high, dry inter-Andean plateau 11,500 to 14,000 feet above sea level, and in dry intermontane valleys between 6,600 and 10,500 feet. Most people inhabit settled communities, some organized into *ayllus*, within cultures that follow the rhythms of the yearly agricultural cycle. Their highly developed symbolism and rituals are captured in haunting and emotive music, sophisticated ceramics, and some of the finest and most intricate textiles the world has ever seen (Zorn 2004; Stobart 2006).

It is a common Andean saying that "reciprocity begins with a gift," reflecting the concept's centrality. Reciprocity stems from the balance and complementarity between male and female; both are seen as necessary to create a whole. In usually scattered communities, people collaborate on group tasks through communal work arrangements such as *ayni* and *mink'a*. Community leadership rotates yearly, and while the man is the nominal leader, his female partner replaces him when he is away or ill.

Thanks to the *ayllu* structure, the Andes' different ecological regions were historically highly integrated, from the arid, almost treeless highlands to scrubby, dry valleys and dense, lush tropics. Trading was active among all three through wide-ranging kinship networks. The region is the original home of the potato, with over seventy varieties of colorful tubers, from bright yellow to deep purple, found in Andean markets. Much of the culture has historically revolved around llamas (pack animals and meat), alpacas (wool), and the wild vicuña (wool). Bolivia still has the largest number of llamas in the world.

Andean cosmovision combines animism with a deep respect for nature. The sun, moon, the highest mountains, and phenomena such as lightning and thunder are all venerated. Viracocha is seen as the creator of all, and the earth mother, the Pachamama (*pacha* means earth, *mama* is mother), the personification of fertility and growth, is a living being. Ancestors are also worshiped, as it is believed the dead actively ensure the well-being of the living. They are considered the creators of the *ayllus*, and reverence is extended to ancestral places of origin. Frequent religious and social festivals accompany the natural seasonal and agricultural cycle, with music and dance central to festival ritual and participation.

Space and time are two simultaneous realities expressed in the same word, *pacha*, unlike the separation common in Western cultures. Time is also perceived as cyclical rather than linear. Consequently, the past and future operate differently than in Western culture: rather than the past being "behind" and future being "ahead," the past lies in front because it has been experienced and is known. This suggests the importance of a return to a known past as a means of comprehending the future (Nuñez and Sweetser 2006).

The collective wields greater weight than the individual, resulting in a low tolerance of deviant behavior and outsiders. While in Western cultures, worth is usually measured by individual achievements, in the Andes, people are more likely judged by their community contributions. Such an orientation exerts a strong social control over individual behavior, and criticism centers on individuals but not the community or collectivity (Nash 1993).

My Parents as Local Authorities

One December afternoon when I was nine, I was helping my mother and sisters herd the sheep and llamas back to the house. We heard someone playing a *pinquillo*, accompanied by a drum and with the occasional sounding of an ox horn known as a *pututu*. My mother grabbed my hand and, leaving my sisters to corral the animals, hurried back to the house. We spotted my father with two neighbors, all dressed in red ponchos, on the path approaching our house. My mother rushed to quickly set up a reception table, with an *inkuña*—a special fabric—laden with coca and a small bottle of alcohol. My mother understood, having seen the red ponchos, that my father had been named *jilakata*, the maximum political authority of the *ayllu*.

The *jilakata* played a critical function in administering the community's property. To officially transfer the office, which happened every year, it was not only necessary that my father accept, but also that my mother was willing to assume the complementary role of *mamatalla*. The *mamatalla* replaced the *jilakata* if he went away or died during the year of his authority and assumed the mantle of command with his complete responsibilities and powers.

This was an important event for a number of reasons. It implied an enormous cost for the family and additional risk as well. What if things didn't go well during my father's one-year term as *jilakata*? What if he was away or sick or for some reason he couldn't fulfill his duties and my mother had to act in his place? For these reasons, to finalize the agreement, my mother as well as my father was part of the ceremony. During the transfer, my mother broke into a flood of tears, not only because she was proud but also because she worried about taking on such a big responsibility.

Given that the government had so little presence in our daily lives, we were largely self-governed. Responsibilities rotated in a system where positions were assigned according to age and experience. To gain use-rights to communal land, community members were expected to assume local authority roles during their lifetime. Unlike urban authorities, where, for example, a man receives a salary to serve as a mayor, in our community each family had to use its own resources to perform the required job. In some cases the community offered some support in tending the family herd or ensuring that crops were sown if an authority was away on business. But to act as a local authority demanded a sacrifice, a cost to be borne in support of the community and the *ayllu*, similar to the obligatory taxes that the citizens of modern cities are required to pay to support schools, roads, and police. In this setting, the goal of public service is not to steal from the people and get rich, but to lend services to the community to ensure a continuity of local government and, in return, receive the full rights of a community member.

Before he was named *jilakata*, my father had fulfilled other community obligations. One of the most important *cargos*—which literally means loads—was that of *khawasiri*, and as with the other *cargos* in the *ayllu*, when it was his turn he had to dedicate his time to it, as the survival of the entire community depended on him; if he was away, his wife stepped in. The *khawasiri* was the local authority responsible for the success of the agricultural cycle, which required two important tasks. First, the night before we began to sow our crops, he coordinated a rite to guarantee the year's harvest, and protect our fields from frost, hail, and drought, all of which were serious potential threats, given the high risks associated with Andean agriculture. To protect the crop he called a *yatiri*, a religious healer, to make an offering to the Pachamama, the earth mother. The following day the *khawasiri* hosted a meal for all the members of the community, who brought their musical instruments to celebrate the planting.

During the agricultural cycle itself, the *khawasiri* had to protect the fields from frost, hail, and violent winds, any of which could destroy our crops. When it threatened to hail, for example, he ran to the top of the hill, where he launched a stick of dynamite with a sling so that the explosion stopped or scared the hail away from the crops. He also had to prevent the stock that freely roamed the hillsides from entering the small plots of potatoes or other scattered crops that were not fenced. We planted crops across a number of different fields and staggered the planting so that if one plot was hit by hail or a late frost, only some of our harvest was affected. Because the small plots were dispersed, those caring for the stock could not always keep them out. When that happened, the *khawasiri* negotiated a fair settlement for any damage.

The *khawasiri* finished his term each year after the potato harvest. When the crop of our basic staple was plentiful, the *khawasiri* held his head high and was respected by the community. When the harvest failed, whether because of drought, too much rain at the wrong time, hail, or heavy winds, people blamed the *khawasiri*, saying that he had acted badly or had failed to properly carry out the blessings required for the crop.

The *comisario*, the second authority in the community after the *jilakata*—a man typically served as *comisario* before assuming the role of *jilakata*—acted as the *jilakata*'s assistant. If the *jilakata* wanted to call someone to a meeting he gave a *chicote*—a small whip and the physical representation of the *jilakata*'s authority—to the *comisario*. The *comisario* went to the community member, handed him the *chicote*, and said, "The *jilakata* wants to see you." The man picked up the *chicote* and was obliged to return it to the *jilakata*.

During the year my father served as *jilakata*, he was the principal contact with public authorities outside the community, whether of other *ayllus* or of the provincial and departmental governments. For example, he had to collect payments from community members and personally take them to Oruro to pay tributes to the state.

He was also responsible for administering local justice. That year a man in the community stole three llamas from a family in another *ayllu*. The victims came to our house accompanied by their *jilakata*. They insisted that they would consider the entire community thieves if restitution wasn't made, and demanded that the thief be put to death. My father immediately summoned the thief, as well as other men from our community, to a trial. The next day about thirty people arrived at the school, which served as our community meeting center. Although children were excluded, we formed a human pyramid outside to watch what was going on through the window. As I was the smallest, I climbed to the top and related what I could see to the others below. The authorities of the two *ayllus* sat at the teacher's desk, and on the floor directly in front of them lay the skins of the three recently slaughtered llamas. The thief, his hands and feet lashed together, was suspended by a rope from one of the roof beams, from where he was obligated to make his statement. The rest of the room was filled with other community members. As I recounted the scene to my friends, a man rushed out of the meeting and chased us away. I don't know what happened next, but it appeared that the authorities of the two communities were able to resolve the problem and the thief made adequate restitution.

Another day two men accused a young man of stealing dung, essential for fertilizer and cooking fuel. My father called the *comisario*, who fetched the accused, who adamantly denied the theft. As he was a minor, his father was at his side. My father had the young man face the wall where the *bastones de mando*—the staffs that represented the authority of the community—were hanging and swear that he had not done anything wrong. Although the accusers were unhappy with the outcome, my father dismissed all parties. The following day, the boy's father showed up in a state of desperation. During the night his son had fallen seriously ill, and, afraid he was going to die, he confessed that he had not only stolen the manure but lied about it. My father immediately reconvened the trial, and, with the promise to replace the stolen goods, the boy recovered almost immediately.

In some cases *jilakatas* are unable to resolve problems within the community. During the annual celebration of the *ayllu*, which involves a lot of alcohol, two men got into a drunken fight and one man was knifed. All attempts to settle the problem through mediation failed, so my father accompanied the two men to Huanuni, the provincial capital, where he turned the case over to government authorities.

When he was *jilakata*, my father had to practically give up all his other activities. My mother did a whole lot more, including most of the agricultural work. When the year was finally over, it was a relief for them, although they knew it had been an honor that had significantly improved their status within the community.

My First Visit to the Mines

The first time I left my community I was about eight or nine years old. My father decided I was old enough to accompany him when he moved a pack train of llamas to the mines. My mother opposed the idea, as she thought I was still too young. My father, as head of the family, usually the case in rural families, overruled her, even though I remember they fought about it. We left at about seven in the morning with more than thirty llamas loaded with dung to sell in Llallagua. We herded the animals along narrow paths for about eight hours without stopping.

When my father realized I was walking slower and slower, he asked, "Are you tired?"

I looked at him, puzzled, "What do you mean?" as I really had never felt the symptoms of exhaustion before.

"Do your feet hurt?"

"Yes, they do and so do my calves."

He smiled at me, "That's being tired."

Even though we were only about an hour short of Llallagua, we rested.

Just before we arrived in the city two women approached my father, "We'll buy your entire load."

My father declined their offer, "I've already promised it to someone else."

The women started walking alongside us, pressuring my father to sell them the dung. He ignored them, but they didn't give up until we ran into the woman my father had promised the load to. At the time I did not know who these women were or what they could possibly want with so much dung. I later learned that they made *chicha*—corn beer—to sell to the miners. At this time, the mining centers had neither gas nor electric stoves for cooking, and, as there were almost no trees due to the altitude and lack of rain, dung was the fuel of choice.

Before entering the mining camp itself, we faced a control post. The watchman on duty registered our entry. The woman got angry and yelled at the watchman, "What do you have to do this for? This entire load is my property."

As we crossed the last ravine before Siglo XX, which was surrounded by hills and gullies, I saw a long line of white walls with red roofs covering the entire hillside in parallel rows. I had never seen anything so big; it was even larger than the trains that I had seen pass in the distance. "What are those?"

"They're houses."

I couldn't imagine how a house could be so big that it covered the entire hillside. My father explained that, rather than a single house, they were actually many houses attached to each other.

In the valley below us, I noticed some large green things I had never seen before. My father explained that they were trees. Although I had seen plants growing all my life, I couldn't believe a plant could get so big. I tried to ask my father why no one had harvested them, but he was busy with the animals and had lost patience with my constant questions, "Pay attention to the llamas and don't worry about such things."

We reached the woman's house, and my father unpacked the llamas. In the evening, we ventured out for a walk. It was the night before Bolivia's Independence Day, August 6. For me, everything was new and marvelous: streets full of more people than I had ever imagined, electric light that

25

transformed night into day, houses with lots of glass windows and mirrors, men—certainly ex-miners—who were disabled, without feet or arms. I watched the holiday parade, dazzled by the floats and fireworks. As this was my very first night in a city, I assumed it was always like this.

The next day we headed out early. My father told me to keep my eyes open because you could always find something in the streets. I found a drinking glass, and my father found twenty pesos—almost a full day's wages. Later, my father left me to care for the llamas in a field that had a view of the mining camp's school. I was struck by the number of boys and girls with white school coats, who first lined up outside the school and then marched to the town's main plaza. As they passed by me, many of the children handed or threw me candies and cookies. At first I piled them up in my hands, and then as more came, I filled up my poncho until I had no more room. Although I couldn't imagine the wealth they had just given me, I grasped that this was the way holidays were celebrated in the mines.

When my father saw all the stuff I had gathered, he laughed. He helped me carry my harvest, and later we loaded the llamas and headed home. When we were almost there, my feet became so inflamed that my father had to carry me the last few miles. I remember that my mother was furious. The next day, even though I was still in pain, I doled out the candies to my sisters, who were happy, if awestruck, at so many sweets.

Chapter 2

Moving to the Mines

HISTORY OF MINING

Bolivia has always been shaped by the promise, the greed, and the agony that drive mining. Even before the Inka invasion in the fifteenth century, mining was important locally, but once the Inka were firmly in control, Bolivia's silver regularly traveled north by llama train to decorate Cuzco's ornate Temple of the Sun.

The mine the Spanish discovered at Potosí in 1545 became the richest silver mine in history. The settlement quickly grew larger than either Paris or London, packed by the turn of the seventeenth century with some forty thousand fortune-seekers from all over Europe. Its Cerro Rico (Rich Hill), known as Sumaj Orcko (Beautiful Mountain) by the Inka, provided more than half of world production of silver and gold for over a hundred years. This wealth paid off debts the Spanish crown owed to northern European bankers, partially fueling Europe's industrial revolution and transition to capitalism (Klein 2003).

Mining continued to dominate much of Bolivian economic and political life during the Republic. In the late nineteenth century tin production soared in northern mines, including Siglo XX–Catavi, and proved strategic for the nineteenth-century industrial expansion of both Europe and the United States. Demand spiked as technological advances expanded the use of tin to preserve foodstuffs precisely when Europe's principal source of tin in Cornwall, England, was exhausted.

By the early 1900s, three tin mining firms, Patiño, Hochschild, and Aramayo, collectively known as the Tin Barons, consolidated an almost absolute control over Bolivia's export economy and political apparatus. Between 1896 and 1917 tin quadrupled in price, driven in part by the First World War, when tinned food permitted soldiers to suffer in trenches almost indefinitely. The Tin Barons' fortunes mushroomed. Simón Iturri Patiño, who rose from humble indigenous origins to become one of the world's richest men, owned his most important mine at Siglo XX (Twentieth Century), the site of much of Félix's story. During its first thirty years

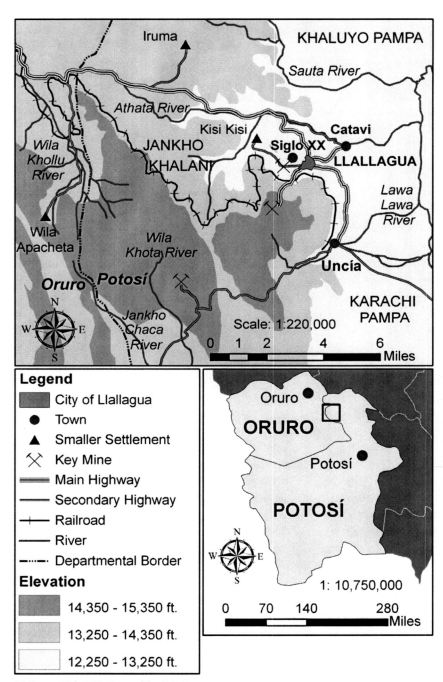

Llallagua–Siglo XX. Prepared by Eric Fox.

this mine alone produced 6 percent of the world's tin from among the richest veins ever discovered, some as wide as ten feet (Klein 2003).

By the end of the 1920s, Siglo XX was riddled with over ninety miles of tunnels, and exploration expanded at a feverish pace. Production plummeted during the 1930s global depression, and miners were laid off by the thousands. But just as world tin prices recuperated, the mines were hit with a labor shortage precipitated by Bolivia's Chaco War with Paraguay. Women were recruited to work underground for the first time. Companies had little choice but to hire married workers, which they had previously resisted so as to avoid providing family housing and services (Nash 1992).

By 1950, the mining complex of Siglo XX–Catavi and nearby Llallagua comprised Bolivia's seventh-largest urban area. Llallagua, a Quechua word, means "the spirit that makes potato harvests abundant," for prior to mining, the potato was the staple that underpinned the local economy.

More and more of the miners who flocked to Siglo XX were like Félix's father—campesinos from the windswept altiplano in northern Potosí near the mines, rather than those who, in previous generations, came from the Cochabamba valley. The position of miner was increasingly handed down from father to son, a strategy that helped families retain their urban housing.

The Family Moves

After the 1952 revolution, previously employed mine workers were allowed to return to the jobs they had lost. As my siblings and I were growing up quickly, our parents worried about our education. But my father was reluctant to return to the mine because the work had been so miserable and difficult. He kept asking my mother, "Do you really want me to die in that mine?" But my mother insisted, "If you won't go, I'm going anyway with my son. I'll work there and put him in school." Just like all campesinos, my father believed that if we left our land, we would never return, and this meant we would lose it. And for a campesino, land is everything.

They argued for some time. It was very clear that because I was a boy, it was more important to educate me than my sisters, who were thirteen and fifteen at the time. This discrimination against girls' education in rural Bolivia is widespread for two reasons. First, the historical division of labor means that a woman is most valued for her domestic abilities. But when a woman marries she leaves her parents' home and is incorporated into her husband's household, usually in a different community. It is the male child who stays at home, and it is he who inherits the goods and land rights, while the daughter only takes with her things that her parents give her, such as clothes and utensils. Parents believe that girls will serve others, so they choose to invest in their sons, who will, hopefully, care for the parents in their old age, although in reality it is often the youngest unmarried daughter who assumes this role. Second, older daughters are needed to take care of the house when the parents travel in search of work, such as when we moved to the mine. In rural Bolivian families many people, mostly the men, migrate, sometimes for a month or two, other times for years. They send back cash to complement the family's agricultural production, and women run the farm.

From my ninth year on, my parents lived with one foot in the mine and the other in the countryside. My two eldest sisters, Cristina and Cursina, were responsible for everything in Wila Apacheta. They stayed there until they married and followed their husbands: Cristina to the town of Vinto, outside of Cochabamba, and Cursina to Cochabamba itself.

My mother first took me to the company school at Siglo XX that the state mining corporation, called COMIBOL (Corporación Minera de Bolivia), ran, but the authorities would not let me enroll. "This school is only for the children of full-time mine employees," they told her. So instead, I was sent to Jaime Mendoza School, which was for the rest of Llallagua's population. The difference in schools was significant for my family, because children at the mining company school received breakfast with bread, milk, oatmeal, cheese, and butter, as well as school supplies, while students at state schools received nothing.

My mother must have complained to my father about the differences, because he finally, but reluctantly, agreed to go back to the mine. He got a job quickly after he gave a lamb to a company employee for writing him a letter of reinstatement, as he had lost his job for political reasons.

Now that the mine was state-controlled, my father told us, things had changed for the better. Before the 1952 revolution, the foremen strictly controlled the workers. They punished absenteeism and kept the workers constantly on the go. He said that when the miners rested, the foremen were allowed to hit them to force them back to work. My mother told a story of taking food to her father, who labored in the mine tailings when she was small. She saw a foreman hitting him and when she asked him why, he shrugged, "Because I took a break."

It was a big shock to leave the countryside and move to the mining camp. The first day I attended school, I wore my rural clothing, without a white school coat but with my traditional cap, a *chullo*. I arrived a bit late because I didn't know which classroom I was supposed to be in. The school secretary showed me where to go, and when I arrived I noticed that the other children were already writing quietly. As I crept in, the teacher said something to me, but I didn't understand a word, as he spoke Spanish and I only understood Quechua and Aymara. When I didn't do what I was told, he got angry and grabbed my *chullo* and threw it on the floor. As this is considered an insult, I picked up my cap, stuck it on my head again without saying a word. At that point, he realized that I didn't understand Spanish and asked the other students, "Which one of you speaks Quechua?" While nearly all of them did, only one child from the last row dared to admit it. The teacher ordered him, "Come here. Tell him what I said." The child translated, "The teacher says that to enter the class you have to take your *chullo* off and sit down."

I continued to feel intense culture shock, in part because the teachers were openly hostile and discriminatory to me and other rural children in the school. Fortunately, I only stayed there a year.

My mother could not find a job, so after school we hung around the company store offering to help women carry their groceries home. They paid us with a bit of bread, sometimes with some sugar or rice, and we lived from this. Sometimes when I carried everything, they paid me in money. My mother had planned to weave *aguayos*, or blankets, because, like most rural women, she was an excellent weaver. But it was very difficult to get started because she couldn't find anyone to help her.

MINING NATIONALIZATION

When President Víctor Paz Estenssoro announced mining nationalization on the dusty, dry pampa near the Siglo XX mine in 1952, miners believed that an exit from their perpetual misery was in sight. The Bolivian Mining Corporation (COMIBOL), a semi-autonomous enterprise, was created soon after to run state-owned mines. COMIBOL rapidly became the largest of Bolivia's state companies, responsible for 65 percent of all mineral production (Dunkerley 1984).

The mines the government inherited, however, were close to exhausted. World demand for tin had dropped, and the newly nationalized companies had been decapitalized, as owners, who feared that nationalization was imminent by the late 1940s, had stopped reinvesting in exploration and maintenance. As well, COMIBOL's initial marketing opportunities were severely curtailed, not only because the Tin Barons controlled contracts with international markets and foreign smelters, but also because the United States began to sell off the stockpiles of tin it had accumulated during World War II (Gall 1974a).

With 97 percent of Bolivia's foreign exchange stemming from minerals, COMIBOL not only was the linchpin of the economy, but also under enormous pressure to generate income for the new government. But the state enterprise also quickly turned into a source of jobs for the party faithful. While the number of miners rose steeply at first—by about a third—after 1956, COMIBOL's administration became increasingly bloated, and the ratio of underground to surface workers shifted from over 2:1 to 1:2 by the late 1960s (Gall 1974b).

To satisfy the demand to generate income, COMIBOL adopted a short-term perspective that focused on exploitation, with little reinvestment in either exploration or technological improvements. Since 1952, not one new state mine has opened.

Housing

The social situation in the mine had improved a bit since the revolution. Housing, for example, was better because several new camps had been constructed, although there were still shortages. Occasionally a family had a tiny house to itself, but it was much more common that two families would somehow cram into each one. When we first arrived, we lived with a cousin of my father's, Angel, who had a rented house. It was thirteen by ten feet, and, as part of the rent, the owner required him to keep twenty guinea pigs in the house. We never got to eat a single one, even though we lived with them for at least half a year.

My father learned from some of his friends in the mines that a vacant house lay at the settlement's edge because a miner had recently died from black lung. The miner had built it himself, half of stone, half of adobe, with an earthen floor. It was about six and a half feet square and had a small separate kitchen. We lived there three years until we could secure company housing.

My father was pretty *machista* [sexist], and occasionally beat my mother when he was drunk. This kind of treatment of women was very common among mining families. Because my father was adept at playing many different musical instruments, he was very sought after to play at parties, where everyone was urged to drink to excess. And certainly he flirted with other women, which made my mother, who loved to dance at parties, very jealous. Eventually she stopped going with him.

A miner had to be a long-standing employee, and married with several children, before he could get a house. Even after we finally got one we lived with another cousin's family. Even though he, too, worked in the mines, he couldn't get his own house. A special settlement called Villarroel, in honor of the president assassinated in 1946, was built after the 1952 revolution. Only families that had eight children or more could live there, and one of the families we knew there had sixteen children. Our house was close by this settlement.

The settlements had no parks, and school offered the only recreational activities we had. We often played war between the different settlements. For example, my friends from Villarroel fought the kids from Salvadora [female savior] Camp with stones, arrows, and slingshots. Generally, each time our fathers came back from work, they found one of us with a busted head or bloody nose. The workers insisted that the company build soccer fields to give us something else to do. We followed the construction with interest, and when they were done we gave up war and dedicated ourselves to soccer. This was a great distraction for the boys, but the girls didn't have this option and spent their days at home helping their mothers.

Our family lived for twenty-six years in the mining settlement. We had the right to have a house as long as my father worked for the company. The moment a worker left, the staff of the social benefits department removed the family by force, putting their things out into the street and handing the house over to a different worker. Generally, people left the settlement when a miner died if there wasn't a son who could take his place, or if he was fired for union activity. As most miners were originally from the countryside, the only option for a widowed family was to pack up and return to their community of origin, because in the mines they had neither a house nor an income.

School

After my father returned to the mines, I was able to go to the COMIBOL school in the morning. But I had difficulties learning the language and in assimilating what I was being taught, so my father enrolled me in the state-run night school for nonminers as well. This meant I only had midday free. But the night school teachers were really dedicated and gave us extra classes when needed. Sometimes they even invited me along with other students to their houses for additional instruction, which helped us a lot.

The company provided us school supplies and textbooks. When we went outside to recess, we left these on our desks. One day when I came back in, I couldn't find my textbook anywhere. As it was the end of the day, I couldn't tell my teacher because he had meetings, so I had no choice but to head home without my book. Because I feared they would be angry with me, I didn't tell my mother and father either.

A few days later, the teacher announced, "We are going to practice reading. Those who do well can go home early, and the rest will have to stay for extra practice." One after another, the good readers left, and the rest slunk back to their seats. I hung back because I didn't have my book. At the end of the afternoon, only I and another classmate who had also lost his book remained. The teacher asked me, "Where is your book?"

"I lost it," I admitted.

He made me read from his book, but because I lacked practice, I couldn't do it well. I read the passage over and over until I mastered it. The teacher was stern, "When you practice, you read well, but without a book you will never improve." He handed me a letter for my father that requested he appear at the school the next day. My father was illiterate, so he asked me what the letter said. I rather reluctantly told him, "The teacher wants to see you." After his session with the teacher, he was really angry, as much because I had not let him know I had lost the book as because we needed to buy another.

The night class I attended was at a grammar and vocational school that offered basic technical literacy in electricity, automobile mechanics, and carpentry. As we had neither tools nor machines, the teachers only taught us theory. Many of the students in the night school were street children who were orphans or didn't live with their parents and were considered juvenile delinquents by the company's social services department. Many were well known to the police but were so poor they had little choice but to rob for a living. When I first started in that school, I didn't realize this. But because we were hunting for a house, I visited the company social services office with my father, and there I saw photos of several of my classmates posted on the wall.

Even in the night school, students were treated differently because of their names or the color of skin. The rural children, who had last names like Mamani, Quispe, Condori, and Mita, were treated worse than the children of criollos, who are people of Spanish origin, or a mixture of Spanish with indigenous people, and who had names such as Álvarez, Linares, and Gonzales. Generally, the urban criollos at my school were children of teachers, engineers, and company employees.

My school performance suffered not only because neither my mother nor my father could read, so I had no help with the homework, but also because no one in my family spoke Spanish well. The difference with other children whose parents spoke, wrote, and read Spanish constantly was huge. We had to make a double sacrifice to learn as well as the criollo students.

During this period, my mother returned to the countryside with my younger siblings, who needed more care. My father stayed on at Siglo XX for a year with just me. Later my mother returned with Germán, my younger brother, so that he could study too. Years later, Carmen and Margarita, my younger sisters, were born at the mine and went to school in spite of being girls, as we were influenced by the attitudes of our neighbors, who all sent their daughters to school. But even more important, they went because our family situation had improved economically. We no longer needed their labor, because we depended far less on agricultural production for our survival.

Juk'u

When I was sixteen and finished the sixth grade, I started to work. As my father earned very little, I had to help my family. Other boys from the mining camp told me, "If you want to dress well and earn some money, we know the best place for you." That's how I started as a *juk'u*—mining the exhausted veins of the state mines without a legal concession. Although *juk'u* implies thievery, we just didn't see it that way. We didn't think that we were stealing minerals but were simply mining without permission, a practice that continues today.

We saw ourselves as miners, not robbers, working to make a living to help our families. Nonetheless, it was illegal and highly dangerous: at night we snuck into isolated areas to work rock faces that the state miners had abandoned. My parents, although they knew how hazardous it was, couldn't object, as they didn't see that I had other options.

Illegal production of minerals was a fact of life in the mines. When I began as a *juk'u*, the Trotskyist party, the Revolutionary Workers' Party (Partido Obrero Revolucionario, or POR), had organized groups to work as *juk'us*. This activity served to strengthen the party and partly solved the tremendous problem of unemployment in the district. But among the people I knew, these Trotskyists were viewed poorly because you had to join their party in order to participate in their *juk'u* groups.

My friends and I didn't get into the hill through the primary entrances of Siglo XX, Cañiri, or the Patiño mine that were routinely used by the union workers. The mountain is honeycombed with passages and abandoned entrances, which had been blocked off with cement and stones when the veins ran out, and because these were never completely sealed, we could break in. Dams formed in the front of the walls, and water, which continually drained from the mine's interior, created pools about four to five feet deep. Security was lax, because the company managers argued that nobody would be brave or desperate enough to climb over the walls and cross the freezing pools of water to gain access to the mine.

We never ever went in alone; it was just too dangerous. At about ten o'clock at night, in groups of four or five, we crept up to an abandoned entrance and clambered in, sneaking out at about five in the morning. To keep our clothes dry we stripped down to our underwear outside the mine and waded or swam through the frigid water. Once we crossed the pool, which was about twenty yards wide, we dressed and descended deep underground. When we worked closer to the surface, the temperature was only about fifty degrees, but in the lower levels, it got really hot, between eighty and ninety-five degrees, so getting wet wasn't really a problem. It was always harder to leave, because as we came out of the warm, humid mine, we had to take our clothes off to go through the icy water, and then suddenly we were outside in the dry, freezing cold. The mines are at about 15,500 feet above sea level, so at five in the morning any day of the year the temperature was well below freezing. It was torture, after working all night, to strip down and wade through freezing cold water carrying our clothes and a twenty-five- or fifty-pound bag of the mineral we had cut out of the vein. The cold was indescribable, and it took hours to shake it off.

Juk'us and Informal Mining

In the face of recurring economic crises provoked by low international tin prices during the 1950s and '60s, COMIBOL's Siglo XX managers quickly figured out that it was cheaper to purchase mineral removed from the mine illegally by *juk'us* than to have it extracted by unionized workers, even though they officially maintained a policy committed to preventing unregulated ore extraction.

Juk'us, a Quechua word meaning "night raptors" (with the connotation of thieves), worked abandoned areas under perilous conditions. They were scarcely a new phenomenon. Few haciendas existed in the agriculturally impoverished north of Potosí, and for generations indigenous men had migrated to the mines during the agricultural off-season, to work as *juk'us* or in other informal jobs. By 1964, nearly half the mineral production at the Catavi concentration plant was listed as obtained "from other sources" (Gall 1974b).

Nonunionized work abounded outside the mines as well. In the 1960s, from dawn to dusk, nearby riverbeds were swarming with men, women, and children, sometimes working as family groups, sometimes in cooperatives, scratching through the tailings and surface deposits to find bits of scrap mineral. As global mineral prices, not production cost, determined payment, these informal miners barely made enough to eat while COMIBOL profit margins were as high as 400 percent on their production. The 1960s surge in informal mining gave birth to mining cooperatives, which function more as small businesses than as collaborative enterprises, and currently absorb the largest numbers of the country's mine workers.

Informal workers are divided into three groups. *Veneristas* work low-grade alluvial deposits in mountain streams and hillsides much as was done in ancient tin mines in Cornwall, England, while *lameras* extract mineral from the liquid waste flowing from the concentrating plant. *Palliris*, who began working after the mid-

1950s construction of the "sink and float" concentrating plant, absorbed many of the women working inside the mine who had been displaced by men with tacit union backing (Nash 1993). These women and their children—often widows and orphans—rummage for ore in the slag heaps that tower around mining districts.

Following the late 1940s abolition of bonded labor, local campesinos, like Félix's father, flocked to the mines, and Llallagua grew quickly as *jukeo* production exploded after the '52 revolution. Many of the narrow veins of ore they worked had been overlooked during Patiño's era.

The *jukeo* boom generated new prosperity for the town of Llallagua. Storekeepers bought stolen ore in exchange for food, and then often resold it back to the company, garnering profits of 100 or 200 percent. This was such an important supplement to miners' income that even salaried miners smuggled ore to sell in town.

The singular importance of the *jukeo* reemerged during the commodity boom at the beginning of the twenty-first century. The fragility of semi-industrialized mining operations and the cooperative organizational structure create constant pressure to regress toward more rudimentary mining and environmentally destructive technologies and working conditions in order to maximize short-term profits.

Mining in the Bolivian state mines is dirty and dangerous even under the best of circumstances. Where we worked, the danger was amplified, especially in the abandoned caverns formed by "block caving." In this system, miners follow the veins off a central passageway and blast large sections of rock out of an area rich in minerals. The miners remove the ore through a narrow gallery that forms a bottleneck. As the miners dig into the face, the roof of the cavern formed by the blasts slowly collapses under its own weight. After an area is exhausted, the tunnels are unstable, and miners avoid them. As *juk'us*, we mostly worked the veins relatively close to the passages where the pillars holding the cavern's ceiling had partially collapsed and around the perimeters of the caved-in areas, because that's where we could find the richest ore. But these faces were inherently unstable, and sometimes we walked for twenty or thirty minutes only to find that the face we had dug the day before had disappeared.

Cave-ins were one of the greatest dangers, because a block could easily fall as the load shifted or a ceiling could collapse even as we worked. If a ceiling caved in on a worker, which happened frequently in the large state mines, the body was never recovered. Numerous workers were lost in the mine forever, gone without a trace. I experienced one cave-in during the time I worked as a *juk'u*. Suddenly, we felt a slight tremor, like a small earthquake, and we scrambled out of there as fast as we could. A minute later we felt more tremors and then heard the ceiling collapse, rock filling the area where we had been digging.

37

While we lost our tools and didn't get any mineral that day, we felt incredibly lucky that no one was killed or injured. When we realized we were safe, we looked at each other and began to laugh, first softly and then hysterically, as if we were crazy. We joked that we would have died without the chance to get married, or have a woman and kids. And, as I was the youngest, they teased me, "And it would have been worse for you—you're a virgin and don't even have a girlfriend." While we didn't say anything to our families about the accident, we repeated the story to our friends during the following weeks. Our friends and other *juk'us* took the story seriously, but the younger ones also interrupted with jokes.

Minerals are found incrusted in narrow, threadlike veins. To free the ore, we drilled small holes in the rock by hand with a hammer, a five-inch chisel, and a twelve-inch steel bar with a diamond point, driving the chisel into either side of the vein. It took about a half hour of hard work to drill a five-inch hole, taking turns among the group. Normally we drilled two holes and then put half a six-inch-long stick of dynamite in each. We used fuses that gave us just enough time to race out before the explosion. After we dynamited the ore free from the mine face, we gathered it into sacks, repeating the process until we had bags stuffed with ore, often drilling two or three sets of holes during a single shift. If we were lucky and the rock was soft or fractured, with a single stick of dynamite everyone could fill their sacks and we could go home early.

We considered the veins public property, and different teams of four or five young men worked the same ones. If we found another group had arrived first, we had to wait our turn. Typically we hung around an hour or two. And when we finished, others filed in after us because somebody was always in line. As the others worked, we chewed coca and speculated about where we could find other veins, or we checked for the location of the mine security officers. Sometimes we waited an entire shift and never got a chance to work the face, forcing us to go home empty-handed. Some young men needed to make a quota, and, if they weren't able to find enough mineral during the night, they had to stay for another twenty-four hours until they extracted the fifty to seventy-five pounds they needed. These guys were more ambitious than I. Usually I got about twenty-five pounds of ore and sometimes only ten to fifteen. Even if I didn't get anything, there was absolutely no way that I would remain in the mine for twenty-four hours straight. Because I lived at home and had no family of my own, I didn't have the urgent needs that drove some of my friends.

We talked a lot with the other *juk'us*, as conditions changed constantly. We told each other which galleries contained the best minerals, where there had been cave-ins, and where the security patrols were active. We worked inside the mine two or three times a week, because getting the ore was only half the battle. Then we had to concentrate it and sell it. First, we ground it into a fine powder with a hand mill. The mill consisted of a stone, about forty inches long and twenty inches high, shaped in the form of a half-moon, with iron handles on each end. It was mounted on a sheet of iron and weighed over four hundred pounds. We stuck the ore on the sheet and then rocked the stone back and forth like a seesaw to pulverize it. A skilled worker could grind twenty-five pounds in two hours. The next stage was to wash the ore and separate out the heavy metals from the fine powders in a hand concentrator. This took another hour. Then we washed the ore to finish the concentration process and dried the mineral on canvas. If the ore was rich we ended up with as much as eighteen pounds of concentrate from twenty-five pounds of rock.

Doing this dangerous work had a real impact on me, because I realized that I could die at any moment. This pushed me to live only in the moment, because I had no real future. Most miners felt this way. The result was that often they drank everything they earned, because they wanted to show off that they were men with money and because they wanted to forget the terror of the mine. We had an amazing solidarity with each other as *juk'us*, because we knew that one mistake and someone could lose his life. Each of us was responsible for the survival of us all.

We had two ways to sell our mineral. One was through a private buyer [*rescatiri*] who offered us a very low price. He gauged how desperate we were, and the more we needed the money, the less he paid. But sometimes when we had no choice, we sold it to him. The second way was much better. We turned the mineral over to a miner with a legal claim to exploit a small, shallow vein—these workers are called *veneristas*. The *venerista* then sold the ore to the company. As the entire mining district was full of minerals, these miners worked small deposits close to the surface where minerals had been exposed through erosion or a volcanic intrusion had forced minerals to the surface. Another group who sold minerals directly to the company was the *palliris*, mostly miners' widows who rummaged through the mine tailings searching for mineral overlooked in processing. Other women called *lameras* picked for mineral in the wastewater coming from the mine. But we rarely sold through them, preferring the *veneristas*, who, although they took advantage of us, could possibly offer us work in the future. As well, they provided us a certain amount of protection, because if we sold through them and later had a problem, they backed us up with the authorities and told them we were their workers.

But the *veneristas* also robbed us, because they paid us only half of what they received. So we were doubly exploited—not only from the low price of the mineral that the company paid the miner, but also because intermediaries took advantage of us.

Before the revolution, almost all of the mines were owned by only three families. After 1952 mineral rights reverted to the state. The many *juk'us* were joined by other people who smuggled ore out of the state mines or stole it and then sold it back to the state company through the *veneristas* like we did. If we were found with ore, whether as rock or as concentrate, the police assumed that we were thieves, and so we played a continual game of cat and mouse with them, as the police regularly patrolled the mine to shut down illegal activity.

Once we were outside, we carried our mineral to a hiding place. We often stored it far from the heart of the mining camp to throw the police off our trail. But we weren't always successful. One morning, hauling sacks filled with rough stone from our night's work, we were surprised by two policemen. They rudely demanded to see what we had in our bags, which all of us knew were filled with ore. I had a friend with an expensive Swiss watch, and as he moved to open his bundle, his sleeve slipped up his arm just enough for the policeman to see it. My friend saw that the watch had caught the policeman's eye, so he put down his bag, took the watch off his wrist, and offered it to the cop. Pleased with his new acquisition, the policeman waved us on.

Laborer for a Venerista

I worked almost a year as a *juk'u*. Then I was a laborer for a *venerista* for several months. This man was a neighbor who lived in a dilapidated house he built himself of stone and adobe. Like the other *veneristas* he had a legal concession on the edge of the state mine. He paid me a minimum daily salary, without social or medical insurance or benefits like contributions to a pension fund. I did everything for him. I hauled heavy bags of mineral out of the mine; ground, concentrated, and dried the ore; and even carried it to the company to sell. As well, if the veins disappeared, I worked for free until we discovered others, because otherwise we couldn't earn anything. He treated me well because I was experienced and his only laborer. He promised to help me get authorization from the mining company when I came of age so that I could become a *venerista* myself.

Through him I was introduced to other men working under the same contract system: one of them was a deaf-mute. I became very fond of him, and we helped him whenever we could. A lot of the miners could communicate with this man, who had never gone to a school for the deaf but instead had invented his own language through gestures. He was the clown of the group; during the rest period he made us laugh with his jokes and exaggerated physical humor. Everybody loved him, and he had a special role. As there were no services available to people with disabilities, usually the family, friends, and neighbors around them assumed the responsibility for their care.

I was proud to be a miner from the moment I started as a *juk'u*, even though I was only a kid of sixteen. As miners are often looked down on as drunks, crazies, or communists, sometimes it was hard for the miner himself to feel good about his identity. But I realized how important the miner is to the country's economy and in its social organizations, so I never hid being a miner from anyone. I felt that every person has the right to work and working made me a citizen who was supporting my country's development through my productive labor.

Chapter 3

The Army

Enlisting

In 1964 I turned eighteen, and all around me young men from the mining camp, including some of my neighbors and *juk'u compañeros* [buddies or mates], talked all the time about joining the army. We perceived the army as a rite of passage; we always knew who had gone, and if someone knew how to handle a gun. After we had served the obligatory year, when we were at fiestas either in the mines or the *ayllus*, we invariably asked young men of our age where they had served during their military duty. Lots of soldiers also got a small tattoo to identify their division, and it provided them something that connected them to the broader society. This sense of camaraderie was another part of what motivated us to fulfill our military duty.

If you hadn't completed your service, you didn't have much right to participate fully in fiestas, because you were considered remiss in your duties. If such a man asked his girlfriend's parents for her hand, they would refuse, as the boy wasn't considered an adult. Just as important, you couldn't get a job with the mining company or other state-owned companies without proof of army duty. For me, the combination of the social pressures and the need for my army discharge papers before I could apply for a mining job propelled me to sign up as soon as I could.

Twice a year the army took on new recruits, and at the first call in 1964 I traveled alone for the first time in my life to Oruro, where the Camacho Artillery Regiment base was located. Once there, I found a tremendous line that snaked more than three blocks around the base. Some people had even slept on the sidewalk.

I joined the end, and a soldier asked to see my birth certificate. He peered at it and announced, "You're too young to sign up. Come back next year."

I was shocked, "What? You're my age and you got in. Why can't I?"

He wouldn't even let me get back into the line. He insisted, "You have to be twenty. It's the law." Then he paused for a moment and continued in a low voice, "But you know what you can do? Have someone falsify your birth certificate. It's not hard."

I was disappointed, because I had traveled so far and hadn't even been allowed to stand in line. I felt ashamed to have to go back home at this point because I had left saying, "I'm going to join the army." I had never seen anyone return before. But I had no choice but to swallow my pride and reluctantly make my way home.

I asked a friend who had served for advice, and he convinced me that it was easy to falsify my papers, so I went to a Civil Registrar close to my house. I nervously approached the secretary. I said that I needed a birth certificate, but I wanted them to change the year of my birth so I could join the army. Completely unruffled, she took me into the office of the registrar, who examined my birth certificate. He asked, "Do you have thirty pesos?"—an amount roughly equivalent to two days' wages for me.

I handed over the money and he told me, "Come back tomorrow and you'll have a new birth certificate." The next day I picked it up and overnight I had aged two years!

I kept working as a *juk'u* for another three months while I waited for the next call. In Oruro, the very same soldier was at the back of the line, and I showed him my birth certificate. He smirked, "I see that you meet all the conditions. Do you have a pencil and a ballpoint pen?" I hurried off to the store to buy them. I handed them to the soldier, and thanks to this petty bribe, he moved me up to the middle of the line.

About an hour later another soldier approached. He said, "If you don't want to wait here and have ten pesos—five for me and five for the officer who will enlist you—you can go in immediately." I handed him the money, because I was getting tired and fed up.

When I enlisted they didn't mention my birth certificate, but sent me straight in for the medical exam. Lots of soldiers were milling around, and a man said, "Get undressed," and I joined a line of naked young men. The medical examiner checked each of us over quickly and asked if we were homosexual. Then we were herded from one line to another, where they checked our height and weight, our eyes, our teeth, and hearing, and finally someone told us whether we had passed. Until that point tension filled the air. Maybe they'd reject me for some reason, and then what would I do; how would I tell my friends? But they simply said to me, "You pass," and just like that, I was in the army. I quickly gathered my clothes and got dressed.

My first act as a soldier was to get my hair cut. There were several soldiers with clippers who buzzed our hair down to the scalp as if they were shearing sheep. Then we had to hang around until the end of the day to get our initial orders. While we were waiting, they had us move adobes and stones from one side of the base to the other and then back again in order to pass the time. In the evening they lined us up and dismissed us until six the next morning.

The next day they informed us we had been assigned to the Seventh Army Division in Cochabamba, the neighboring department. Generally, in Bolivia, people do their military duty far from home for two reasons. First, because if soldiers served where their families lived and a conflict erupted, the officers worried that the soldiers might not follow orders to fire on civilians. But there's another reason. Sending soldiers to a different department gives them the opportunity to experience someplace else. Young people living in places like the mines or the countryside rarely have the chance to travel. So they take people from the altiplano and send them to the valleys or lowlands and vice versa. This serves as part of a nation-building project to give people a better sense of what it means to be Bolivian.

People who have some money or have connections in the military will often do their service where they live. Even if the relative is only a sergeant, he can talk to a colonel or another officer to have his relative stationed closer to home, as it is easier for the family.

At this time, indigenous people and campesinos were not allowed to study in the military academy. There weren't any officers with names like Mamani or Quispe. This changed only when, shortly after he was elected in 2006, Evo Morales assisted a group of indigenous people to enroll in the military college to show that he was serious about change.

We were dispatched the next day. This time my father accompanied me to Oruro to see me off. He had little confidence in the army and the way they treated their recruits and was nervous about my leaving. He had been grabbed by army recruiters when he was transporting mineral by llama during the Chaco War. Fortunately, before he was formally inducted he managed, unlike many other peasants, to escape back to his community.

The night before I left I didn't sleep. I was nervous because I really had no idea of what I was getting into and how things might turn out. The next morning, we were up early and loaded into military troop transport trucks that deposited us at the central train station, where we all clambered aboard empty cargo wagons. We squeezed in—there were at least five hundred of us in the first group. Once the train was stuffed full, we started off. It took us all day to get to the Seventh Division base in Cochabamba.

Basic Training

The following day they sorted us according to our skills. Very few of us had any real abilities, but some were tailors, bar or restaurant workers, gardeners, office workers, or students. Part of the reason for this exercise was so that they could pick recruits who could provide services to the officers. For example, if a recruit had experience tending bar, he might be assigned to work in the officers' bars; gardeners often worked in officers' gardens or on the grounds of the base; and barbers cut the officers' or soldiers' hair. I remember one fat colonel saying, "I need agricultural workers," and with that he took twenty-two recruits, mostly peasants, to work on his own farm. They spent their year of service working his land, receiving no instruction, military or otherwise—then they were discharged.

I told them I was a student, which was good because the skills I had acquired in the mines didn't serve for anything in the army. In any case, it was never wise to admit to being a miner, because even though the army needed us to fill the ranks, the officers considered us their natural and eternal enemies. They thought that the miners, who led the revolution of 1952, also destroyed the army, which had only recently begun rebuilding due to U.S. pressure. They considered us communists and, therefore, enemies of all Bolivians. I was assigned to basic military training with the majority of the troops.

When we started they combined our group with recruits from Cochabamba, many of whom were taller and lighter-skinned and had been selected to stay with the Seventh Army so the division commanders could put them in the front ranks when we paraded. That way it didn't look as if the division was made up only of indigenous people. At first I thought they were the sons of professionals and that they spoke Spanish well. But as I got to know them, I realized that they were Quechuas, and mostly illiterate. I was surprised, because where I was raised only the doctors, lawyers, engineers, or schoolteachers were white or mestizo. The rest were darker and smaller indigenous Quechuas or Aymaras like me. When I asked where they came from, they answered the Cochabamba valley. But their parents, when they came to visit, looked just like the campesinos I knew in the altiplano. We questioned them, "How is this possible?" They explained that they came from haciendas, where the white landowners, or *hacendados*, had fathered many children with the women who worked on their land, a practice that only ended after the 1952 revolution. I was stunned to realize these blond campesinos were the illegitimate children of local landowners.

I was surprised by the way the military tried to indoctrinate us with anti-miner sentiments. They told us whenever we did something wrong,

"You're acting just like a miner!" The majority of my comrades from Oruro, who were miners, were stung by these comments. We never said anything, as we could have been punished: forced to run carrying three or four rifles, or made to sleep in a cell or bathroom without blankets. As the officers represented a specific class, they felt that it was okay to beat miners, and they turned on us with their fists, feet, or the butt of their guns. Sometimes officers would slander the great mining union leaders like Federico Escobar or Irineo Pimentel. They screamed at us, "You look like those communists Escobar and Pimentel."

They didn't limit their insults to the miners, but also denigrated indigenous people, whom they considered ugly and stupid and the root cause of the country's slow development. They hated *indios* [Indians] even more than us and treated them even worse. But their indoctrination was incomplete. There were always soldiers who refused to shoot the miners or peasants in confrontations, and sometimes these soldiers, instead, were killed by their own officers.

The hatred between the miners and the army had historical roots in the repeated massacres during the period before the 1952 revolution, when the country was run by the Tin Barons. When we saw the soldiers kill our people or shoot innocent civilians, it was as if we were at war. But in reality, these stories were things told to us by our parents, and not something we had experienced firsthand.

The first enemy we miners saw was the common soldier, not the person who gave him orders—whether that was a military commander or the President of the Republic. We felt the same about the police, because the police always acted hand in glove with the government. After nationalization, most conflicts involved the government, and when they couldn't win with simple arguments they turned to the police and the army to maintain order.

Even though the miners suffered at the hands of the military, we still loyally did our service. The world of the miners was very small, and few of us had a good sense of Bolivia as a nation. Soldiers who were sent to the mines to repress us always came from other parts of the country and didn't understand that we, the sons of miners, had been sent to other areas—maybe even their communities—to do the same to their families. The pressure to prove our manhood through military service was so strong that it overcame the hatred that miners or peasants had against the armed forces. But the *libreta*, the certificate that showed one had completed the compulsory military service, was even more important. With it, a young man could get a job in the mines or government, marry, or go to school. Without it, everything was more difficult.

The young soldier, 1964. From the private collection of Félix Muruchi.

THE MILITARY

Despite Bolivia's long history of military coups, its armed forces are technologically unsophisticated and relatively small in number compared to those of neighbors such as Chile and Peru. They total about thirty thousand troops, with the army serving as the largest unit (Gill 1997).

When the military fails to meet voluntary enlistment targets, it forcibly conscripts soldiers from rural areas and poor urban neighborhoods (CIA 2007). Most conscription is carried out in the countryside—currently, some 92 percent of the troops come from rural areas even though less than half the population lives there. Abuse of recruits has been widespread (U.S. Department of State 2003). Despite this, many young men, often under the age of eighteen, enlist voluntarily for the yearlong service, which has been seen as a rite of passage to adulthood since the 1952 revolution (Gill 1997). A significant inducement to serve is the preferential treatment they gain for a range of government jobs: in Félix's case, it allowed him to apply for a job in the mine.

Bolivia has lost over half of its territory to its neighbors since it declared itself a Republic in 1825, but over the past seventy years virtually no military threats have emanated from the five countries that border it. Rather, the Bolivian military has focused on the perceived internal threat created by its own citizens demanding social and economic justice. A popular saying notes that the only war the Bolivian army has ever won has been the war against its own people.

Because the armed forces have consistently backed elite interests against Bolivia's majority, one of the 1952 revolution's chief goals was to dismantle the military and replace it with local militias. Worried that the new government would embark on leftist policies, the United States made its future aid contingent on reconstructing the armed forces. The recurring economic crises of the 1950s convinced the new government that it had little choice but to acquiesce. Substantial U.S. assistance permitted the armed forces to rebuild rapidly, and in 1964, with the Barrientos coup d'état, they plunged the country into eighteen years of almost continuous military dictatorship. These regimes were conservative for the most part, although some of them expressed nationalist and populist inclinations (Dunkerley 1984).

The military governments did not dismantle the foundations of the 1952 revolution, leaving the nationalization of the mines and increased voting rights intact. Instead, they substantially increased patronage and crony capitalism. They pirated resources for themselves and allocated land (especially in the eastern lowlands), provided mineral concessions, and granted tax exemptions and credit to supporters and family.

General René Barrientos sprung a coup on November 4, 1964, against Víctor Paz Estenssoro in his third term as president. Barrientos, the sitting vice president, publicly insisted that he supported the 1952 revolution and merely sought to restore it to its "true path." In fact, he abolished all unions, curtailed the wage gains of miners and other workers, while privileging the private sector (Lora 1977). The reduction of miners' wages, combined with a surge in international tin prices, improved the economy, and COMIBOL realized its first profits ever in 1966. Barrientos's preferential treatment of the private sector facilitated the expansion of medium-sized private mines, along with foreign firms such as Gulf Oil, which was granted substantial petroleum and natural gas concessions.

Barrientos invested considerable time in consolidating his support among Bolivia's campesinos, mobilizing his considerable charisma and command of Quechua to convince them that he would never permit their return to semifeudal estates or loss of the other hard-won freedoms of the revolution. In exchange, they agreed to support the military, forging a "campesino-military pact" that subordinated the campesino militias formed during the revolution to army command. This arrangement infuriated the miners and others in the labor movement, who suffered a great deal under the dictatorship (Dunkerley 1984).

Félix's narrative about the 1964 elections reveals the complications in holding democratic elections in countries like Bolivia. As he describes, voter manipulation and fraud were endemic, and it would take more than a revolution such as the one in 1952 to overcome them. Because of the blatant fraud, combined with a history of elites that consistently jockeyed for power, the frequent conclusion of miners and campesinos that they had little option but to forcibly overthrow such regimes comes as no surprise.

The 1964 Elections

I voted twice for the same candidate in the 1964 national elections when I was in the army. Three days before the election, women from the Barsolas, the women's arm of the MNR, named after a woman mining leader who was killed in the 1942 Catavi massacre, registered us to vote and then gave us ballots for the MNR slate. They provided us false addresses and told us, "If there are any problems, and someone asks you where you voted, tell them you went to the polling station closest to your address." My comrades and I signed the book, and we all voted for the official presidential candidate, Víctor Paz Estenssoro. We cast ballots the second time on election day itself. In the morning the bugle sounded to form up the troops. An officer shouted, "Those of you who have civilian clothes can take the day off on the condition that when you come back you can prove that you voted. You already know who you are to vote for."

I dressed and hurried off to visit my sister Cristina, who lived near Vinto, twelve miles outside of Cochabamba on the road to La Paz. She and her husband moved there when he left the mines. They had a tiny store and a small piece of land—about one-quarter of an acre—where they planted carrots, beans, corn, and other vegetables. She had four children, but one died of diarrhea at the age of six.

When I arrived, she told me the authorities were checking house by house to ensure everyone voted. Soon after, they turned up at her door and accompanied us to the polling station in the main plaza. There was no pretense of a secret vote, and, in fact, the only ballots at the electoral table were those for the MNR, the official party. We signed the book, held up the ballot so the electoral judges could see it, and stuck it in the box. Then I put my little finger in the bottle of ink, staining it to prove that I had voted, which was the most important part of the exercise to me. The election observers were already half drunk, celebrating their triumph. Later we found out that Víctor Paz Estenssoro won 93 percent of the vote in the first round: a landslide. That night the officer on duty examined my finger. The soldiers who didn't vote, but just spent the day wandering around the city, were punished and forced to sleep in the bathrooms.

For me, voting wasn't an act of fulfilling a social obligation, but simply following orders. I felt used and manipulated. As a miner, I had my candidate; if given the chance, I would have voted for the head of the miners' union, Juan Lechín Oquendo, for president and for another important mining leader, Federico Escobar, for vice president.

The elections took place during the first phase of military training, which consisted of three things, the most important being the use of arms, whether a Mauser, machine gun, or mortar. We also learned to march for military parades and civic functions, and, of course, we engaged in physical training, which included acrobatics: building pyramids, learning to do somersaults, flips, and other gymnastic moves.

We had one opportunity to display our skills during a daylong event in which we swore our allegiance to the nation and the flag. We formed into ranks very early, and they kept us there all day long, with no food and not even the chance to use the bathroom. It was ironic that after this symbolic civic event a number of soldiers returned to the barracks having wet themselves, as they had been refused the basic right to urinate.

Military Life

After I finished the first phase of military training, I was assigned to supervise the kitchen and food preparation for the troops. One day I was asked to bring a sample of the food to a visiting commander. Our breakfast consisted of *sultana*, a drink made from the shells of coffee beans, and a piece of bread. The commander was surprised to see how small the bread was; it was a little over five ounces. He asked me if that was what we had been giving to the soldiers, and I responded affirmatively. He then said the *pan de batalla* [standard bread] should be about eight ounces, and he made me sign a statement about the size of the bread. One morning the next week I was surprised to see the bread was larger than before. I later learned that the base's commander had been stealing wheat and selling it, and, because of my statement, he had been suspended. For me this demonstrated military honor on the one hand and military corruption, which was much more common, on the other.

In October 1964 we were ordered to prepare to reinforce the Camacho regiment, who were in a confrontation with the miners of Siglo XX and Huanuni on the plains of Sora Sora, outside of Oruro. The miners were fighting because they felt that the MNR had betrayed the 1952 revolution. The order was rescinded, however, when the officers realized our regiment was composed primarily of miners. The officers feared a mutiny if soldiers were ordered to fire on fellow miners who might be our relatives.

The clash between the military and miners and peasants in Sora Sora ended in a massacre at the hands of troops from the Oruro regiment. Dozens of peasants and miners, along with four soldiers, originally from Cochabamba, were killed in the worst confrontation since the revolution. They brought the soldiers' bodies back to the Seventh Army Division base to hold the wake. When the mothers of the slain soldiers saw their children's bodies, they attacked the commander of the guard on duty, pummeling him with their fists, screaming, and blaming him for their sons' deaths. Although it was a painful moment, I felt some degree of satisfaction, because at least someone was speaking the truth directly to military personnel.

The Barrientos Coup, November 1964

Tension in the country had grown steadily since the fraudulent election of June, and the massacre at Sora Sora set the stage for the military coup. The army had lost any faith in the civilian government, which was incapable of maintaining the peace. The third of November we were scheduled to be discharged. We had turned in our guns and our bags were packed when the base commander suspended our discharge and returned our weapons.

The very next day, commanders from all over the country descended on our base to plan the coup d'état that would propel Bolivia into eighteen years of military rule. General René Barrientos Ortuño, the sitting vice president, as well as the godson by marriage of President Víctor Paz Estenssoro, was the instigator of the coup. That day I was assigned to stand watch outside the commanders' meeting. When it was over, they had reached consensus to support the coup. Foreign officers participated: I think there was a uniformed group from Argentina, and others, including a group I thought were gringos.

When the commanders first entered the meeting room, I tried to guard the door from the inside, as I was curious about what was going on. But they kicked me out, and I couldn't hear anything from my post in the hallway. After the meeting, we were ordered to hold our base's colonel in an office for several hours, as he apparently was not willing to support the rebels. I don't know what happened to him, but I suppose that after he realized the coup was inevitable, he decided to join in, but even so, shortly after he was replaced by another colonel. This experience taught me that the military was not monolithic and that it suffered from internal conflicts. I understood that when an institution takes a public stand, it is not something spontaneous, but rather the result of infighting and negotiation.

By that point, the majority of Bolivian citizens were completely disenchanted with the twelve-year-long MNR government, which hadn't achieved much change even though it had taken a revolution to put it into power. It had roundly failed to deepen the revolution or improve life for the majority. Campesinos were anticipating that the 1953 Agrarian Reform would be applied more broadly to the entire country, and that hadn't happened. Miners had seen very few improvements. In the cities, people were also frustrated. For all of these reasons, many people supported the coup.

Some of the people who had been defeated in 1952, including right-wingers, conservative factions of the military, and other rich people, reorganized to reclaim the property, power, and position they had lost during the revolution. These factions always waved and saluted us as we marched by, saying how good it was that the military was assuming power. Some people, mostly from the upper middle class, including representatives of fascist student groups, visited the base to express their support. In some cases they even accompanied us on our patrols through the city and joined in when it came time to beat a crowd into submission or arrest protesters.

As common soldiers, we were primarily responsible for maintaining a security perimeter when we were sent into poor neighborhoods. The officers carried out the actual operations, as they were more committed to the army and had greater responsibilities. They usually asked the tallest soldiers to follow them as they moved through a neighborhood, taking prisoners and beating up others who resisted. Most soldiers would not do very much, but there was always one or another who took to the task with relish, and I and the other soldiers hated them for it.

One day a soldier—I think he was a miner from Colquiri—walked through a group of prisoners kicking them, just like he would if he were an officer. At that moment we couldn't do anything to control him. Later, when things calmed down, we returned to the base, and he bragged how proud he was of what he had done. We were furious. "How could you have behaved so badly?" we shouted. Then a group of us who hadn't followed the repressive orders pulled him aside and beat him fiercely with the same rage he displayed toward the campesinos.

They sent us to the Valle Alto [upper valley] region of Cochabamba, which included the villages of Punata, Tarata, and Cliza, as General Barrientos sought to pacify the area by encouraging campesino leaders to come to terms with the new government. About a month after the coup we went to Punata, which had long been a stronghold of MNR support, to establish control before Barrientos arrived. Many campesinos there still had their arms from the 1952 revolution and were actively mounting resistance to the new government. They formed peasant militias, with their own military bases under the banner of the campesino unions. The campesinos fired on us, leaving several wounded, and almost daily we struggled to control the area by capturing campesino union leaders, members of the MNR, and communists. When we picked someone up we transported him back to the municipal building in Punata for interrogation.

To most of us, the majority miners, our role in the military was becoming increasingly clear: it was to protect the interests of the army, not the country. Sometimes we even made jokes about it. Before, I perceived the army as a single entity, but I was learning to distinguish between the soldiers, who were there because they lacked options, and the commanders, who earned a lot of money and used the military to pursue their own personal interests with the support of a small national elite.

But we still had to defend ourselves if we were surrounded by angry campesinos, even though we didn't support the coup. I was clear, "If they attack, we've got to fight back. There is nothing else we can do." At one point I was assigned to guard Barrientos's large and beautiful house in Cala Cala, a wealthy neighborhood in Cochabamba. One night—I can't remember if we were really attacked or if it was simply part of a training exercise—we heard gunshots, so we fired back in self-defense.

Sometimes campesinos came to the base to ask for help or to report communists in their towns. They told officials, "A group of armed campesinos have gotten together" or "there is a stash of guns in [such and such a place]." They revealed this expecting to get some payment from the officers. But if we got there and found nothing, the officers became enraged. They'd yell, "For having lied, you're under arrest." But they only held these informants for a couple of hours before releasing them.

In Punata, the unrest continued. Gregorio López was the principal campesino leader detained. As I was assigned to guard him, I brought him a soft drink, and he told me that the only reason he was being held was because he was a campesino leader. They called him Muruloq'o, which means the man with the old or deformed hat. When his wife and daughters, who all wore *polleras* [traditional skirts with multiple petticoats], visited him, we found a revolver hidden in one of his daughters' wide skirts. Once he heard this, Barrientos hurried off to talk with Muruloq'o in his cell, realizing this was a man not to be trifled with.

I think they must have paid him a lot of money, for after he met with Barrientos, Muruloq'o called for a meeting in the principal plaza of Punata. Hundreds of campesinos spilled out on the surrounding streets. Someone had to pay for their transport, their food, and *chicha*. Barrientos spoke in Quechua to the crowd and, with Muruloq'o at his side, was able to convince many campesinos to support the dictatorship.

At one point Muruloq'o addressed the general in front of the crowd. I remember his words to this day, because they foretold the pact that would be formed between the military and the campesinos. "My general, you need to have faith in the campesino *compañeros* [comrades], because we are more responsible than the university students who support you now but who will turn on you tomorrow." His words sent a chill through me, because I realized how some people can change from one day to the next. In effect, he was handing over a whole mass of people to General Barrientos. It showed me the importance of the union leader's role and the possibility of betrayal when social control from below is lacking. Sad to say, this situation has not changed much in Bolivia. Too many leaders look out only for their own personal interests.

The same thing happened in Cliza, in Quillacollo, and in other places as well. Barrientos first spoke with local leaders and then cemented the relationship on a more personal level. I remember once in Cliza, after he'd spoken in the main plaza, he went for lunch with the local campesino leaders. Afterwards he disappeared into a back room with the daughter of one leader to enjoy his "dessert" for half an hour while his entourage waited outside. The same thing happened in other towns as well. I later learned that Barrientos commonly demanded that a young *cholita* [indigenous woman] should be waiting for him wherever he traveled. When he died, the general had dozens of children whom he'd recognized legally, and at his funeral many of his "widows," as the newspapers referred to these women, were in attendance.

It took a month for the new government to stabilize the situation, because some degree of resistance from miners and campesinos and members of the MNR continued. Gradually party members decided to come to terms with the new government, so they could ensure that the military wouldn't harm them.

PART TWO

The Mines

Introduction: Life in the Nationalized Mines

After the 1952 revolution, the huge Catavi–Siglo XX mining complex located near Llallagua, some two hundred miles south of La Paz, quickly became COMIBOL's largest operation, just as it had been for Simón Patiño. The ratio of dependents to miners was very high—about 4.5:1—reflected in the large families like that of Félix, whose parents had thirteen children, eight of whom survived beyond infancy. Wages in the mid-1960s amounted to about eighty cents a day, supplemented by subsidized foodstuffs at the company stores (*pulperías*).

Work underground was organized hierarchically, with the driller—whose equipment weighed as much as 150 pounds—holding the highest status. Miners' daily lives were shaped by the knowledge that death or serious injury was just one misstep away. Even the lucky miner faced inevitable death from black lung. Miners usually died before they were forty—leaving their widows and orphans without means of support. This reality was often dulled by the consumption of alcohol, leading to rampant alcoholism, at an estimated incidence of over 50 percent of the male population. It contributed directly to frequent physical abuse of women and children and indirectly to increased malnutrition, as resources for food, medicine, or clothing were spent on drink. A more constructive way to cope was to immerse oneself in the deep-seated tradition of collective resistance and struggle for better wages and conditions (Nash 1993).

Not only was mining incredibly dangerous, but life in the settlements was far from easy. In the 1960s, a company doctor reported that 40 percent of children were badly undernourished and that 15 percent of all babies died before they were one year old (Gall 1974b). Families were crowded into tiny unheated houses, often having to share with another family, as Félix's family did when he was young. Everything had to fit in one room crammed with two to three beds for six to eight people. Most kitchens were outdoors on the small porch.

With a large number of children, water supplied by a neighborhood tap, and bathrooms in overcrowded communal latrines, women led lives shaped by domestic chores. They spent long hours chatting together as they lined up at the *pulpería* every other day waiting to pick up subsidized food, the only way to ensure a single check came close to buying enough to feed the family. Caloric intake was generally less than what is required for healthy lives (Nash 1993).

COMIBOL schools were better than other state schools, but even a poor state school was out of reach for much of the rural population. Nonetheless, miners' children were frequently packed seventy-five to a small classroom, with some sitting on the floor and few with books.

Within this often desperate world, miners and their families forged a subculture with deep bonds to their community and their union, the Federation of Bolivian Miners' Unions (Federación Sindical de Trabajadores Mineros de Bolivia—FSTMB—commonly referred to as the Miners' Federation). By 1961, women had formed a Housewives Committee of Siglo XX (Comité de Amas de Casa de Siglo XX), which played an important role in increasing pressure on COMIBOL for better conditions, and in strengthening the FSTMB. Their contribution often went unacknowledged, however, due to the strong machismo of both miners and their representatives.

Left-wing political parties heralded the miners' union as the vanguard of Bolivia's proletariat, and played an important role in fostering a sophisticated class consciousness among miners. But indigenous rituals also held a central role in their lives, and before 1952 were used by owners attempting to make them more compliant. Miners made regular offerings (*ch'allas* and *k'araukus*) to the god of the mines, known most commonly as the Tío, but also as Huari or Supay, to ensure his continued benevolence. As left-wing parties and the union gained prominence, these ancient rituals played a critical role in reinforcing class consciousness (Nash 1993).

By the mid-1960s almost five hundred miles of tunnels pockmarked the inside of the Siglo XX mine, but the average grade of ore had dropped significantly. What remained was steadily removed by the "block caving" method of blasting low-grade masses of mineralized rock, allowing the extraction of greater volumes with far less manpower. The addition of a "sink and float" concentrating plant raised the mineral content of ore entering the mill, contributing to COMIBOL's profits when tin prices rose between 1965 and 1975. When tin prices dipped after the Vietnam War, COMIBOL lost money once again.

For decades after the 1952 revolution, COMIBOL's share of national production dropped steadily, as new initiatives in mining—for lead, zinc, gold, and silver—were all in private hands. Three companies dominated from the 1960s on: COMSUR (largely owned by two-time president Sánchez de Lozada until 2005), EMUSA, and International Mining, which together accounted for about 75 percent of total production. The remaining 25 percent was produced by cooperative mines, generally small, rudimentary, often family-run operations. Much of this production leaves the country as contraband through Brazil, providing the government no tax revenue at all.

Chapter 4

Joining the State Company

Getting a Job

Once the new government gained control of the Valle Alto [Cochabamba's upper valley], my discharge papers arrived, and I headed home. I was happy to leave the barracks. Military service had allowed me to learn a little bit more about the world outside the mine. Both in my own eyes and those of the community, I was now an adult.

Before joining the army, I had kept up contact with my family's communities, and when I went to fiestas there, I met people of my age who had already completed their military service. They had always looked at me and my friends as if we were still children. Sometimes we saw old men who hadn't served when they were young, and people always made fun of them. Just knowing I would never suffer such treatment made me feel good, and I returned home with my head held high.

With my new maturity came a new attitude toward work. I no longer wanted to labor as a *juk'u* or even for a *venerista*, because I realized that formal work in the state company was much better. I had seen other ways of life and was determined to move up in the world. And I had the essential prerequisite for a state job, which was the military service booklet.

Workers in Siglo XX were hired through the union, so I went off to speak to Don Gilberto Bernal, the permanent secretary. "Yes, we are signing people up, but you need to make the arrangements with *compañero* Federico Escobar, the worker control representative," he said, pointing to a nearby door. This reflected that a certain level of worker control still existed in the mine despite the Barrientos coup.

At that time, the MNR and the Catholic Church had joined forces to keep the communists from fully controlling the union. Irineo Pimentel, the general secretary, had their support, and it was no secret that he was there to contest power with Federico Escobar. To reduce tensions and infighting,

Mining union march when Federico returned, 1961. From the private collection of Félix Muruchi.

Federico invited Pimentel, who had a separate but adjoining office, to combine efforts. One concrete measure of their collaboration was that they cut a hole in the wall connecting their offices, which served to increase symbolic, as much as material, cooperation. However, each maintained his own list of unemployed workers, which allowed them to build separate bases of support within the union. I first went to Gilberto Bernal, as I knew that he worked with Escobar, who I thought better represented miners' interests and who I knew was more popular than Pimentel.

At Escobar's office, six men were seated in a line of chairs against the wall waiting their turn to talk to him. I listened curiously as the workers asked for advice or support on work or family problems, and Escobar paid careful attention to their entreaties, answering each one with authority and confidence. When my turn came, I enthusiastically blurted, "I want you to add my name to the list of miners looking for work."

He just stared at me. "I'm sorry. We're not signing anyone else up because there simply isn't enough work. Besides, you're young, not like the other *compañero* who was just here," he said, pointing to an empty chair. "He has six children, so his needs are clearly greater. We have to find him work first."

I stood there, dumbfounded and fixed on the spot, because it never occurred to me he would refuse my request. I plaintively responded, "But I've just completed my military service." Something in my manner affected Escobar, and he looked at me long and hard. Then he picked up a piece of paper, where he wrote down my name and said, "Take this to the secretary, she'll add your name to the list."

There were about 640 people ahead of me, but because I lived at home and my father supported me, I had lots of time to go to the union hall every day, where, with 500 other unemployed men, I waited patiently for the newest list to be posted. Even though I realized I would not be hired immediately, I had to show up every day. If I missed a roll call, they dropped my name to the bottom. For two months, I showed up five days a week, first in the morning and again in the afternoon.

One day *compañero* Escobar announced, "All those who are unemployed should organize themselves to travel to the COMIBOL offices in La Paz and demand work. We'll take you in one of the company trucks." After naming a commission of six representatives to negotiate with the company, we set off the next day in one of those huge British Leyland trucks they use for hauling mineral. Many of the men weren't able to get ready in time, so in the end only 320 of us traveled to La Paz. I had already moved halfway up the list.

MINERS' UNION

Bolivian miners have always resisted their exploitation. As far back as 1923, the dense crowding in the camps provided fertile ground for organizing efforts. But repeated repression and massacres of hundreds of workers meant that the union— the FSTMB—was not recognized until 1944.

Juan Lechín Oquendo, a machinist, a star soccer player in the miners' league, and then a member of Bolivia's sizeable Trotskyist party, the Revolutionary Workers' Party (Partido Obrero Revolucionario, or POR), assumed the leadership of the Federation, a post he held for forty-three years. In 1946, the FSTMB adopted the Pulacayo Thesis, promoted by the POR, which closely followed Leon Trotksy's guidelines for a worker-led revolutionary government.

The FSTMB played a defining role in the 1952 revolution, which, along with revolutions in Mexico and Cuba, was one of Latin America's most profound. The FSTMB spearheaded the consolidation of what would become a formidable labor confederation—the Bolivian Workers Central (Central Obrera Boliviana, or COB).

The COB forced the new middle-class government to make good on its promises to nationalize the Tin Barons' mines. As part of a cogovernment deal between the COB and the government, Juan Lechín assumed one of five worker-controlled posts as the mining minister and shifted his loyalties to the MNR. He later served as Bolivia's vice president in 1960 before abandoning the party in disgust at its right-wing drift and forming the Revolutionary Party of the Nationalist Left (Partido Revolucionario de la Izquierda Nacional, or PRIN).

A system of worker control (*control obrero*), designed to grant union representatives some degree of veto power over management decisions in state-owned enterprises, was introduced by presidential decree in 1953 and took root unevenly in the mines between 1955 and 1963, functioning most successfully at Siglo XX (Gall 1974b). While the Office of Worker Control exercised a watchdog role over COMIBOL funds, its representatives had no participation in decision making, and only one union representative served on each local management board. Attempts to extend the system to other sectors failed.

We arrived after hours on the road, dusty and tired, at the headquarters of the Miners' Federation in La Paz, and we camped out in the large meeting room, which gave it the appearance of a military encampment as we spread our bedrolls on the floor. I remember sitting in the room studying two murals by Miguel Alandia Pantoja, a famous Bolivian artist. The paintings, ten to fifteen feet high and twenty to twenty-five feet long, portrayed the struggles of the miners before the 1952 revolution. Unfortunately, they were destroyed after the 1980 coup of Luis García Meza.

The day after we arrived, Juan Lechín, the head of the Federation, met with us. We immediately told him that we had decided to undertake a hunger strike if we were not given jobs. In the early 1960s, the Housewives Committee of La Paz had used hunger strikes with some success, and by the middle of the decade they were incorporated into social movement strategies. Lechín looked us up and down and commented, "You must be the group that Escobar sent. I'm sure Pimentel will send his own group shortly, but we'll arrange a meeting for you with the president of COMIBOL."

After Lechín left, leaders of the local unemployed workers' union showed up and told us that if we wanted to find work, we had to join their federation, which would cost us five pesos per person. They were all very well dressed in suits and ties; we stared at them in disbelief and responded, "Why should we join your union? Our problem is far more urgent than yours. Even if you are unemployed, you obviously still receive some income from your union, and so you can hold out longer." We couldn't figure out any reason to join, as our union was based in Siglo XX, not La Paz. We figured they just wanted to collect five pesos from each of us.

While this was the first time I had come to La Paz, I didn't have any chance to see the city. Every day we were busy in meetings, being interviewed, or filling out forms required both by the union and COMIBOL. After three days, we were summoned to a meeting in the COMIBOL offices. The building had been owned by Patiño before the 1952 revolution and was the fanciest structure in La Paz. The main entrance was built in polished black granite, with beautifully detailed revolving doors. We walked through the lobby, which was completely done up in marble, and it seemed that we were the only people who weren't dressed in suits and ties, but there were enough of us that I didn't feel out of place. The meeting was held in the wood-paneled auditorium on the third floor, and even though more than 300 of us filed into the room, there was space for more. When we were seated, the president of COMIBOL, Lechín, and other mining leaders took the stage, and the president announced a plan to survey and sample Siglo XX. He said this new project would allow him to hire 390 additional workers.

We were overjoyed, and with agreement in hand, we returned to Catavi in the back of the truck, standing squeezed together for the freezing twelve-hour trip. But we neither got tired nor felt the cold, because we were so excited that we had won the right to work. A couple of days later, they posted the list of those of us who had been hired. The first fifty names included the neediest men with families and children to support, and young, single men like me were down at the bottom. But they systematically went through the entire list, and, after a few months, on April 15, 1965, I started work as a miner.

Life in the Mining Town

The entire area was brimming with minerals, and there were tin mines not just in Siglo XX, but also in Uncía and Catavi, where the company's main administrative offices were located. The Siglo XX mining district was divided into two sectors: the camp and company administration, and the mine itself. The city of Llallagua bordered the mining camp. Together, they comprised the combined metropolitan area of Siglo XX–Llallagua, which at that time had about 120,000 inhabitants. Some 5,000 families lived in Siglo XX, each with an average of five children, so about 35,000 people in all. My family lived in the Salvadora Camp, a half-mile from the principal mine entrance of the Siglo XX mine, at an altitude of 12,200 feet above sea level.

Siglo XX

Norman Gall, an American political scientist, wrote a vivid description of Siglo XX in the mid-1960s that we have excerpted here:

The Siglo XX (Twentieth Century) tin mine is cradled among sullen, rusted hills that rise from the altiplano—the highland desert of scrub and stone. . . . [The road runs] through the mining camps themselves: steep, gullied streets threading a mass of decayed adobe warrens with corrugated metal roofs that glisten in the altiplano sun and are loaded with stones so the wind won't blow them away. It passes the old concrete movie house that is poised like a Greek temple at the edge of a precipice, overlooking the ramshackle structure of the "Sink-and-Float" pre-concentrating [sic] plant next to the mountainous gray-green dumps of waste rock that bear witness to 70 years of continuous extraction.

The road finally dissolves into the Plaza del Minero, the center of communal life at the mine. [It] is dominated by the heroic statue of a bare-chested, helmeted miner raising a rifle aloft in his right hand while pressing a pneumatic drill into the ground with his left. The statue commemorates Bolivia's 1952 Revolution, but its bold, angular lines point merely to a three-story concrete facade painted with a riot of rival political slogans: the headquarters of the miners' *sindicato*.

All the installations in sight were built before the mines were nationalized in the Bolivian revolution of 1952, save for the union headquarters, the only permanent building on the plaza, its facade . . . pocked with bullet marks. The windows are still broken from last September's battle [1965], in which some 50 miners, soldiers and policemen were killed and more than 100 were wounded.

[A] small army of boys gather each afternoon around a huge rack of comic books—Spanish translations of Superman, Batman, and Donald Duck—displayed beneath the communist posters adorning the *sindicato* headquarters and rented for a penny a half-hour. Many of the unemployed wander into an old, concrete movie house where the admission charge is two cents—like nearly everything else here dating back to the Patiño days. . . .

Bowler-hatted Indian women sell ice cream, cotton candy, and glasses of *chicha* next to the miner's statue. Near the market stalls across the plaza there is a constant flow of altiplano Indians in dusty ponchos and floppy sheepskin hats who bring potatoes and firewood on clusters of llamas to sell at the miners' houses. These Indians gradually melt into the mining community—as porters in the marketplace and peons in the marginal workings greatly swelling the local population. (Gall 1966; used with permission)

The settlement was called Salvadora, because when Simón Patiño, the first Tin Baron, was just putting the mine into production, the principal vein abruptly disappeared. Patiño was desperate, on the verge of abandoning the mine and returning to Oruro bankrupt. According to popular legend, late one night he descended into the mine and forged a pact with the Tío, the god of the mine interior. An enormous vein suddenly appeared before his eyes, larger than had ever been found, and it was called La Salvadora. With the increase in demand for labor to work the new vein, an additional neighborhood was built, which was baptized Salvadora as well.

Approximately 1,700 people crowded into the settlement in small adobe houses, each one about 650 square feet, divided into a 13-by-16-foot living room, a 6.5-by-10-foot bedroom, a 6.5-by-6.5-foot kitchen, plus a small patio. This was considered an adequate house for a family with eight children. Families with only three or four children had even smaller houses. Electricity switched on only at night and for an hour at midday. There was no indoor plumbing or sewer system. The entire settlement had only one latrine, with twelve compartments for men and an equal number for women, which was located about two hundred yards from my house. Two public taps served the entire settlement, one of which was one hundred yards from our house. To fill canisters with water, generally we had to wait in line for about five minutes.

We bought our food from the *pulpería*, which was a kind of supermarket only for mine workers. Four items were subsidized: rice, sugar, bread, and meat. Other articles like vegetables and clothes were sold at market prices. It wasn't necessary to pay in cash; if there was a mine worker in the household, the family was registered with the store, but each worker's family could only shop every other day.

The worker's wife was responsible for stocking the house and taking care of the children. My mother usually got up at four in the morning to prepare food for my father before he left for the mine. When I began working, she did the same for me. On Tuesdays, Thursdays, and Saturdays, right after we headed out the door, she hurried to the company store to stand in the long queue for the necessities, finally returning at midday. She spent half the morning in separate lines for bread, meat, rice, and sugar. While she was out shopping for food, the older siblings helped the younger ones to prepare for school.

In the bedroom, we shared three beds. My parents had their own; the children slept two, three, or even four to a bed in the other two. Because the house lacked a proper ceiling, and just had a tin roof, it was tremendously cold, so aside from being a necessity, sleeping together kept us warm.

Military Occupation of the Mine

About a month and a half after I started work, General Barrientos launched his political assault on workers, directing his ire principally at the miners. On May 7, 1965, the government decreed a new Mining Code, which undermined the gains of the 1952 revolution. Its principal objective was to privatize the state mining company, and the union with its combative leadership presented the most substantial obstacle. The transnational companies imposed this measure on the country so that they could improve their access to new mining concessions. With this law, the reprivatization of our national wealth began. It also heralded the formal creation of mining cooperatives.

The government immediately ordered massive firings of miners, and particularly union leaders. Officials first lowered salaries by 25 percent and deployed both legal and physical force to confront protesters. The government recalled all recently discharged soldiers to active duty. Faced with the high probability of a bloody massacre, mining leaders had little choice but to flee into exile, most of them to Argentina. Federico Escobar escaped to Chile, and others stayed in the country, but hid underground. In some cases they escaped to their communities of origin in the countryside.

Some weeks later, in July, *compañero* César Lora, a well-known union leader, was assassinated. He was a high-ranking leader in the Revolutionary Workers' Party (Partido Obrero Revolucionario, or POR) who worked in the Beza section inside the mine. He was brother to Guillermo Lora, a great national intellectual. Another *compañero*, Ribota, was also murdered, and his body was later found with signs that he had been tortured.

By September we could no longer tolerate the constant abuse of the national police. The government justified the increased police presence as aimed at controlling the *jukeo* and declared a state of siege in the mines, arresting people for no obvious reason. Sometimes the police accused those who were being jailed of being *juk'us* when they weren't. And sometimes as we left the mine entrance, they checked us over for contraband mineral.

On Saturday night, September 19, 1965, a confrontation erupted between police and students at the secondary school where I studied at night while working in the mines during the day. When we left school at 11 p.m., the police refused us passage through the main plaza of Llallagua—most of us lived on the far side of the plaza in the mining camps of Siglo XX. We were exhausted—many of us had worked all day and then gone to study in the evening, and not going through the plaza meant a far longer walk home. Despite our exhaustion, this infuriated us, and we started to hurl rocks at the police, who reacted by setting off tear gas and firing their guns. We rapidly retreated, but several students were arrested and others wounded. This made the miners, both students and nonstudents, even angrier, and we decided to take to the streets again on Monday, even though it was clear that the military was trying to provoke a confrontation to justify their occupation of the mines.

The media called us communist agitators, and government officials proclaimed it was their duty to remove the troublemakers to ensure public safety, so they sought to install handpicked union leaders who would represent state rather than worker interests. They arrested three principal leaders—Filemón Escobar, another leader whose name I don't remember, and Isaac Camacho, who disappeared in 1967 and was assassinated. His remains were never recovered.

On Monday, September 21, 1965 [National Students' Day in Bolivia], we learned, as we were heading off to work, that as many as 200 workers had been pulled out of their houses, arrested, and some even shot and killed. We were enraged rather than frightened. We organized emergency meetings in every section inside the mine and announced a walkout to demand freedom for the detained union leaders and workers. Several family members of those arrested told us that the prisoners were being held at the police station. We decided to march there, but before we took to the streets we raided the warehouse where dynamite for underground blasting is stored. The aboveground workers joined the 1,200 underground miners. We were close to 3,000 strikers in all.

We all had sticks of dynamite strung across our chests like old-fashioned cartridge belts as we marched together to the Miners' Plaza. But suddenly we realized that almost all our leaders had been arrested, and so we had no one to address the crowd. We were accustomed to having a leader direct the assembly, and so no one dared speak and, honestly, no one had the skills to forcefully address the crowd either. Finally we convinced *compañero* Vargas to lead the meeting. Of course, he didn't have the oratory power of our leaders, and instead gave a simple talk about our arrested comrades in the jail. The assembly demanded they be freed by noon. Meanwhile, groups of strikers surrounded the police station. My section was assigned to the west part of the jail. The younger students were responsible for keeping us informed about the ongoing negotiations. At noon the police still refused to meet our demands, and in fact, we discovered that the prisoners had been moved to Oruro.

We had agreed that if we couldn't free the prisoners, we would attack and break the military's siege. There was no lack of people willing to initiate the offensive against the police, who by then had climbed on the roof of the jail to better control the area. One of my comrades set off a stick of dynamite near the city hall, and the police, more out of fright than anything else, I think, began to fire.

We only had dynamite against the rifles, machine guns, and grenades of the police, but our numbers gave us an advantage. I felt all fired up that this was our chance to free the prisoners. We had a great sense that we were right in our demands, and this, along with our superior numbers, and the feeling that we were braver than the police, gave us the strength to attack the jail even though we were largely unarmed. The immediate goal was to wrest guns away from the police so we could arm ourselves and engage in a more equal combat.

As miners, we were accustomed to danger, as we lived under an indeterminate death sentence: the only question was whether we would die in a mining accident or live long enough to fall victim to the slow drowning of black lung. So we confronted the police fueled by rage and without fear. In retrospect, perhaps we were not conscious of what we were going up against; however, in the heat of the moment, and with the knowledge that we were part of a group of 3,000 fighting for our brothers' freedom, we advanced. We simply did not consider the consequences.

We were steadily closing in on the jail, forcing the police to retreat, when I realized that shots were raining down from the hillsides. We had been surrounded by the army, who were attacking us from behind. At just this moment, I felt a sharp sting in my left buttock, and then wetness from blood flowing down my leg. I think it was probably a piece of a grenade that hit me. I gradually backed out of the combat in the direction of the river and headed home as quickly as I could by way of the Río Seco (Dry River), the only place out of sight of the army. At that moment I was not so much worried about the wound, which turned out not to be serious, but rather about the brutal massacre that was about to take place.

My poor mother was horribly frightened by the nearby sounds of battle and was enormously relieved to see me. So as not to worry her more, I didn't tell her about my wound and instead headed to one of my cousin's houses. He was a nurse, and he expertly bandaged me up. A bit later, and much more relaxed, I returned home.

During the course of the afternoon, the company, with police support, forcibly evicted a group of workers from a Patiño-era army barracks that had been turned into informal housing. They quickly loaded the miners, along with their few belongings, into trucks and hauled them off to schools and other locations. About five o'clock, along with a newly arrived contingent of soldiers, prisoners from the confrontation, with their hands behind their heads, were forced into the now-vacant barracks.

Military units, originally from Santa Cruz, who had landed at the Uncía airport before attacking us from behind, were the ones who transported the prisoners. The event, which left more than thirty people dead and hundreds wounded, including miners and police, was called the September Massacre. Many of the prisoners were detained in the district and others moved to Oruro. This was the beginning of constant military occupations of the mine. Once they began, no one had any desire to work, and so repeated radio announcements demanded that we go back. For three days we held out, but eventually we had little choice but to return into the mines when the company threatened to fire anyone who didn't show up.

Chapter 5

Union Activist

THE COB

The Siglo XX mine and Llallagua served as the crucible for the revolutionary politics that characterized much of Bolivia's social movements during the twentieth century. Félix's story is at the heart of the struggle of organized miners at Siglo XX for better wages and conditions, which provided the spark for resistance to exploitation all over Bolivia and underpins the militant social movements of today.

For thirty-five years after it was founded in 1952, the Bolivian Workers Central (Central Obrera Boliviana, or COB), under the leadership of Siglo XX machinist Juan Lechín, embodied the aspirations of Bolivia's poor and working classes. At first it served as a counterbalance to the state, defending the interests of those who had fought during the 1952 revolution for structural changes. It cogoverned in a minority position with the MNR until 1956, successfully advocating the revolution's most radical changes and blocking conservative government initiatives.

Unlike labor movements in most countries, the COB played a role in Bolivia extending far beyond mere work-related issues despite frequently fractious internal divisions related both to politics and to turf. The COB successfully fused demands for labor rights with the struggle for civil and social rights (Dunkerley 1984). Its statutes provided that the miners—considered by Marxist ideology to be the vanguard of the working class—should always lead the organization. This made the Federation of Bolivian Miners' Unions (FSTMB) inordinately powerful.

Within the miners' union, several left political parties vied for control, including the MNR, which had led the 1952 revolution, and the Trotskyist Revolutionary Workers' Party (Partido Revolucionario Obrero, or POR), formed during the 1940s. The Bolivian Communist Party (Partido Comunista de Bolivia, or PCB), founded in 1950, was initially far less important largely because the Soviet Union, which supported many communist parties around the world, neglected Bolivia until the 1960s, when it made significant inroads both in the FSTMB and the COB and the POR declined in importance (Alexander and Parker 2005).

By 1964, increasingly frustrated with the PCB's domination by urban in-tellectuals and the proclivity of other left parties to form opportunistic electoral alliances with conservatives, several mining leaders in Siglo XX joined the fledgling Marxist-Leninist Communist Party (Partido Comunista Marxista-Leninista, or PCML). Its head, Federico Escobar, was an influential union figure who held the controversial and influential post in charge of Control Obrero (Worker Control). He died mysteriously in 1966 after being transported to La Paz for medical treatment. After his death, a statue of him was erected in the Miners' Plaza in the center of Llallagua in the pose he was best known for: delivering an impassioned speech to his fellow miners. After Escobar's death, the PCML allied with Chinese Maoists, and its members were identified as *chinos* (Chinese), in contrast to the PCB, whose strong ties with the Russian Communist Party led its members to be called *rusos* (Russians).

At no point were the differences and infighting among the various left parties more pronounced than during the events that led up to the death of Ernesto "Che" Guevara in 1967. Che arrived in Bolivia with the hope of sparking a continental uprising. While publicly welcomed by the PCB, his virtually unannounced launching of guerrilla warfare in eastern Bolivia was resented by the party, which insisted that a revolution in the country must be led by Bolivians. Sectarian differences meant the PCB blocked the assistance offered by Félix's party, the PCML, although a few people did abandon the mines to fight with the tiny guerrilla force. For his part, Che Guevara, despite his differences with Moscow, was only willing to work through pro-Russia parties and never fully grasped the depth of nationalist sentiment entrenched in parties like the PCB throughout Latin America (Anderson 1997).

During this entire time, Bolivia suffered under the military dictatorship initiated by the 1964 coup that effectively brought the country's revolutionary experiment to an end. General René Barrientos legitimized his rule in a 1966 presidential election, winning 63 percent of the vote with backing from conservative politicians, businessmen, and campesinos, who threw in their lot with the generals to guarantee they would not be forced back into semislavery on private estates.

Barrientos's newfound legitimacy emboldened him to increase the intensity of his assault against labor, which had begun with the 1965 Mining Code. By 1966, Barrientos had cut the workforce, abolished *control obrero*, and installed a military officer as COMIBOL's director. Miners' militias were disarmed, union leaders forced into exile, and strikes forbidden. Military occupation of the mines occurred with regularity. The most brutal took place in 1967 during celebrations of Noche de San Juan (San Juan Night), June 24, when giant bonfires are built throughout the highlands to heat the Pachamama (Earth Mother) on the year's coldest night. Barrientos's troops' bloody invasion of Siglo XX mine and the mining camps caused the largest massacre in Bolivian history.

But despite the repression, Barrientos could not completely silence the labor movement, and miners stood at the forefront of the growing opposition. Mobilizing around a recurrent sore spot among Bolivian radicals, the miners were particularly outraged by his proposal to sell natural resources under favorable terms to foreign firms.

By the time Barrientos died in a helicopter crash in 1969, the military firmly controlled the country. However, officers committed to "revolutionary nationalism" managed to take over the government. They argued that the military was obliged to move the reform process forward because civilian efforts had failed. Two short-lived regimes, the first under General Alfredo Ovando, who headed the military under Barrientos, and then General Juan José Torres, sought alliances with the COB. Ovando nationalized Gulf Oil in 1969, and Torres threw out the Peace Corps in 1971, moves that infuriated the United States. But their governments were weak and unable to forge the widespread support necessary to expand reforms.

After the September Massacre, the regiment commander claimed absolute authority over the entire district and imposed a state of siege. We could not walk in groups even as small as two or three and needed special authorization to be in the streets between nine at night and six in the morning. The military controlled everything. We returned to work listlessly with hearts bursting with sorrow. Too many of our fellow workers weren't on the job but were wounded or dead, in prison or deported.

A few months later, General Barrientos attempted to increase his government's legitimacy by holding general elections. This decision led him to withdraw the army from the mines until the elections were over.

For me personally, the events that began with the September confrontation with the police, through the military occupation, to their withdrawal from the mines, really got me thinking. I had seen too many innocent people imprisoned, fired from their jobs, and even assassinated, and I wondered, "Couldn't the same thing happen to me at any time?" I realized, with the eyes of a nineteen-year-old, that if this was our destiny as miners, I had to do something. I decided to become politically active, which meant participating in the union, our one political instrument. But realistically I wasn't prepared to be a union leader, as I lacked information and skills.

At that point, I was in my third year of secondary school, taking classes at night. They taught us technical skills complemented by a completely distorted history that reflected neither our context nor our reality. Some of the best teachers had been fired, jailed, or persecuted for their union activities. We desperately dreamed of expanding our horizons, so we approached certain teachers and asked them to recommend books.

But there was nowhere to buy any books. The military had sacked everything when they invaded the district. Soldiers went house to house and carted off anything considered even remotely suspicious, including books, pamphlets, fliers, and booklets that explained the revolution of 1952, the Communist Party, and Trotskyism—burning everything inside the barracks. To fill the void we would have had to travel to the big cities of Oruro, La Paz, and Cochabamba, which for a mine worker on subsistence wages was close to impossible.

The result was that we were totally unprepared ideologically. At the same time, there was a vacuum in leadership. Miners who appeared suspicious or took initiative to speak out were watched and reported on by informants inside the mines. The police raided their houses during the night and accused them of being communists because they spoke out against the government. They were often arrested or fired and, if they were considered especially dangerous, deported to the eastern part of the country to internment camps. Sometimes this frightened them so much that they became either company or government agents so that they could return home to their jobs. A palpable fear prevailed in the community, creating a psychological terror that inhibited any kind of free speech. I realized at this point that my only option was to keep studying, and I continued night school. At least there I could meet other people, whether miners like me or craftspeople or just young people who shared my views.

Joining the Party

I wrote up some fliers and drawings about the student march of September 1965 and had them printed with my own money. I was hoping to encourage other students to participate in the student organization. As well, I wanted to be a candidate in the student elections where I studied. Teodoro Choque, one of my fellow students, congratulated me. "It's great that you printed those fliers," he told me. "You know what? Students taking these types of initiative are meeting to organize study groups to discuss our problems and the political situation. Some are students from this school and others come from elsewhere in the district. Would you like to come?"

"Of course," I said. As I recall, four students from my school expressed interest. At the meeting, Teodoro told us, "Look, to change things in our society, we need to join a political party. It is the only way we can become better prepared. I am from the Marxist-Leninist Communist Party, and I can put you in contact with party leaders." Domitila Chungara de Barrios was in charge locally, and we all agreed enthusiastically to meet with her.

Domitila was already well known as a leader of the Housewives

Committee of Siglo XX, and one afternoon Teodoro took the four of us to her house. When I first saw her I thought she was like any other housewife— more a mother than anything else. But when she began to speak, I was immediately swept along by her passion, her clarity of expression, and her commitment. She made me feel that a revolutionary triumph was possible. She informed us that we could join the youth division that was meeting the next Saturday. "Come then and we will formally incorporate you," she said. Although this was a quick process, I was excited and felt that I was on the verge of filling a hole that I had been carrying around in me for a very long time.

I asked her to explain what the party was about and who was involved. She explained in general terms, "We are the Marxist-Leninist Communist Party of the line established by Federico Escobar. He's our first secretary, and you'll need to speak with him as well. But he is not here, he's in exile. When he arrives, we'll introduce you."

For me, because I was still not totally convinced, I intended to talk with the party head when he returned. I thought I would just go along to the meeting to check it out. When I arrived, I saw there were young people, women, and some of Domitila's sisters; Margot and Marina are the ones I remember. But the person who had the biggest impact on me was a young man from La Paz, Raúl Quispaya, a well-trained political activist. He led the meeting and explained a good deal about the party line and its objectives. His description convinced me to join the youth movement then and there.

He explained, "In this area, we will hold a youth meeting, and you need to prepare for this by reading the materials like *The Communist Manifesto* that the party has provided. You will understand the party's philosophy and how the working class can seize political power by studying this document." He made sure each of us had a copy.

He also urged, "The way to continue the struggle is not just by reading and participating in the party, but also by acquiring military and ideological preparation, because the triumph of revolutionary history in the world and in our country will only happen through armed struggle." This position clarified history for me and reflected the reality I knew and lived. At that point, I didn't think much about different ways to achieve political power. In my country, power had more often been seized through armed conflict of one kind or another than through the ballot box.

Two communist parties actively competed in the mining districts at the time, but they represented considerable differences. Basically, the PCML believed that the only way to guarantee the construction of a profound revolutionary process in favor of the disadvantaged was through armed struggle, while the PCB believed that it was possible and desirable to achieve structural change through peaceful means.

The political cadre clarified that the PCML had only just been formed in April 1965 by Federico Escobar and other PCB militants who were disillusioned by the deceptive practices of the PCB. Besides, the PCB was led by people from the upper middle class, and it was widely believed that the party depended on the economic as well as ideological support of the Soviet Union. In contrast, Federico's party was headed by a mining union leader from the same social class as we were and didn't have a defined international ideological orientation. After Federico's death, the party affiliated itself to Communist China and Albania, and we became known as *chinos*—Chinese—for our affiliation with Maoist ideology.

When the meeting with Domitila ended, I introduced myself to Raúl Quispaya. He asked me, "Where do you work and live?"

"I work in the Siglo XX mine and live in the Salvadora mining camp. My name is Feliciano." Only later, after I had joined the party and had been arrested once, did I adopt the name Félix as a way to mask my real identity.

"Really?" he said. "I would like to work in the mine too. But for now, be sure to read the manifesto and then we can discuss it." So I read the party's document, but I didn't understand much of it, which frustrated me, but didn't discourage me from wanting to learn more.

Raúl impressed me because he was such a simple and straightforward young man and didn't have many of the prejudices common among miners. He wasn't sexist; for example, he cooked and was not ashamed to grab a vegetable bag to go shopping or carry pots in the street, activities considered women's work. He wasn't racist, either. Instead, he was respectful of the customs of rural indigenous people, and he was dedicated to understanding other people. He was a confident young man and optimistic about his political work. I liked him a lot. He was still at school, but I really admired his way with words and that he was so well informed. He later joined Che Guevara's guerrilla movement and was killed by the military with other members of Che's group at Ñancahuazú in eastern Bolivia in 1967.

I formally joined the party and became an active member early in 1966. Given the military's deportation and imprisonment of so many union leaders, the movement was in the throes of a real leadership crisis, and the demand for new activists grew. My decision to join the party wasn't like joining a sports club, given the risks. I decided that in order to better serve workers I needed to be a party militant, but not just in any party. The large traditional parties like the MNR and the Bolivian Socialist Falange (Falange Socialista Boliviana, or FSB) were right-wing and didn't represent workers' interests. For the miners, the most important parties were the Trotskyists like the Revolutionary Workers' Party (Partido Obrero Revolucionario, or POR), the PRIN, and the PCB.

Nonetheless, I preferred the PCML, not only because it was new, but more importantly because its leader was a miner. In the mines the political parties were the only universities we had: the places to acquire training as a political leader. Shortly after Federico Escobar left the PCB to form the PCML, the majority of miners followed him because they supported his vision. At the international level, the orientation was also socialist, but a true socialism, like the one Federico promoted, and not the type of demagogy or idealized and unrealistic socialism that the other so-called socialist parties stood for. I was absolutely convinced that this system could solve the social problems of the world and my country.

My brothers Germán, Max, and, later, Willy also joined the party—Germán actually joined before I did. Probably Willy and Max joined because Germán and I were involved. For our parents, it was a real worry that their sons were militants in a left political party. Normally few women joined, and my sisters never showed any interest. In hindsight, I now think that they weren't interested because they were more realistic. My younger brother Germán joined when he was a secondary school student leader, and I think he spoke several times with Federico at his house. Federico was held in the highest esteem, not just because he was a miner, but also because he was considered honest and capable, as well as someone we felt would carry out the historical objectives of our class to establish a government led by workers.

I also decided to dedicate myself to political activity because I had been wounded during the September Massacre, and, as a miner, I could die at any moment whether in the mines or on the streets. I thought it would be better to die fighting for a cause than as a victim in a mining accident. I was convinced that an honorable death defending our sacred rights to work, life, and country would be welcome.

Sometimes at night all the young people in the party hit the streets to paint graffiti. We prepared the paints at Federico Escobar's house, and there I first spent a little time with his daughter, Emilse, who was part of the party's youth wing. We'd mix red and black paint—the party's colors—with gasoline to stretch it further. Generally, we covered the entrances to the mines or the workers' offices with slogans like "Reject the government's measures," "Get the military out of the mining district," or "Fight for national liberation from the U.S. imperialist yoke."

Teodoro, my school friend, assumed the leadership of our group. One day he let me know that Comrade Federico Escobar was arriving. He had snuck back into the country at the beginning of 1966, although as soon as he surfaced in Santa Cruz he was arrested and imprisoned again. They tried to bribe him, but he refused and was finally released because of the enormous pressure the miners brought to bear on the government. He was keen to meet with the young party members, and I was tremendously excited to finally get to know him.

Teodoro called eight of us to a tiny house that we all crammed into, waiting impatiently to meet Federico. I worried, as the house lacked adequate security measures, because it had only one entrance and one exit. Then all of a sudden Federico Escobar filled the doorway, accompanied by two young men. He looked like a typical Aymara miner—short and broad-chested. His hair was wavy and he had thick lips, which made him look like the dancers from the Morenada in Carnaval, so his nickname was Macho Moreno [tough dark guy]. While he had enormous charisma and inspired respect and confidence, I always had the impression that he was a simple man who didn't go out of his way to seek attention.

He shook our hands one by one and then addressed us, "I don't have much time. I realize I don't know many of you. Some I'm seeing for the first time, and I want to be certain you understand the following: I have been told that you want to be part of the youth division of the Marxist-Leninist Communist Party. I can tell you that to be a communist—a true Marxist-Leninist—is a difficult task. Of the eight of you who are here, I am sure that only two or three will be able to bear the sacrifice that is required. It is worse than what Jesus Christ suffered. I respect your desire to commit yourselves to this kind of sacrifice, because being a party militant means that you must study and be well prepared, you have to always do the best you possibly can, and you must be a good leader. If you achieve this, you will be persecuted, arrested, exiled, and perhaps even murdered. You just don't know what you are getting yourselves into." We were all very moved by his speech.

Then he rushed off and we never saw him again. A few months later in November 1966, just after All Saints' Day, we heard on the radio that we awoke to every morning that Federico Escobar had died in La Paz. Everyone was sure he had been murdered by the government. On the other hand, the PCB distributed fliers that accused his successor, Oscar Zamora Medinacelli, of being the intellectual author of his death. Indeed, it was strange that as the party's first secretary and then later senator and president of the Bolivian Congress at the end of the 1970s, Zamora never demanded an investigation to determine what really happened. From my perspective, Zamora's ascent to the leadership over the long run led to the party's destruction, the culmination of which was the decision to run as vice presidential candidate with the dictator, Hugo Banzer Suárez, in 1989.

Federico's death was a huge loss not only to the district, but to miners all over the country. With it, worker control came to an end. Just a few months after I had met him, I attended his funeral at Siglo XX with fifty thousand people, not only from the district, but from all of Bolivia as well as from other parts of the world.

Intense state repression continued. Informants had infiltrated among the mine workers and were denouncing communists of all stripes to the police. Although they informed on some people, they couldn't simply report everyone who opposed the state, because there wouldn't have been enough room in the prisons for all of us. We felt a real hatred toward the informants, and some people wanted to kill them in the mine or lynch them in the streets as traitors. The union had decided that the leaders in the mines, and I among them by this point, had to protect the informers not only to avoid bad press, but also to prevent providing the military an excuse to take revenge.

In February 1967, the news came over the radio that Che Guevara and his guerrilla force had arrived in the eastern part of the country. We were tremendously excited that an armed guerrilla movement had taken root, as it inspired hope that we could achieve liberation and the destruction of the national oligarchy that sold the country to the multinational corporations at every opportunity. In the following months, the press announced that the army had arrested Loyola Guzmán, a young student working with the guerrilla movement. The press published photos attributed to her that confirmed Che was leading the guerrilla band.

Various workers who had been fired, exiled, or imprisoned whispered confidentially to us, "We have declared armed struggle and now we have to fight. Our comrade Arancibia, for example, is now incorporated in the guerrilla movement." Arancibia was a workmate of my father. I met him when I was a boy, because when I carried food to my father in the mine, we ate and talked together. My father told me he was a good man and always very supportive of others.

But even though many miners declared, "I too want to go and fight against the military," no one knew how to contact the guerrillas. This lack of coordination frustrated us and convinced some fired union leaders to call a national miners' meeting.

We set to work to organize a large meeting, even though the government explicitly prohibited these types of gatherings, having outlawed the union. The assembly preparing the national meeting resolved to assist the guerrilla movement with a contribution from our salaries. Certainly it would have been better to go directly into combat, but we lacked access to arms. After committing to assist the Ñancahuazú guerrillas economically, we decided the national mining conference would be held at Siglo XX on June 24, 1967, the day after [Noche de] San Juan. Our actions provoked General Barrientos to begin plotting a new military takeover of the mining districts.

On June 23, the mining leader Rosendo García Maisman let us know that he had finally contacted Che Guevara. He said, "Let's go. The war has begun and we're ready to fight." The next day, however, he was killed in the Massacre of San Juan.

San Juan Massacre, June 1967

The bonfire of San Juan, on the night of June 23, is a long-standing Bolivian tradition, in the cities as well as the mines and countryside. It occurs close to the winter solstice, which we believe is the longest and coldest night of the year. To keep the Pachamama, the mother earth, warm, we build bonfires. Before the bonfires were lit that year, I met with the visiting delegates to define the inaugural program for the next day's conference. By the time I got home at about 11:00 p.m., my family already had our bonfire burning.

As we celebrated around the fire, a neighbor came running up shaking with worry, "The military has arrived and is already at the fence. The whole district is surrounded." I didn't pay much attention because I was exhausted, and instead of going to check out what was happening, I stumbled off to bed. My parents watched the bonfire die down, and then they too slept. At about four in the morning, I was jolted from sleep by a lot of noise that many people assumed was the firecrackers everyone normally sets off during San Juan.

I realized I was hearing gunfire, not firecrackers; soldiers were shooting directly on the houses in the mining settlement. I dashed out of bed and peered out the window. Right across from my house, up on the hillside, I saw flashes of gunfire. But it was still half dark, and, because I was groggy with sleep, I foolishly turned on the light. The soldiers responded to the sudden light by firing toward my house. Still not really understanding what was going on, I moved closer to the window when several shots hit the house and some almost came through the window. The rush of adrenaline jolted me awake, and I hurriedly shut off the light and turned on the radio. The announcer was calling for all miners to gather at the union headquarters to defend it from military assault. And then, with this last call, the radio station "The Miners' Voice" went dead. With the fading of the radio signal, I felt like we had lost once again, and that the best course of action was to stay in the house. I hid materials like books, pamphlets, and my father's revolver that he had most of his life, as I thought soldiers might ransack the house in their search for leaders and contraband.

It turned out that not only had soldiers already occupied the union building and the miners' radio station, but they had raided houses of union leaders to arrest or murder them. The mining camp was in a state of total confusion, and it was only as the sun rose that we began to grasp what had happened. The whole district was surrounded by the army, which was engaged in a street-by-street sweep throughout the camps. Soldiers fired left, right, and center on every street, shooting anything that moved. People left their bonfires burning and fled indoors. Even the dogs left to wander in the chaos were shot.

Just as my mother was getting out of bed, a bullet came in through the roof and grazed her head, burning her hair before it sunk into the opposite wall. She was lucky, as a number of people were killed or wounded by stray bullets. As it got lighter, we became more and more desperate to go outside to the bathroom, because in the settlements we had only collective latrines, not individual bathrooms. But it was impossible. Some children who couldn't hold it in snuck out, and others, curious to see what was going on, went too. They were all targets and many were shot, as were those who left their houses to help the wounded. But people took the risk anyway, as for many people it is impossible to see a child, relative, or neighbor lying wounded in the street crying for help and not respond.

In the Massacre of San Juan, the press reported that more than one hundred people were killed. After we buried the dead, we had little choice but to return to work. Once again they had destroyed the union leadership, killing some and arresting others while stepping up surveillance in the mines. We had to be careful if we wanted to keep our jobs, but despite all of this, we were determined to organize again, even though some workers were terrified to be union leaders, because it meant that they could be jailed, killed, or forced into hiding or exile. Nonetheless, some were incredibly brave and assumed the responsibility of serving as a leader.

Two years later in 1969, President Barrientos died in a helicopter crash. This signified a change for mine workers, and we celebrated in the mining camps with music, corn beer, and other alcohol. We danced through the mining settlements and in the main plaza waving the miners' flag. It was a great moment for us. Everyone expressed great happiness and relief. We all felt that we had a new opportunity to organize ourselves and continue the struggle. Many people said that with Barrientos's death, finally God had remembered us.

Work in the Mine

Beginning with the 1965 occupation of the mines, I worked in a section called Diamintina, which involved prospecting the Juan del Valle hill, sampling mineral quality to plan for future excavation. For three months we worked to finish the surface sampling. I then descended into the mine itself. Working inside the mine is frightening: it's like signing a suicide pact with an indefinite term. Eventually everyone contracts black lung, because the air is contaminated by the mix of silica and the toxic dusts dispersed by the minerals during the explosions. The dust is dangerous, as the minerals are rarely encountered in a pure state but always contain a range of heavy metals and poisons such as arsenic.

I worked in the mine for several months as a cleaner, the lowest-status job, reserved for the newest workers. The cleaner works in the passageways and water canals that function as sewers, carrying the tailings and other wastes out of the mine. Because of our work in water, the miners teased us, calling us fishermen. I didn't have to do this long, because the bosses recognized that I was comfortable in the far reaches of the mine and had more skills than most recently hired workers because of my previous experience as a *juk'u*.

I moved from there to work in the interior survey crew. This consisted of taking samples from each vein to figure out its average mineral content. I did this for almost two years, six or seven days a week, working eight-hour shifts in the mine, sometimes with overtime.

At a quarter to five in the morning, the siren blasted from the union building to wake us up. In the camps, women generally got out of bed even earlier. A typical breakfast consisted of a roll with a cup of tea and a bowl of noodle soup. Then the miner headed off with a bottle of either tea or water and some coca leaves, which were indispensable for staving off hunger until he left the mine at three or four in the afternoon. Single miners carried a sandwich with them or ate at small diners just outside the mine entrance.

At 6:00 a.m., transport trucks ferried workers up to the mine, and we headed directly for the timekeepers' window, where we got our time cards stamped before reporting for work, because the window closed at precisely 7:00 a.m. If we arrived late, we lost a day's wages. We then picked up the tools we needed from the depository. In my case, I gathered bags for the mineral samples, three twelve-inch chisels—two normal and one diamond-pointed—a long-handled two-pound hand sledgehammer, and a bucket to put the samples in. All this was stuck into a big bag.

I worked in a team with six people: five operators and one administrator. First we assembled in one spot, where we chewed coca for ten to fifteen minutes, and then we agreed on who would do what. Generally, we were expected to cover an area ten by sixteen feet long, by eight by twelve inches wide, and one inch deep each day. We had to sweep the area clean before we could start collecting samples.

The miners jokingly called us "healers," because sometimes when there wasn't much mineral in the vein where they were blasting, we added some rich ore from a different vein to increase the quality of the samples that the company checked to ensure that the production of the miners hired on contracts rather than as salaried workers was in line with company norms. We did this because sometimes after three months of poorly paid work preparing an area, a contract worker discovered that the average yield from a vein was so low he wouldn't be able to keep his contract. And even though the team administrator controlled our work, we were savvy about how to get minerals from other places in order to "heal" the mineral samples that were sent for testing.

Other workers were on straight salary. If a miner worked under a contract, his pay was based on what he produced, and supposedly opportunities were greater to earn more. But because the commissions the company paid were so low, many of the contract miners didn't make any more than those who worked at fixed wages.

Every Friday, or sometimes the last Friday of the month, it was crucial to honor the Tío [the Uncle] with a *ch'alla* ritual. The Tío is the god who protects the interior of the mine, the miners, and the minerals. The image of the Tío, made from clay, is displayed in the central part of the mine or some other principal production location. The main Tíos are up to six and a half feet tall, red in color, and generally look like devils. They have cigarettes in their mouths, horns, and exposed, erect penises.

To perform a *ch'alla,* we placed as an offering a small bottle of alcohol or other spirits, cigarettes, and coca on the platform where the Tío is seated. It is important to carry some part of the offering to perform a *ch'alla* in your gallery. Everyone individually performs a *ch'alla* in the name of his work group. All miners, no matter what their religious or ideological tendency, believe in and revere the Tío.

Sometimes, working alone deep in the mine, a miner felt as if someone had paid a visit, perhaps a foreman, only to later discover that no one had come by. When that happened we would say the miner had been visited by the Tío. Sometimes the Tío was accompanied by women. At that time, women weren't allowed in the mines, because they were supposed to bring bad luck. The fact that the Tío could have women accompany him without suffering negative consequences demonstrated the enormity of his power.

I remember once a white-skinned, blond worker decided to sit naked beside the Tío in order to frighten everyone else, as a kind of joke. Those who came by and saw him thought he was a ghost or something else equally strange. When one worker stopped by to leave alcohol, coca, and cigarettes, the white man moved his head and indicated towards the Tío with his eyes. The worker was terrified and ran off screaming. Everyone said it drove him crazy, and he had to be shipped off to the psychiatric hospital in Sucre.

An evil goddess resides in the mine, and we called her the Old Woman. She could cause the disappearance of a mineral seam, a cave-in, or an accident. To protect ourselves against her, we allied with the Tío. When we performed a *ch'alla* on a Friday or during a pause to chew coca, we sometimes heard sounds or rock falling from the ceiling. We would speak to her directly and say, "Old Woman, Old Woman, don't bother me."

I worked hard in different jobs in the mine interior until, after three years, I was incorporated into the administrative staff and put in charge of the sample team. Because I already knew all the tricks of my workmates, I was better able to control the section.

In spite of the widespread negative sentiment about miners, I was always proud of my work. During my five years underground, I studied at night to finish secondary school. I left the mine, ate, rested for an hour, and then raced off to night classes, doing, in effect, a double shift. When I finally graduated from high school my ambitions had changed, and I dreamed of becoming a mining engineer or a lawyer. Very few miners had the chance to move up, but I was determined to do so. I was lucky enough to learn some engineering because, after working as a sample gatherer, I was transferred to the technical engineering department and learned how to draw and take measurements.

The Miner-Campesino Pact and My First Arrest

When Barrientos died in 1969, his vice president, Hernán Siles, who had been president from 1956 to 1960 and was one of the MNR leaders during the 1952 revolution, assumed power. As he was a civilian, we had greater freedom, and we started to organize again. During this time, the *jilakata* [community leader] of my father's community, Wila Apacheta, showed up at our house at Siglo XX, a day's walk away. He said to me, "Feliciano, it is important that you come to assist in the community assembly because we are going to reorganize ourselves. We need to define our positions and select delegates for a departmental congress of campesinos in Oruro."

I had stayed in touch with my community, often returning to the *ayllu* for festivals and other social occasions. I had helped in getting a school functioning in Wila Apacheta during the Barrientos years, finding Irma Rodríguez, a private teacher for the children in the community, and raising money to pay her. She had studied at the Oruro Technical University (UTO) and had been persecuted because she was a militant in the PCML. She was much safer in the countryside, because the repression did not reach that far.

The next Saturday, I went to Wila Apacheta, and in the assembly, we adopted the position that the campesinos would join with the miners to continue our struggle, because we had greater strength in numbers. I was chosen to represent the community at the Oruro Department Campesino Congress, which had been scheduled for July 1969 in Toledo in order to ratify a resolution to replace government-supported leaders, who served to ensure campesino union loyalty to the military. The campesinos planned to replace these leaders with an ad hoc committee headed by Macabeo Chila.

In July 1969, I traveled by bus to the congress in Toledo, a town southwest of Oruro, with Valentín Condor, another delegate from Wila Apacheta. We arrived at six in the morning along with other leaders and walked right into the lion's mouth. We were immediately surrounded by police, accompanied by official campesino leaders, who were hitting and arresting leaders as they stepped off the bus. However, Valentín and I initially escaped, as we looked more like miners than campesinos, but then we unfortunately walked into a restaurant where several policemen were eating breakfast.

They looked surprised to see us and demanded, "What are you doing in Toledo?"

I responded with our cover story, "We came to buy material in the market," as Toledo was famous for its *bayeta,* a coarse, widely used handwoven cloth. They believed me at first, but the commander looked a bit dubious and ordered, "Search them, and if they are telling the truth let them go."

They pushed us down the road to the police station, where they rifled through my bag that held my poncho, clothes, and a blanket, nothing else. We were nervous but figured we would be all right, but then they searched our bodies and discovered the hidden fliers about the campesino congress and the miner-campesino pact. This infuriated them.

A policeman hit me with the butt of his rifle and threw me on the ground. "So you only came to buy cloth?" he shouted, looking at documents from the PCML.

They registered my identity card so that they would know who we were, and, as we were considered dangerous, they shoved us into an improvised cell in an abandoned building without a roof. There they beat us as much as they pleased without the bother of being interrupted—in the office there was always the risk that someone would show up and put an end to it. This was the first time I was tortured.

As they beat me, they yelled, "When is Macabeo Chila arriving?" He was the top democratically elected campesino leader in the department of Oruro. They continued hitting me, "Who told you about this congress? Where are you staying?"

Four of them beat Valentín and me, fortunately all body blows, and none to our faces or heads. They tossed me about, and kicked me until I fainted. They did the same to Valentín, and then, much to our relief, they disappeared. After a while I regained consciousness, managed to sit up, and commiserated with Valentín.

They returned a short time later and jeered, "You're still alive? Okay, well now we're going to have to be sure to kill you." Right at that moment, another squad of police herded in about ten more prisoners. The police had no choice but to stop beating us, because there were suddenly so many prisoners that it was impossible for them to kill us all. The new group of detainees had been beaten before they arrived in the cell, and several of them were in pretty bad shape, moaning and writhing in pain.

They kept us there all day. At eleven that night, they decided to move us to the city of Oruro in the back of an open truck. The temperature was well below zero, and of course, the cold was even worse because of the wind. The union leaders helping the police had their faces covered with woolen masks that we called *chullus de juk'u,* and you couldn't see who they were. I had a similar face mask that I used against the cold, and I pulled it on. That meant that no one could see if I was an agent or a prisoner. I realized this when they stopped pushing me with their guns while they continued to manhandle the others. I gradually separated myself from the group of prisoners and sidled closer to the guards. When we arrived in Oruro, I quietly climbed down as they pushed and beat the other captives, shoving them out of the truck. While they were focused on controlling their prisoners, I snuck silently and slowly to the corner so as not to draw attention, but then sprinted as fast as I could around the next corner and jumped in a taxi.

I fled to the house of my sister Cursina's *compadre* [fictive kin], who lived in the center of Oruro. I walked in casually as if nothing had happened, but once safely inside, I quickly told the family my story. Cursina's *compadre* commiserated, "I heard about it on the radio. You have to get back to Siglo XX. The best would be for me to buy you a ticket in my name using my identity card."

He slipped out of the house to purchase the ticket and then smuggled me out of the city. We walked about three miles, past the toll plaza, where I flagged down the bus. I snuck into Siglo XX and went back to work. If I had been away much longer, I would have lost my job as well. This was my first capture as a union leader and my first escape.

Fortunately, thanks to pressure from the campesino and miner groups, we forced them to free the other prisoners. Valentín was confined for an additional three days. I saw him a week and a half later in Siglo XX, and he told me what had happened. They were tortured the entire first night. Police agents and the corrupt campesino leaders had danced on top of the prisoners' bodies. Several years later, as a consequence of this torture, several leaders from my village died, including Valentín, who was younger than I. Even now I feel very sad when I remember this, and at the same time recognize my enormous luck in escaping.

From Coup to Coup

Turmoil continued because President Siles was unable to address the country's fundamental problems. On September 26, 1969, General Alfredo Ovando Candia pulled off a coup d'état and seized office as the president of the military government. But strangely, he started to adopt progressive measures, such as the nationalization of oil through his minister of hydrocarbons, Marcelo Quiroga de Santa Cruz, a very important socialist leader.

The miners seized the opportunity presented by the change in government to organize a national congress at Siglo XX. To keep alive the memory of the leaders killed during the Barrientos regime, we wanted to inaugurate our congress with the dedication of a monument of Federico Escobar that had been fabricated in Oruro. After all, Federico was one of the most lucid leaders of the Bolivian workers movement and the first secretary of the PCML. But we were infiltrated by government agents and spies who told the Ministry of the Interior about our plan. Because we had reached no formal agreement with this new government, it continued to try to control us. Officials wouldn't let the statue leave Oruro, where it was seized by the police.

The entire Siglo XX Miners' Congress declared itself in a state of emergency with the threat of a hunger strike in order to force the statue's release. This was the only way that we were able to finally transport it and install it in the Plaza of the Miner, where it remains today.

The Ovando Candia government didn't last long, and the conflicts and coups continued to be a fact of life. The next leader was General Juan José Torres, who on October 17, 1970, issued a call for popular assistance, particularly from the miners. We decided to grant him our unconditional support because we were tired of the previous governments that all applied the same repressive policies, lowering our salaries and doing whatever the multinationals asked. We yearned for a change that favored the miners and the Bolivian people. Not only did Torres actively seek our help in consolidating his de facto government, he promised to respond to our concerns. Although we didn't trust him much, the situation offered an opportunity to reorganize and, therefore, be better prepared for future struggles.

We asked Torres for arms so that we could provide him greater support, but he refused. At that point, many of us realized that having Torres in power was not enough to ensure a government that responded to the people, as apparently the military carried out a coup anytime it felt like it. Under such circumstances, there was no guarantee that a progressive general like Torres could maintain control of the state. Torres recognized that he needed support, however, and he affiliated himself with the PCB and other opportunistic left parties. At the same time, he isolated not only the radical left parties, like the PCML and certain of the Trotskyists, which weren't as easy to control, but also business owners and the Santa Cruz oligarchy. The latter formed the basis of the opposition that brought him down.

The mining leaders of Siglo XX, and at this point I was among them, were determined to support Torres not only verbally but also through concrete action. In a secret meeting we voted to form a miners' militia and seize the Miraflores police barracks in Uncía. We planned to stage a march by Miraflores, something we had done before, and then overpower the soldiers standing guard at the gates and grab their weapons. To guarantee the mission's success, I was assigned to lead an assault of the barracks from the rear.

A day later, the Miners' Voice radio station announced the march past Miraflores to support Torres's government. About a thousand miners gathered at eight in the morning, and an hour later we were on our way. Just behind the march's leaders we had two large and powerful men to jump the guards at the barrack's gates and a force of about fifty miners assigned to scale the rear wall. We managed to seize the barracks without incident, but by the time my men successfully assaulted the building, the few arms that were to be had were already long gone. My group was furious with me, as they felt we hadn't achieved anything for our efforts.

We captured an officer, however, and demanded that he reveal where the rest of the guns were stored. He was reluctant to say anything, but I kept reassuring him we wouldn't do anything to him if he cooperated, and he finally gave in. We heisted a pickup truck from the barracks, and, followed by a second truck filled with my men, we raced off for Katiri, about twelve miles away. The officer pointed us to a pile of rocks out in the open, and buried beneath them we discovered a stash of about twenty Mauser rifles. There weren't enough to go around, and, just like me, everyone was desperate to have a gun. We argued about who was more deserving, and at a couple of moments it even looked like a fight would break out. I was barely able to maintain discipline, but as I was in charge of the operation, I insisted on distributing the weapons. No one disputed that I was entitled to one of them.

We were ecstatic, not only because we accomplished our mission, but also because we thought we finally had the capability to defend ourselves. Our joy was short-lived when we realized that the guns had no triggers. The policeman demanded that I set him free, as he had fulfilled his part of the bargain. I was furious and shouted that he had promised us weapons, not gun parts. Tempers were increasingly short, and the officer quickly grasped that he had little choice but to show us where the other parts were stashed. We headed about three miles down the road, where the officer pointed high into the branches of a tree where a bundle was hidden out of sight. Sure enough, inside were the pieces to transform our cache from gun parts to deadly weapons. Once we assembled the complete guns, we released the officer and even gave him enough money to catch a bus back to the base. We were like kids with new toys as we jubilantly returned to the union office.

Ciliro Jiménez, a Trotskyist responsible for the miners' militias, declared that the guns should remain in the union offices. We made a list of the weapons, and, as a reward for our efforts, they were assigned to the men who had helped capture them. Jiménez told us that when the union needed to mobilize the militia, the siren would sound and we should report immediately to the union hall. This happened once, but as I lived quite far away, by the time I arrived my gun had been given to someone else. I had lost the one thing that I was sure would guarantee my safety.

The Faculty of Law

In 1970, I got my high school diploma. At that point, I needed to choose whether to stay in the mines or find a way to continue studying. I opted to go to university at the cost of having to give up my stable job in the mine, where I had hung on for five years despite the considerable difficulties of working and studying at the same time. This also meant I had to leave home, because the closest state university was in Oruro, about six hours away by bus.

Because I was determined that other students graduating from high school should not encounter the same difficulties I had faced, I got involved with my friend Tito Burgoa, who had graduated with me, in a project to create a university at Siglo XX. We proposed the idea to the miners' union, which named us to form a commission to study the feasibility with the well-known mining leader Filemón Escobar. We met several times and solicited support from the Roman Catholic Church and other local organizations. Later, we held a national meeting in La Paz that was attended by the COB, the FSTMB, and the Universidad Mayor de San Andrés (UMSA), La Paz's public university. But the coup d'état pulled off by General Hugo Banzer in 1971 meant that the founding of Siglo XX University was postponed until 1984.

I signed up for precollege courses at the University of Oruro, and once I had passed them, I joined the law faculty. I chose law because, unlike engineering, it was possible to study at night and, as I was on my own, I needed to work during the day. Besides, in the mine, I had seen a tremendous deficiency in knowledge about the country's laws and regulations. I was somewhat disappointed, as I would have preferred engineering: I had worked in the mine in the engineering department and had a good level of technical knowledge.

I landed a job as a laborer on the construction of the National Social Security Hospital. I didn't know anything about construction, absolutely nothing, and I figured I would serve as the boy who carried water for the site, the lowest rung in construction work. But they contracted me as an assistant to the head of a finish work team. My first day, I arrived just when the workers were chewing coca together.

The team leader gave me orders, "Take this pail and spade, and prepare some stucco for me," he said, and pointing to the water boy, a fourteen-year-old kid, "He will be your helper."

When we got to the storage place for the stucco, the helper brought me water and realized immediately that I didn't have a clue what to do. "Don't you know how?" he asked.

I said vaguely, "I knew but I've forgotten."

He looked puzzled and said, "I'll do it for you." Fortunately for me, he had been working for quite some time as a water boy. "Here, you make it with four scoops of stucco, half a pail of water, and you beat it together until bubbles come up, and then it's ready."

I picked up this mixture and gave it to the foreman, "Here it is." Without looking at me, he said, "Another one."

Later he asked me to hang the main guides on the wall and cover them with stucco, and I said to him, "Look, I haven't done this work for a long time, and I've forgotten. Could you show me how to do it?" And fortunately, because we were both young, and he saw I worked hard and learned fast, instead of throwing me out, he taught me what I needed to know.

Every Saturday I played soccer with my boss and other workers, and from there we went to drink *chicha* regardless of whether we won or lost the match. One day when we were out drinking, he got into a fight with another contractor, who blinded him in one eye. The following day the fight was mentioned in the police report in the Oruro paper. My boss was happy because it was the first time in his life he had his name in the paper.

At night, I attended classes. As I had a political affiliation, I also attended party meetings for university students with both teachers and students. We decided to organize a slate to run for the elections of the Local University Federation (Federación de Universitarios Local, or FUL), the organization that represented students. I was active in the campaign, and we won. I was made the permanent secretary, which gave me the right to eat in the university dining hall. These responsibilities meant I had to stop my construction work, and I became really involved in the university. Our success in the elections created a base from which we launched a series of activities to involve students in the party, both inside and outside the university.

The political environment of university students was intensely emotional and theoretical. I was weak on theory because I had not read much, and consequently, I was very practical in orientation. This meant that I was considered very radical, because for me the new political model for a man was Che Guevara. I saw him as someone who had put his ideas into practice and had died for his ideals. At that time within the university to be a communist from whatever party was considered as being a traitor to the revolution and Che's guerrilla struggle, because the Bolivian Communist Party had roundly rejected providing him any support. The result was that very few declared themselves communists, and many people preferred to remain quiet so as to avoid criticism.

While I studied at the university, I lived in a rented room behind the Oruro train station. The owners of the house were two sisters who both wore *polleras* [the traditional wide skirt of Quechua and Aymara women] and worked in commerce. They were very strict about the hours for the house, and locked the door at 9:00 p.m. As I often didn't get back from classes until 11:00 p.m., and because the door was blocked off with a wooden log, I had to climb over the wall.

Several months after I became a tenant, the younger sister started to show some romantic interest in me, suggesting that because I was studying to be a lawyer, I should become the administrator for the family's sulfur mine, which had its own bus, cargo truck, and dump truck. At that time, however, I already had a girlfriend, a fellow student named Carmen Flores who also worked as a schoolteacher. When I fled Oruro, I had to leave her behind, but after my first return from Chile, she served as an important contact for information about the resistance.

But even had I not had a girlfriend, I would not have considered developing a relationship with my landlady, because she wore a *pollera*. I would have been ashamed if my middle-class university friends had known that my girlfriend wore a *pollera,* even though my mother wore one. In our circles, no one had a girlfriend *de pollera*. I felt very conflicted about this and mostly just wanted to hide my indigenous roots—everywhere there was enormous discrimination against rural people.

Despite my politics and the contradictions between my personal aspirations and what the party taught, I had a strong desire to escape the campesino-miner world and improve my economic and social status. In the university all women with *polleras* were considered indigenous, and indigenous people were seen as ugly, bad, and responsible for the country's backwardness. I hold a very strong indigenous consciousness now, but at that time I was incapable of defending my identity and my race.

Chapter 6

Bolivia under Banzer

HUGO BANZER

The reformist military governments of Ovando and Torres were swallowed by a coup perpetrated by a coalition of right-wing business interests coalescing around a U.S.-trained conservative military officer, General Hugo Banzer. He received financial support from the U.S. government, which was worried about Bolivia's latest left-wing turn (Baird 2010). It was not the first time that Banzer, who came from a wealthy ranching family of German origin in Santa Cruz, had attempted to seize power. He had been vying for political position since first appointed minister of education under the regime of his personal friend, General Barrientos.

In 1971, Banzer finally achieved his goal, with the support of the United States and the MNR's chief architect, Víctor Paz Estenssoro, and installed the longest-lasting regime Bolivia had experienced in more than a century. Banzer was a graduate of the U.S. military's School of the Americas, and in his first year as president, he benefited from a substantial injection of U.S. military assistance. He also joined Operation Condor, which coordinated intelligence operations and repression among South American military dictatorships (Dinges 2004).

State mine infrastructure continued to deteriorate for lack of investment in modernization and exploration as Banzer diverted resources to support the ever-growing patronage system that propped up his regime. He benefited from fortuitous circumstances: the rise in oil prices during the early 1970s boosted government revenues, in no small measure because petroleum production had surged after the 1969 nationalization of Gulf Oil's holdings. Advantageous market conditions for hydrocarbons and tin, and an increase in cotton production in the east, combined with the small share of the post-1973 petrodollars Bolivia was able to borrow on international financial markets, permitted a reasonable rate of economic growth.

But this prosperity rested on shaky foundations. As with other countries throughout Latin America, the infusion of borrowed petrodollars dramatically increased debt. Government-backed loans for agricultural modernization favored

Banzer's family and friends: the export-oriented agricultural elites in the eastern lowlands near Santa Cruz. The majority of these borrowers, foreshadowing Mexico a decade later, defaulted. Some loans did actually finance agricultural projects but were never repaid, while others provided capital for Bolivia's entry into the nascent coca/cocaine trade. Still other borrowers simply turned the loans around and deposited them directly in Miami banks (Dunkerley 1984).

Banzer relied on the support of about 20 percent of the civilian population from the most conservative elements of the middle and upper classes. Medium-sized private mining companies continued to expand, emerging as the country's most significant business group. Other influential interests were La Paz–based importers and manufacturers, who pushed an agenda of strictly controlled wages and lowered import duties on intermediate products, and eastern lowland elites based in Santa Cruz, with investments in agribusiness and independent gas and oil production. An increasingly powerful Santa Cruz Civic Committee demanded the retention of profits from the region's growing oil and gas industry through vociferous demands for government decentralization.

Public support for military regimes was highest between 1966 and 1974, when the dictatorships could count on campesino acquiescence in exchange for guarantees to land and education. But in 1974, General Banzer miscalculated and ordered troops outside Tolata, Cochabamba, to fire on a campesino protest over price hikes, killing more than 150 people. Campesinos abruptly shifted their loyalties to the opposition.

The Tolata massacre consolidated an emerging indigenist movement in the highlands, under the leadership of the Aymara Katarista movement (named for the leader of the late-eighteenth-century rebellion, Tupaj Katari). Katarismo heralded a decisive break with the government-sponsored unions linked to the 1952 revolution's modernizing project. In the face of over four hundred years of exclusion, early Katarismo promoted an indigenous nationalism that merged class consciousness with indigenous demands. It had enormous influence, propelling the founding of the national Confederation of Campesino Workers' Unions of Bolivia (Confederación Sindical Única de Trabajadores Campesinos de Bolivia, or CSUTCB) in 1979. The CSUTCB joined the COB and steadily gained importance, playing a decisive role in restoring democracy in 1982, even though campesinos were prevented from assuming top COB leadership, always reserved for a miner.

Banzer's antileft crackdown was one of the most ruthless Bolivia has ever seen, and the "little general" from Santa Cruz was widely feared. He banned all left-wing parties, shut down the COB, and closed the universities. With the legitimacy provided by MNR support, he imposed his version of "order" and respect for authority. By 1974, the political parties supporting him realized he had no intention of ever holding elections. Their subsequent protests were met with a ban on all political activity, and many party leaders fled into exile. During Banzer's

1971–1978 tenure, thousands of Bolivians were arrested or escaped abroad, over two hundred were killed, and many more tortured and imprisoned. Félix was among the lucky survivors of the dark period of Bolivia's history known as the Banzerato.

At the beginning of my second year in university, Bolivia again plunged into crisis. J. J. Torres, whom we had backed as president, faced growing threats of a coup. Colonel Hugo Banzer Suárez, holed up in the Santa Cruz barracks with considerable local support, was the protagonist. He united in a conspiracy to topple Torres with various right-wing political parties, including the Bolivian Socialist Falange (Falange Socialista Boliviana, or FSB) [a neofascist party] and the MNR. The plot culminated in a successful takeover on August 21, 1971. During the buildup, I experienced a profound sense of insecurity, because there was no way I could make any plans, personal or political.

In the university, we furiously started preparations. Although we ultimately failed, universities across the country were critical sites of resistance. Just a few days before, the FUL had begun a feverish coordination with organizations in Oruro, including the San José miners' union, factory workers, the departmental branch of the Bolivian Workers Central (COB), and campesinos. As a FUL representative, I hurried off with other activists to rural communities to coordinate. We traveled to Peñas and to Challapata, two communities that explicitly requested our help.

The Banzerato

On the day of the coup I was preparing documents in the FUL offices for immediate distribution in the countryside. One of my comrades frantically called on the phone, shouting, "Get out of there right now! The university is surrounded by the army." I was scared because a day earlier in the UMSA, La Paz's public university, the military had carried out an assault with helicopters that left students dead, wounded, and imprisoned. I rushed to the street door to see whether I could escape, but it was too late. Through the window, I saw troops massed at the main gates. Moments later, a soldier fired a bazooka that breached the university entrance.

Panicked students and administrators streamed out of the building in a vain attempt to flee, but when they realized there was no escape without walking straight into the arms of the military, they poured into the university dining room, where I joined them. We quickly hung a white cloth out the window in hopes that the military wouldn't shoot us or fire a bazooka into the cafeteria. Everyone was really frightened and frantically trying to figure out what to tell the military, and, although the tension was mounting, we patched together a common and coherent story. Minutes later, the military charged in and took us all captive.

Although the soldiers respected the white flag, they ordered us to place our hands behind our heads and kicked and hit us as they marched us onto the patio, where they forced us down on the ground. Then they jerked us back up onto our feet and bashed us with their weapons as we faced the wall. Some of the students cried: they were mostly middle-class kids not used to this kind of abuse. Some of my companions passed out, and then all of a sudden, the soldiers tired of beating us. A group of officers showed up to interrogate us one by one in an improvised office from a written questionnaire. As this assault occurred at lunchtime, we had agreed to say that we were simply in the dining room eating. Some of the interrogators just looked at us in disbelief, but others began to scream, "You are communist agitators," and without asking further questions, started to beat us again. Those of us with political experience were a lot calmer, because we could anticipate what was about to happen. It was a lot less traumatic for us than for the middle-class students, who were absolutely terrorized.

Typically, almost all torture takes place at the moment of capture. Maybe it is because the agents, whether military or police, have spent so much time and energy to catch us that they had worked themselves up into a fury, and beating us discharged their rage. This was my experience every time I was arrested. Sometimes they forced me and other detainees into a special interrogation room. When my statements did not match what the interrogators were looking for, I was often beaten again. They usually had a standard questionnaire that asked things like names and addresses, and sometimes they presented documents or photos. They demanded to know who wrote a certain document, or who was in the photos. They also wanted to identify where the documents had been printed and who provided us access to the printing press. The torture was always worse when they had these kinds of questions.

It was important to try and protect your body. It helped to shout loudly, because this often cut through the torturer's sadism. For many of them, hearing a person cry out made them realize they were beating a human being, and they would instruct the victim to shut up. But screaming gave you a sense that some resistance, even if it was only verbal, was possible. Many times to avoid looking you in the face, they struck you from behind. You always tried to not talk too much and hold off giving them any information as long as you possibly could. Within my political party, we studied how to prepare for torture and learned that it helped to think about other things such as pleasant memories with friends and family. I also figured out that some torturers didn't treat you so badly and discovered that even within an inhuman system, some people tried to behave as human beings.

We slept fitfully that night on the floor of the dining room without any blankets, and apparently they checked to see whether we were actually students. We all worried about what would happen next. The next day I was freed with many of my companions, but they carried off some of the better-known leaders, although it was never clear how they made the decision about whom to free. It appeared that the leaders of the coup were so busy consolidating control that they didn't have time to waste on us.

I rushed home determined to join the resistance, because the news said that the coup was not yet in control in La Paz, and people were fighting fierce battles in the streets. I hoped that perhaps we could do something to support them. Some leaders close to Torres let us know that the general planned to provide arms to miners and university students. Along with other students, I headed to the outskirts of Oruro to wait anxiously for the arrival of miners from Siglo XX and Huanuni who were expected at midday. Once there, we heard that planes and a train from Challapata were on their way with arms on board, and that some people were already heading to the airport. We joined the group going to the train station.

When the train appeared, it shuffled down the tracks at about six miles an hour, but didn't stop. We thought perhaps that the drivers didn't know where they were supposed to stop. So the *compañeros* farther down the line blocked the train's path, forcing the train to a halt. But to our horror, soldiers poured out and immediately began firing at us, killing three people. The train wasn't carrying the arms we needed; rather, we had been tricked, and it was full of well-armed soldiers sent to crush the resistance.

We scattered in the direction of the Vinto foundry, which was on the way to the airport, where we expected a plane to land with the promised arms. Just as we were getting close, we spotted a cargo plane approaching from the east. As it landed, soldiers streamed off, firing on the waiting miners, killing, wounding, and capturing many. We were really frightened. By that time, mercifully, night was falling, and we took advantage of the darkness to straggle back to the city, heading for the offices of the San José miners' union. A lot of miners and university students planned on spending the night there, figuring that if we were attacked at least we could defend ourselves together. In any case, the coup was not completely consolidated, so we still hoped to mount a counterattack. We arrived quite optimistic, but as we listened to the radio we realized that we were losing, and the group's confidence steadily dissipated.

The military had arrested almost half the miners between those who had surrounded the airport and those at the train station. We later learned that they were cruelly tortured that night. We realized that it wasn't safe to stay in the union building and hurried home to friends and relatives.

In retrospect, it is clear that the commander of the Challapata regiment betrayed us and cast his lot with the military uprising. We later learned that Banzer's group paid a lot of money to buy the allegiance of army commanders, as it would have been difficult even for the army to capture the prefecture or the Second Army Division regimental barracks. On top of all of this, the Camacho regiment had taken control of Oruro. At that point, with neither arms nor a military organization, we had little option but to withdraw. We had been defeated, and we were terribly demoralized.

The next day I went to find some *compañeros* who were arriving from Siglo XX. We headed off to assist those who had been wounded or taken prisoners the previous day. The commission we organized to negotiate their release was successful, because the military lacked the space to hold everyone. The prisoners were released on the condition that they returned to the mines and to work.

In La Paz, sporadic fighting continued the following day, but it was impossible to join the resistance because all the roads were patrolled by the army. President Torres fled to the Argentinean embassy and from there into exile.

Resistance under Banzer

Among Banzer's first acts was to close all universities for two years. From one day to the next, I was unemployed and without a future. As I had spent the first year taking pre-university courses, I was just finishing my first year of law school, but I hadn't taken my final exams. My dream of becoming a lawyer was gone. I felt incredibly depressed, as my life had been turned upside down. Once again I had to start from zero; I was just one more unemployed Bolivian.

Forced to rethink my plans, I first decided to try my luck in the Yungas, east of La Paz, on an undeveloped twenty-four-acre piece of land my parents had purchased with the money they made from selling their llamas when they moved to Llallagua. During this time, I tried hard to maintain my relationship with Carmen, who was still in Oruro, but the distance and poor communications made it very difficult.

I planted potatoes, yucca, and *balusa* potato, as well as custard apple, mandarin oranges, and orange trees, and even some coffee. But I didn't stay long—only about three months—because it was going to be very difficult to make a living: there wasn't a permanent house, just a small hut, and no access to drinking water. I would have had to work long and hard to improve the land to make it productive—some four to seven years before the fruit trees started to bear fruit—and even then the market value of the crops would never have been worth the work I put into producing them. This is the reality of life for small-scale campesino farmers all over Bolivia to this day. I finally came to the conclusion that my only option was to return to the mines.

The political situation had calmed during the months I lived in the Yungas, and I hoped to return to Siglo XX both to work as a miner and continue my union and political activities. I knew that it would be difficult, as I did not have a job waiting for me, and it was becoming harder and harder to get on the payroll. However, I contacted Gilberto Bernal, whom I knew well by then, and we talked about work possibilities. We agreed that while he couldn't get me a job over the short term, I would do clandestine work for the union, until he could help me find another job.

Shortly after taking power, Banzer had outlawed all forms of collective social organization. This was aimed in particular at the unions, not only those of the miners, but of urban workers and campesinos as well. Defiant as always, the miners committed to keeping the now-outlawed unions alive and using them to fight for the return to democracy. We soon decided to organize a national miners' meeting.

As I could travel all over the country, and the union only had to pay my expenses, my first project was to contact other union organizations to start building clandestine networks. While I didn't receive a salary, several comrades put in small amounts of money to cover my travel expenses and support my organizing efforts. I traveled to Colquiri, Matilde, and other small mines to inform people that we were organizing a meeting in the Huanuni district to determine our response to the military government's decrees. I also went to Cochabamba to contact the strongest industrial union in Bolivia at the Manaco shoe factory. Everywhere I went, the leaders received me with enthusiasm, because a visit from a union representative made them feel a little less alone and isolated in their struggle against the dictatorship. In some places the leaders were under constant surveillance, so we had to be especially careful.

Finally, some local mining leaders decided that we needed to contact the top leaders of the COB, who were in exile in Chile, where Salvador Allende had won the presidential elections under the banner of the Unidad Popular (Popular Unity). My party put me in charge of this mission, and I traveled to Santiago with my comrade Gabino Limachi, another university student from the mines. We had to move about secretly, as not only did we lack passports and airfare, but by then we were relatively well-known activists and government surveillance was extensive.

We traveled by train from Oruro to Antofagasta, which was an important commercial corridor for Bolivia's international trade. Some of my contacts were businesspeople without documents who constantly made the trip to Chile, and they served as our guides. "When the border patrol passes by— either in Bolivia or in Chile," they told me, "you need to hide under the seats." They covered us with merchandise. I felt a fair amount of confusion during this trip. On the one hand, I was terrified that I would be imprisoned or killed. But on the other, I was filled with curiosity and excited that I would get to travel and know another country. During the border controls, I could see the officers' feet as they passed by. Psychologically, I had decided to see the whole thing as a children's game of hide-and-seek, and this helped me stay calm. We avoided the controls and arrived in Antofagasta at night after a long and tiring day of travel and headed to our contact's house to sleep.

The Chilean city of Antofagasta was totally different from anything I had ever known. It was surrounded by desert, but what struck us most was the sea. The very first thing we did was to go to the beach and walk by the ocean.

The city was far richer and cleaner than any city in Bolivia, and we didn't see any poor people in the downtown area. But once we climbed up a hill for a bit, we could see the poor neighborhoods, defined by small, precarious houses dotting the hillside. The people everywhere were mostly not indigenous, but either mestizo or white.

We contacted several comrades who generously accompanied us to Santiago. We reached comrade Juan Lechín, the head of the COB, and requested his support for the national miners' congress. He wrote a message to be read at the meeting, and other leaders in the PRIN, his political party, also sent messages and documents with us. I was proud that I had been charged with this mission, and it made me feel quite important.

Gabino and I didn't return together; he ended up staying longer in Santiago. I returned through Tambo Quemado, which was more difficult because there were fewer vehicles on that route, which is now the Pan-American Highway. But it was safer, as there was far less police control. I hitched a ride with a truck up to the Lauca River at about 13,200 feet above sea level and then walked for three long days to reach and cross the border.

I traveled with a Bolivian truck driver, also returning from Chile with his family. He was not a political refugee, but had fled the country rather than face the consequences following a multiple-fatality accident on the road to the Yungas. Like many Bolivians, he hoped to make some money in Chile. But because of the economic crisis he hadn't done well and was struggling on foot with his entire family—his wife and four children, all under ten years old, and his mother-in-law. For me, it was useful to have the company, because I didn't know the route and group travel was safer. I shared the little food I had with them, because they had nothing. We crossed the border, walking through the night to avoid the border controls both in Chile and Bolivia.

Once across the border, we flagged down a bus that was jammed full of passengers en route to Oruro. I was carrying a gallon jug of wine I had purchased in Chile to make me look more like a regular passenger. Seeing that there was no room at the back, the driver said to me, "Leave the wine jug here, and I'll keep an eye on it for you."

Depositing it by the driver, I squeezed myself into a corner. After ten hours of bumping along an unpaved and potholed road, we finally pulled up to a customs checkpoint in Oruro. Two agents clambered onto the packed bus. "Okay," they demanded of the driver, "what are you smuggling?" The driver replied with an innocent look on his face, "Nothing, boss. Actually I brought you some wine." "Let's see it," commanded the agent, "because otherwise I'm going to go through everything." He looked quite pleased as he picked up the jug.

Completely without thinking I yelled out, "Hey, wait a minute, that's my wine! I paid five pesos for it!" The passenger next to me elbowed me in the ribs and whispered, "Shut up, I'll pay you six."

Happy with his wine, the customs agent left.

It wasn't until we stopped in Oruro that I realized that the bus was stuffed full of contraband. Even the seats were simply pieces of material draped over bundles of merchandise. With my jug of wine, I had paid the import taxes for the entire load.

The miners' congress was held after I returned from Chile. It was clear to the PCML leadership that the party lacked young leaders, so they decided to send six comrades abroad to study as part of a long-term party-building project. My younger brother Germán, who was working in the mine then, was among those chosen, not only because he was a good student and leader, but also because he was in considerable danger due to his contact with the National Liberation Army (Ejército de Liberación Nacional, or ELN), a short-lived and failed guerrilla movement that lasted about six months in 1970. But before he resigned from his job, we headed to the union leadership to ask that they support my request to replace my brother for family reasons.

This may seem strange to people in other places, but in the Bolivian mines, a job was not just an individual good; rather, it belonged to the family and could be inherited. Although this was not inscribed in law, it was the usual practice. Most commonly, when a worker died or fell ill with black lung, either his wife or oldest son took his place. Germán's scholarship was not only a great opportunity for him, but it was a relief for me because it would have been almost impossible to get a job any other way as unemployment was rampant. Besides, the mine management under Banzer was far stricter than in previous regimes and actively sought to cut the number of workers as much as possible.

Right before General Augusto Pinochet's 1973 coup in Chile, Germán moved to Santiago and applied to study at the University of Chile. As soon as he arrived, he could see that a coup was probably coming, largely because he had just experienced the same thing in Bolivia. When the coup finally erupted on September 11, it depressed us all, as we saw that workers' movements were suffering defeats, not just in our country, but all over Latin America, and we worried that the possibilities for change were getting increasingly slim. It definitely put a damper on my enthusiasm for political work. Nonetheless, the Siglo XX miners held a huge solidarity march with the Chilean people, and everyone contributed a day's wages to support them.

I was obviously very worried about my brother. He was imprisoned in the Olympic Stadium in Santiago, and we found out months later when a letter finally arrived that he had been sent to the Democratic Republic of Germany [East Germany]. He had tried to go to Albania because of the ties between the PCML and the Albanian Communist Party, but when the Chilean authorities asked him his preferred country they didn't hear him correctly and wrote down Alemania [Germany] instead of Albania. He ended up in East Germany, where he continued his studies in economics and married a German woman. He still lives there, although now working in marketing. He has also written a biography of Evo Morales in German and Spanish.

I returned to taking samples in the Siglo XX mine and, with others, immediately began to organize resistance to the Banzer dictatorship. I made contact with great political leaders whom I had met when I was in university in Oruro, for example, the dean of the law faculty, as well as various professors who were national leaders of left parties. I quickly established myself as a leader, and within three months I was elected delegate of my section of the mine to the Siglo XX union.

At the beginning of 1975, the military carried out an unprovoked late-night raid on the Siglo XX settlement. Soldiers captured and shut down the miners' radio stations, Pío XII and the Miners' Voice, and imprisoned workers and leaders along with some innocent people. We found ourselves living in a permanent state of anxiety, incapable of mounting any resistance because we were under constant attack. This tyrannical state led me, along with other *compañeros*, to realize that we had no choice but to physically resist the military if soldiers came searching for us. I decided that I would defend myself with a gun if necessary. It was the right decision, because at that point, I felt enormously impotent, and I thought that having a gun would make me feel more secure. Under the current situation, there wasn't really any other option. I certainly couldn't count on the government to protect my rights or my life, neither the union nor the party could guarantee my safety, and the possibility of being murdered was high.

Right around that time an opportunity presented itself to buy a gun from a fellow student activist. He appeared after a trip to Sucre and quietly told me, "We have decided to sell the arms we have." Although he was part of a group in his political party committed to armed struggle, I never learned why they decided to sell off their guns. He continued, "I brought twelve rifles and two Heckler assault rifles that can be set for continuous fire with a cartridge belt." He asked me for 1,500 pesos for each one, two months' salary. I, like other miners, couldn't possibly afford such an enormous sum and needed to figure out where to get the money.

A few days before, Marta Laguna, a Bolivian who studied sociology in Paris, had appeared in Siglo XX. Marta was in constant contact with Bolivians exiled in France after Banzer's coup, who were all aware of the political situation we faced. As she was visiting her family in Bolivia, the exiles asked her to contact the miners leading the fight to restore a civilian government. Marta had never been to the mines before, because she was the daughter of a wealthy family from the Bolivian oligarchy. When she came to Siglo XX she asked to interview me, among other union leaders, about the national situation.

Because I realized she had money and was politically committed, it occurred to me to ask her if she would help. I explained, "Look, I don't earn very much money, and I need 1,500 pesos to buy a gun. Can you lend me the money?"

"Let me think about it for a minute." She paused and then continued, "Yes, but you've got to promise me you really will buy a gun and not spend it on anything else." I left and raced off to buy the gun and a cartridge belt. I immediately felt more secure, because I knew I could defend myself if I had to. I told other miners that guns were available, and others followed my example. Marta Laguna headed back to La Paz to stay with her family. A few months later I heard that she had been arrested and deported to France.

In the 1975 union elections I was nominated for secretary of conflicts on a list of candidates headed by Comrade Gilberto Bernal. Although the union was well organized and political, it also presented certain disadvantages. We often spent more time trying to sort out the internal and ideological contradictions than reorganizing an open front against the military dictatorship. Although our party won the 1975 elections, members of other parties, including the Trotskyists, the Communist Party, and the Left Revolutionary Movement (Movimiento de Izquierda Revolucionaria, or MIR), prevented us from taking office and sabotaged us. As happened far too often, they insisted that the elections had been fraudulent and that we hadn't completed the necessary prerequisites and so on. As well, the government perceived the PCML as particularly threatening because we not only were the most powerful party nationally at that point, especially in the mines and universities, but we also absolutely refused to compromise with military regimes.

Prisoner Again

In June 1975, the COB organized a secret congress in a church parish hall in Oruro, and the union selected me as one of the twenty-five or thirty representatives from around the country to attend. While the government had outlawed all such meetings, many national-level leaders returned secretly from exile to participate. The plenary session was just getting under way when we heard a great racket outside: dogs barking and people screaming. But we didn't pay much attention because we were very focused on the inaugural event. Just as the secretary of the COB, René Higueras del Barco, was speaking, a uniformed officer, an armed policeman, and a man in civilian clothing stormed into the room.

The officer said, "Gentlemen, remain calm. This congress has been suspended."

At first when I saw the policeman, I assumed that the COB had armed people to protect the congress. Because no one paid him any heed after his pronouncement, the police officer shot off his gun above his head and shouted, "Everyone! Stand up. Move over against the wall!"

Once again, everyone ignored him, as we thought we were safe because we were in a parish hall and the military mostly left the Church alone. He got furious and grabbed the man closest to him and started to beat him. That was when we realized we were in trouble. At that moment soldiers flowed through every door and started to beat us with their gun butts. There was no way to escape.

We were all taken prisoner; we later learned that one of our own had been the informer, although we never found out who. They arrested more than thirty people in all, and, as they didn't have enough personnel to beat us all at once, we were separated into smaller groups and marched to waiting vehicles through a gauntlet where we were struck by soldiers from both sides. In Oruro, officers rummaged through our belongings as they processed us. It was the first Saturday of the month, which meant I had just received my salary, and, of course, they pocketed my wages. They also took our belts and even our shoes before shipping us to La Paz, where we were placed under the custody of the Ministry of the Interior, which was located behind the Congress building, a colonial adobe structure. It was filled with dark caverns, and its doors had high iron gates.

Two foreign nuns and a priest were among the prisoners, as well as several innocent people who happened to be in the wrong place at the wrong time, including a young man, dressed up in a suit and tie, on his way to a wedding. He got very depressed, because he had to stay a week and couldn't understand why he had been picked up. They also arrested a young couple on their way to the parish to take catechism classes. Fortunately, they freed these two immediately.

In the Department of Political Operations (DOP), which was the modern part of the Congress building, located just off the Plaza Murillo, La Paz's main square, the interrogations started. They tortured us one by one. They screamed, "Where is Juan Lechín Oquendo? How did he get into Oruro?" They knew he had come in secretly and wanted to uncover our networks. I thought they were just making this up in order to justify our detention, because we had lost all contact with Lechín.

"Who made you a delegate to Oruro? Who paid you? How much did they pay you?" As no one had paid me, but rather I had covered the costs of the stay and travel with my own funds, I didn't say a word. This infuriated them, so they beat me again. I knew they would continue torturing me until they got the information they wanted.

They were systematic, and clearly specialists in torture. In most interrogations there were three men: the good cop, the bad cop, and a reporter—while other people sometimes came in and out. The intellectual, the good cop, asked me questions, tried to persuade me, always seemed sure that I was about to tell them something. As well, he tried to convince me, "If you tell the truth, you can go free." When I didn't answer, the bad cop moved in and hit me. He'd say to me, "If you don't speak, I'll kill you."

The good cop interrupted, "No, that's not necessary. He's going to speak, because he is a good fellow with his whole life in front of him because he is so young." They'd ask me again, "Why did you go to the COB congress? Who paid you?"

I told them that no one gave me money.

The bad cop said, "See, what'd I tell you? This one won't say anything." And he kicked me in the stomach hard enough to send me and the chair I was sitting on careening backwards across the floor. In a hard, tight voice, he came up close to my face and shouted, "If you don't talk, if you don't tell me the truth, this is how it is going to go for you." He grabbed his revolver and pointed it at my head. "I am a patient man, but my patience is wearing thin, and I'm going to be forced to shoot you."

I responded, "No, no. I swear I am telling you the truth."

He hit me again, this time with his revolver, and I fainted. From that point on, I don't remember much of what happened. I vaguely recall being stretched out on the floor and then forced to get up again.

The good cop pondered out loud, "Maybe he's telling the truth."

After they took down a few more pieces of information, I was returned to my cell and left alone until the next period of questioning. I was a wreck physically and psychologically. I was really anxious about what would happen, and the mistreatment I had suffered made me want to cry. One of my cell mates saw this and asked me, "What did they do to you?" I couldn't answer him, but I cried in his arms for a long time until I finally was able to share with him what I had suffered.

Another interrogation took place when my worried mother showed up to try and see me. She and I only speak Quechua together. When they heard this, the agents demanded we stop talking and announced, "No, this meeting cannot take place until there is an interpreter." In La Paz, it is not so easy to find a Quechua interpreter, because most people speak Aymara. So while we were waiting, I took advantage of the situation to speak with her a bit in a low voice. "Mom, how are you?"

She told me, "I headed for the university as soon as I got here to figure out where I could find you and where to get permission to see you. The students there gave me a piece of paper with all the information. That's probably why they are angry."

Later, because they couldn't find an interpreter, they wouldn't let me speak with her. Right afterwards, they took me into the torture room, where three agents awaited. They employed the same methods as before. "We know that you are operating from here inside the jail. You're making fun of us. You are rewriting documents and getting them circulated in the university. Tell us, who are you sending them to? Who is paying for all this? Who is doing the printing? Where is the print shop?"

I swore to them that I didn't know anything about any documents. The bad cop started hitting me like he had before. He kicked me and threw me across the room, along with the chair. The chair broke, and he grabbed part of a leg and used it as a club to beat me some more.

One of them said, "Look, you have to come clean and tell us about this. And then you have to respond to all the other questions you haven't answered."

I was barely able to say, "I know you want more information, and please, believe me, I want to tell you the truth. But I have not written any documents, and I have no idea where the printing press is that you are looking for. I don't have any money to print documents."

The persuader said to me, "Okay, we'll stop this session. Go and think about it carefully. When you have everything figured out, you can come back and finish your statement."

The bad cop said, "Wouldn't it just be better to kill him now? He seems really committed to the cause, and I doubt we'll ever get anything out of him."

The good cop looked me directly in the eye and said, "No, this one is going to do the right thing."

Two agents helped me back to my cell. I was half crippled, because they had hit me in the foot.

I spent about three and a half months imprisoned in the DOP without communication with anyone outside the prison, aside from the brief visit from my mother. Then they stuck me for another three months in San Pedro prison, in the center of La Paz, where common criminals are held. When I got out of jail my friends in the mine told me that they had demanded my release. They insisted to the company, "Let him go. If not, we're going on strike." I think the police eventually set me free because it was easier than dealing with a strike.

The rest of the prisoners remained in San Pedro, because their organizations were not as strong as my union. A member of the Miners' Federation came to pick me up when I left the jail, but because I had lost some of my regular awareness on the street, I nearly got run over by a car one block from San Pedro prison. Before I was released, I had to sign a document saying I would no longer participate in union or political activities. But it had no effect on me. I immediately reported to work in the mine and the resistance. As a union leader, as long as the workers continued resisting the oppression of the government and the company, I felt I needed to display an optimistic and determined front. After all, they had made huge efforts to free me, and I had to repay their support.

A national FSTMB congress was called in the Corocoro mining district on May 1, 1976. Our principal goal was to replace the leaders of the federation, because they were bowing under General Banzer's pressure and undermining the struggle for democracy. Once the congress got under way, many of the older leaders who were about to lose their posts began to cry. I had no idea why, because after all, from my limited experience, it seemed that being a leader was really dangerous. But later I found out they were in tears because they stood to lose the one benefit that came with holding office: the payments the government provided to sabotage the struggle against the dictatorship. The new leaders were unwilling to cave in to the government and, in fact, organized the resistance with even greater force. The situation turned far more dangerous for the government, because now it faced a dynamic and uncorrupted opposition.

Some fifteen days after the 1976 congress, General J.J. Torres was assassinated in Buenos Aires by Bolivian agents in an action that was part of Operation Condor. The next day the union denounced the assassination, and the government proclaimed that it would occupy the mine. We blocked all the roads entering the district, but we couldn't prevent the tanks from getting in. The government's goal was the arrest of all union leaders.

Some leaders escaped by squirreling themselves away deep in the mine or fleeing to surrounding communities. Another union leader, Raúl Sánchez, and I were fortunate enough to be able to conceal ourselves within the mining settlement for almost two weeks in a tiny room bolted from the outside. It was horrible, and somewhat ironic: we suffered being locked in a room the size of a cell in order to maintain our freedom. After a while I needed to change my hiding place, because I couldn't stand the confinement any longer and was fed up with the isolation from my political comrades. I snuck out at night, but first I had to go home to pick up some clean clothes. Luck had it that an agent spotted me in the road, but naively I didn't think he would follow me immediately.

I rushed home. My mother was enormously relieved to see me alive. "Thank God you are all right," she whispered. "I thought you had been taken prisoner. Someone must be watching the house."

I answered in a low voice, "Yes, I know, but I'm not going to stay. I just came to pick up a jacket."

I hurriedly said my good-byes, and she asked worriedly, "Where will you go?"

"I'm going to Cristina's house." Cristina had remarried after her first husband, who was also a miner, froze to death after a wedding. He had gotten drunk and fallen asleep beside the road on his way home. This actually is something that happens fairly frequently, given the altiplano's low temperatures. Her second husband was also a miner, and she lived with him and her four children, three from her first marriage.

"In that case let Wilfredo take you," she suggested. My younger brother Willy was eleven or twelve years old, and his presence could help provide me a bit of cover.

I now realize that the agent must have followed me, first to my house and, later, to my sister Cristina's in the Villarroel settlement.

I slipped into Cristina's house and promptly fell asleep. At about 4 a.m., crashing sounds woke me. Just as I was getting up to figure out what was going on, I realized I was hearing the roar from tank and military transport truck engines surrounding the Villarroel mining camp although through the darkness I could not easily see where they were.

I raced to the door in hopes I could escape to the countryside. I whispered to those in the house, "I'm off."

But my relatives had seen soldiers all over the neighborhood, and they begged me to stay. My brother-in-law insisted, "There is no way you can get out."

When the sun came up we sent one of my youngest nephews out as a scout. He raced back and told us with panic in his eyes, "They are going house by house, destroying the floors, the ceilings, and the beds searching for leaders."

The next moment six soldiers burst into the house and forced all of us to line up against the wall of the patio. Other soldiers began searching the house. An officer demanded our identity cards.

"I don't have one," I told him. "I'm the brother of the woman who lives here."

"What is your name?"

"Roberto Rojas."

He scanned his list and said, "No, he's not here. But let me call the informant." A spy came in with his face completely masked.

The officer asked him, "Who's this?"

He said, "It's Félix Muruchi." Immediately they grabbed me and started to beat me in front of my sister, my nieces, and my nephews and pulled me out of the house, shoving me into a red jeep. Beside me sat a soldier and an officer, and in the back more soldiers were crammed in.

They gloated, "That's great that we finally caught up with him." They drove to the public baths in Uncía where they had improvised a jail, and beat me again before shoving me into a cell by myself. As I was already a prisoner, I gave them my real name, which seemed to please them because evidently they considered me a "big fish," which is what they called the important prisoners. I didn't think I was that important, but apparently the combination of my previous arrests, my position on the PCML union slate, and my presence at the aborted national congress in Oruro was enough to elevate my status in their eyes. When they learned who I was they stopped beating me. Meanwhile, I recognized one of the agents, who was the relative of a friend.

I called out to him softly, "Beto, Beto, remember me? I want to talk to you."

He was frightened that I had recognized him and at first didn't want to come anywhere near me. But after a few minutes, he snuck back and asked, "What do you want?"

"A favor. Please tell your brother-in-law Nelson where I am and ask him to let my family know." Nelson was a member of our group and worked as a double agent, a camouflaged revolutionary. Beto promised to tell Nelson.

That same afternoon the soldiers hauled me off to the police station in Llallagua. That night they arrested a lot more people and began to torture us in turn. Dr. Juan del Granado, who has been the mayor of the city of La Paz since 1999, was among our group. At the time he was the press director of the Miners' Voice radio station and an official in a newly formed left party, the MIR, that was largely made up of middle-class intellectuals. Because he had a close relationship with the left-wing clergy at Siglo XX, he had borrowed clothes from a Canadian nun in an attempt to hide. But this didn't work, and when he was arrested, he was shoved into the cell dressed as a nun.

I was positively identified by a government agent, one of my workmates from the mines, whom we had given the nickname of "Governor." He expressed concern, "Hello, Félix. How are you? I've been looking all over for you so that I can help you."

I knew full well he was an informer, so there was no way I was going to reveal anything. He pressed on, "Just tell me what you want so we can help." I didn't utter a word, because I was determined not to help him identify me. After a few more tries, he shook his head in exasperation, and the police threw me back in the cell.

The next morning at six they transported a small group of us—Juan del Granado, Teodoro Campos, and another grassroots mining worker and activist from the Communist Party—to La Paz, in chains and with hoods over our heads. On the way we were able to talk a bit and lament how we had been defeated. We all thought we would likely be imprisoned for a long time, but in spite of all this, we all expressed our determination to continue with the struggle.

We arrived in La Paz without incident and were dispatched to the office of the minister of the interior on the Avenida Arce [Arce Avenue]. There we were pushed up to the third floor, and the four of us stood chained together in the hall. I was shackled to Dr. del Granado with my face to the wall.

Right then, we heard banging and a woman yell, "Open up. I want to go to the bathroom." An agent accompanied her past us down the hall. She recognized Dr. del Granado and said hello. On her way back, she slipped him a note and some money. As I was chained to him, I saw everything.

He read the paper, and then looked at me and whispered, "You know, Félix, I am going to be freed in a little while." He handed me the money and said, "You are going to need this more than I will. Share it with the others."

At that point I couldn't tell how much money it was, but later counted out six hundred pesos, the monthly salary of a miner. This generous act of solidarity on the part of Dr. del Granado moved me deeply.

As he predicted, twenty minutes later an agent barked his name, and we had the handcuffs removed. Dr. del Granado bid us farewell, "Good luck. I hope it goes all right for you." The three of us were forced to stand in the hallway another hour, and then, one by one, we were called in to make our statements. I was first. Two soldiers pushed me downstairs to the basement, where I was shoved into an office with a civilian and two officials from the air force.

The civilian wasted no time. With a sheet of questions in his hand he began: "Why were you arrested?"

I answered, "I have absolutely no idea."

"What activities are you involved in?"

"I am a union leader in Siglo XX."

"Who are the other leaders of the union?"

I told him the legal composition of the directorate.

Then the political questions started: "What party do you belong to? Who is your leader? Why did you get involved in political activities in the district?"

I answered, "Our activities are strictly related to the union, all on the basis of the resolutions, meetings and congresses, and the existing regulations."

They kept repeating to each other, "This is the one." I assumed this was because I had been arrested three or four times before.

They dragged me to another room, which I figured was the torture room. At that moment, another official popped his head in and told the interrogator, "The minister wants to speak to you."

So they left me sitting there alone. Half an hour later, the same interrogator came back, pulled a piece of paper out of the typewriter, and told me, "Here, sign your declaration." Then they transferred me to the DOP, and from that moment on the torture stopped.

PART THREE

From Exile to Exile

Chapter 7

Exile in Chile

A "Guest" of Pinochet

They stuck me in an isolation cell, but just a few minutes later an agent pushed open the door and told me politely, "We are letting you out to the bathroom and to visit other prisoners."

I found my way to an open courtyard for some air. Someone else was there, a young prisoner who spoke with an accent from the Chaco region in southeastern Bolivia. He walked straight over to me and asked, "Did you just arrive?" I answered yes and said, "What are you doing here?"

"I've been here six months," he answered. "I'm so bored. Look, I want to talk to you confidentially about something serious because there is no one else around."

"Okay," I replied. "What's up?"

"Ever since I got here I've been looking for a way to escape. I've figured out a plan, but it'd be easier if there were two of us. I'm going to make my move tonight, and I need to know if you want to come. It's your opportunity. You're young like me, and it doesn't make sense for us to waste our youth in a place like this. Let me tell you how we'll do it."

From the patio he pointed up to the administrative offices windows on the second floor that also faced out onto the street. "We can climb up into the office through that window. I know how to open it, and I've already checked it out by climbing up there once. It's easy. Only one agent with a gun sleeps there. He always keeps his gun in front of him, so it's not hard to grab it. If you help me, we can make it work. Between there and the street, we'd only have to pass one more guard who is at the main door to the outside. He is usually asleep in the office, and he doesn't even lock the door."

"Okay," I said, "but I just got here and can't give you an answer right away. Let me think about it."

"All right, but let me know soon," he replied. "But whatever you do, don't tell anyone else."

The more I thought about it, the more obvious it became that the other "prisoner" was really a government agent trying to set up an escape attempt to give them a pretext for assassinating me. I knew that a man has to plan his own escape—it's not something he can leave to anyone else. Success is never guaranteed, and it's critical to know every possible detail so as to maximize the odds. Two dangers arise with these types of escapes. First, they hand the police an excuse to kill the prisoner, which was common in Bolivia. Second, the authorities can let you escape in order to follow you to discover your contact networks and other political activists.

A little while later the man appeared at my cell, all smiles as he asked, "Have you decided?"

I had figured out that it would be better not to confront him directly, but rather invent some excuse. I said, "Look, it's like this. The government considers me a big fish, and as I've been in jail before, being here isn't such a big deal. I'm pretty sure I'll be sent into exile so I don't need to escape."

The young man said, "Okay, let's drop it because it'd be more dangerous for me anyway, as you're a big shot. Just promise me you won't tell anyone. I'm going out early tomorrow morning." I never saw him again.

Later that night, at about 3:00 in the morning, two agents flung open the door, waking me up. "Muruchi," they ordered, "get up. Put your things together." But I had nothing to get ready because I didn't have anything.

They grabbed me and pushed me across the patio. They shoved me into a dark cavelike room full of other prisoners. The agents handcuffed me to one of them and left the room. The person I was chained to asked, "Who are you?" I didn't answer because he hadn't said who he was, and so he asked me again, "*Compañero*, who are you?"

I shot back, "Who are you?"

"I am Fausto Arce."

"Fausto! Hello. I'm Félix Muruchi."

Fausto was a university student from the public university, the UMSA, in La Paz. I met him when he visited Siglo XX, as he was also a militant in the PCML. His father, Adrián Arce, was an ex–union leader in construction, who had been assassinated in La Paz by the military police during the Barrientos dictatorship.

A little later, agents came with a small flashlight and a paper with illegible text and demanded that we sign it. We scribbled our names without being able to read what the document said. At about 4:30 in the morning, the two agents appeared again. They grabbed the two of us, covered our heads with hoods, and yanked us out to the street, where they shoved us into a jeep and ripped off our hoods. The windows of the jeep were blacked out so it was impossible to see anything. Four other people were already in the vehicle: Walter Villagra, a university leader from Oruro, as well as Jorge Moya, a student leader from Tarija, Rodolfo Siñani, a national leader in my party, and Tomás Bayrón, a university leader from La Paz. Two more prisoners were pushed in, we were handcuffed to each other in pairs, and the jeep took off.

Slowly the vehicle started to make turns, then more turns, and then even more turns. Suddenly it began to climb, and we started speculating about where we were going.

One said, "It looks like they are sending us into exile."

Another wondered, "Maybe the vehicle is going up and we are in El Alto."

"Couldn't we be going towards the Yungas? If it isn't internal exile, then we're being deported."

The vehicle continued to climb, and we concluded we were heading towards El Alto, which sits above the city of La Paz. Shortly after the road flattened out, the jeep stopped. Agents opened the door, and, still chained together, we struggled out and were forced up some steps. At first we didn't realize that we were climbing up into an airplane because it was still so dark. Inside, other people also handcuffed in pairs were already in seats. More prisoners arrived until there were about twenty of us and the plane took off. Nobody had told us anything, and we had absolutely no idea where we were going.

But it soon became clear that we were heading west. This scared us half to death, and we asked each other anxiously, "Why are they taking us to Chile?" General Augusto Pinochet was in power, and we had all hoped that the plane was going to Peru, where there was a relative degree of freedom. We would have felt much safer there.

CHILE AND OPERATION CONDOR

When U.S.-backed General Augusto Pinochet staged a brutal military coup on September 11, 1973, bringing Chile's democratically elected socialist government to a tragic end, Bolivians in political exile from the Banzer dictatorship in Chile were forced to flee the country. Some, like Félix's brother, were caught by the dictatorship and sent farther from home.

But Pinochet's involvement with Bolivia did not end there: it persisted through the intelligence and operational coordination among South American dictators known as Operation Condor. This 1975 arrangement was the first time that militaries in Argentina, Brazil, Chile, Bolivia, Paraguay, and Uruguay—which had been at war with each other more than once in the past—coordinated activities.

It later expanded to include Peru and Ecuador in a more peripheral role. One of Operation Condor's first actions was the Chilean military's assassination of two Bolivian exiles in Santiago.

Initially conceived as a response to revolutionary movements committed to armed resistance, Operation Condor expanded into a multicountry secret "antiterrorist alliance" that targeted democratic opponents to military governments. The six military regimes employed secret prisons, torture, murder, kidnapping, and "disappearances" to track down dissidents outside of their own countries. At least thirteen thousand people were killed and hundreds of thousands were imprisoned in concentration camps through Operation Condor operations (Dinges 2004).

One of Condor's most high-profile actions was the assassination of Bolivian ex-president Juan José Torres in Buenos Aires after the military coup there in 1976. Some twenty-three Bolivians in exile in Argentina disappeared, and six Argentineans were picked up in La Paz and shipped back to Argentina for execution. But thousands of others underwent what Félix describes—capture, torture, and, for the lucky ones, exile.

In Argentina and Chile, the campaign against the democratic opposition reached a massive scale: thousands of people were killed and even more were forced into exile. Regimes tracked down opponents who had fled to other countries, and an international assassination squad killed dissidents in Italy, the United States, and France. Long denied by Washington, the U.S. role in what was called the "dirty war" came to light with the U.S. State Department's 1999 declassification of some CIA documents related to Chile under General Pinochet. They reveal how Nixon's national security advisor Henry Kissinger actively pushed the United States to assist the Chilean military (Dinges 2004).

As Pinochet's regime became more consolidated in the mid-1970s, more of the opposition was subject to internal exile, or what the government called *relegación*. Dissidents were banished to remote parts of the country for up to three months, although this could be extended. These exiles had no right to trial or judicial appeal. One of the destinations was the island of Chiloé in the south, where exiles had to report to police twice a day and survive as best they could, often through a Minimum Employment Program, which paid them about forty dollars a month to carry out menial labor. In 1980, some of the *relegados* founded an NGO in Chiloé, the Office for the Promotion of Development in Chiloé (Oficina Promotora del Desarrollo Chilote, or OPDECH), to address the unmet needs of the poor who had seen state services evaporate under the dictatorship. The organization continues today.

During the time that Félix was exiled in Chile in 1976, Banzer's regime began to face serious economic difficulties. Petroleum production declined sharply, and COMIBOL was operating once again at a loss, despite high mineral prices, as income was marshaled to subsidize other state expenditures. Cotton production in the eastern lowlands also dropped because of a fall in world prices.

The plane landed in Antofagasta, Chile, in a heavy coastal fog, something that was completely unknown to most of us. Most likely they stopped to refuel, and an hour later we were in the air again headed south. About three o'clock in the afternoon, the plane landed in Santiago. We were shoved onto a bus, still handcuffed together, and taken to the offices of the Ministry of the Interior, where we were marched inside. They finally freed us from the now extremely painful handcuffs and kept us there until ten at night, taking our statements one at a time before transporting us to a secret prison in a very big house.

This prison housed women and even children. We were strictly forbidden any contact with the other prisoners and could only observe each other from a distance. The next day the agents informed us, "Representatives from the UN High Commissioner for Refugees are on their way to visit you. You must elect representatives to speak with them." We chose three—Doctor Beltrán Otorrino, a well-known doctor from Potosí, and the other two lawyers. The UN representatives only wanted to know if we were being treated adequately: nothing else was on the table. We were prisoners in a foreign land with a legal system that limited our rights. We tried to demand our return to Bolivia, but our entreaties fell on deaf ears.

That very same night we were put aboard a bus that headed south. We traveled all night, and, at about five in the morning, they removed four prisoners from the bus. A few hours later, at about six or seven, we pulled into a small town and four more men were taken away. Sometime later we got to Puerto Montt, and they put those of us who were left on a boat to cross the channel between the mainland and the islands of the Archipelago of Chiloé. We traveled all day, and in every town they deposited another four people. We never saw any of them again in Chile, except for Jorge Moya and Walter Villagra. Finally only three were left: Fausto Arce, Rodolfo Siñani, whose nickname was Rodo, and me.

Puerto Quellón, Chiloé Island

At 6 p.m., we reached Puerto Quellón, the southernmost town on the island, and they dropped us at the local police station. The commander looked us over dismissively, "We have no cells for you to stay in." The jail was already full.

"You are going to be privileged. In a few moments, you will be moved to a boardinghouse in Quellón." He offered us some tea and explained, "You can go free here, but we will maintain strict control over your movements." He let us know that two other deported Bolivians were already in Puerto Quellón. Then, along with another policeman, he accompanied us to the boardinghouse, where we met them: *compañero* Víctor López Arias, an executive of the FSTMB, and Raúl Rosales, a worker from Catavi mine. Raúl was not a political activist, but had been picked up simply because he was a lodger in the Miners' Federation building in La Paz while he was studying.

Before he left, the officer asked the women who ran the inn to provide us some dinner. We each gulped down two full servings of a seafood soup, our first complete meal in almost a week. The women laughed, seeing us eat so much.

We were puzzled, "What's so funny?"

Smiling shyly, one of them explained, "Here, we think that seafood soup is an aphrodisiac, and with you taking so much of it, you are going to be keen on having sex."

Rodolfo laughed, "Well if that is true, then we can't be held responsible, because you are the ones who gave us the soup!" We felt really good to be able to joke and laugh after all that we had been through. Waves of relief washed over us, and we began to unwind in a setting where people were free.

The women told us that we could lodge there as long as we stayed in Quellón, but we would have to pay for our room. As we didn't have any money, we couldn't make arrangements beyond the first night, when the three of us crammed into a single room. We kept asking each other, "What on earth are we doing here?" but exhausted, we fell asleep, agreeing, "We'll figure it out tomorrow."

The next day the owner of the pension offered us breakfast, and afterwards we headed straight to the police station. The police commander explained the rules that governed our imprisonment, "You are under our complete command and control. You must follow national laws set by the current government of General Pinochet. Any infraction, any attempt to break these laws, will be sanctioned according to Chilean law, and let me tell you, the sanctions are drastic. I hope that our relationship will be cordial and we won't have any problems."

We had to appear every morning at seven on the dot to sign in at the station. Afterwards we could go off to work. The officer made it clear that we were expected to look for a job and that we should check with every business in town. Then at lunchtime, supposedly a time for a break, we had to return to the station again to sign in. And finally, for the third time each day, we had to sign the book yet again at six in the evening.

The other two Bolivians, who had arrived a week earlier, were already working as casual laborers in a small carpentry shop. Speaking to them and their bosses, we quickly realized that it was not going to be easy to find jobs in a small town like Quellón.

Chile had a system of short-term jobs, designed for the unemployed, which paid a minimum salary. These laborers were called "plan workers." I think money for the program came from international institutions. While it was a public program, it was implemented through various private organizations and, on occasion, the Catholic Church. The two Bolivian exiles who arrived before us were employed in this way. However, there were no more positions for plan workers in town. As the police had ordered us to find work, we went to the parish to see if there was something we could do there.

The nuns said they didn't have any work, but asked us what skills we had. We told them, "We can do any kind of manual work. We could even take care of your garden."

From that point on, whenever we spoke to the lieutenant at the police station, we told him that we were fixing the parish garden, but the truth was that we worked there only one afternoon. A couple of days after we arrived, the same lieutenant put us in touch with a government representative from Santiago. This man informed us that an urbanization plan was under way to map the streets in Puerto Quellón, and they needed technicians for the job.

"Let's see if I can arrange for you to help," he told us. I was offered work as a draftsman because of my experience in the engineering department in Siglo XX. Fausto, who had studied engineering, also had the necessary technical skills. We explained to the representative how we would proceed, presenting a rough work plan as we spoke. We convinced him we could do the job, and he hired us on the spot. He even gave us the basic information and materials we needed to get the project off the ground. We started working on it, but he never returned and our efforts were in vain.

During those first days, the women at the boardinghouse, backed by a guarantee from the police, provided our food. About a week after we arrived, while we were busy drawing, a representative of the United Nations High Commissioner for Refugees turned up. She was an Argentinean, Ms. Herrera, and had contacted us independently of the police.

She explained, "As you don't have jobs, the UN High Commissioner will pay a minimal amount to cover your food and lodging." She left us some money and told us, "You can live here or somewhere else, but find a place where you can settle in." After a search, we rented larger and more comfortable rooms.

Once we moved, two women accompanied by a beautiful young girl showed up. The first thing they asked was if one of us was a physician, because the town was so small that everyone had heard that five deported Bolivians had arrived and one was a doctor. One of the women said, "I want to talk to the doctor in private about my daughter's health." But the supposed doctor was Rodolfo, who had never studied medicine in the university and wasn't even a nurse. He had, however, read widely about medicine and taken some first aid courses as part of training within the guerrilla movement during the period when Che was in Bolivia.

Nonetheless, Rodo made an appointment to examine the girl at her house. Once the women left, the landlady revealed that the young woman was a local beauty queen. All three of us went along to the appointment, above all because we were really curious about this beautiful young woman. But when we arrived, the woman asked Rodo to accompany her to an inner room, which sparked even more curiosity. After about fifteen minutes, he emerged looking a little disconcerted and handed the woman a list of medicines. While she hurried off to buy them, we asked him what was going on. At first he refused to say, telling us the woman had sworn him to confidentiality. But we kept pressuring him until he revealed that the young woman had advanced syphilis and didn't dare get involved with anyone. This frightened us, because we had been warned there was a lot of syphilis in Chiloé and here was evidence of it. We also had heard that the disease had exterminated one of the indigenous groups on the island, the Alacalufes, and we worried that perhaps we would have the same luck. But the medicines that Rodo suggested cured her. It was astounding to us that she was so afraid to visit a local doctor that she nearly died.

I'm from the North of Chile

Puerto Quellón is a fishing village. At ten at night, the fishermen headed out to sea, and by six the next morning they were unloading their catch. As they had fished all night, the women sold seafood during the day. The people there believed that women shouldn't fish, which I regarded as a silly superstition until I remembered that in Bolivia we didn't allow women into the mines, as we believe it brings bad luck. In Quellón, the goddess of the seas is called Pincoya, and she is considered very jealous. When a woman dared go fishing, the goddess made the fish and other sea creatures disappear. So only men could be fishermen, and they sustained the family. But the risks for fishermen were extremely high, and if a man drowned or got rheumatism, which was endemic, a family was thrown into crisis. And, of course, women had little choice but to marry to ensure they had someone to provide for them and their children.

One morning I got up early and headed for the coast, although we were prohibited from visiting there, as they were afraid we would try to escape somehow. But that early no police were about. Out on the sea, I spotted a boat rowed by a woman returning with the night's catch. At the back, a man sat lounging. As the boat pulled up to the shore, the woman jumped up to her knees into the freezing water and then unloaded the huge mound of seafood. At this time of the morning in the middle of winter, the air temperature was well below freezing. Stepping into that water was a kind of torture. As I watched, the woman did everything, finally carrying the man on her back to the shore so that he could avoid getting his feet wet.

I thought perhaps he suffered from poor health and that this was the reason the woman had unloaded the catch. I must admit I didn't offer to help, because the cold was too much for me; I couldn't imagine putting my feet into that frigid water. I asked a Chilean who was passing by, "Why did that woman carry the man from the boat?"

The man looked at me a bit puzzled, "Where are you from?"

I answered, "I'm from the north of Chile." I figured it was safer to lie, as it was illegal for me to be by the coast. In the north of Chile, there are lots of Aymaras, so it was conceivable I could have come from there.

"Aah! That explains your question. That's the custom here: women must carry the men in after they go fishing. Look, you can see that other boats are coming in now and it's always the same." He laughed and continued, "You need to get married to a Chilota, because here women will bathe you as well."

What he said was true. I even saw visibly pregnant women do everything.

Some of the people on the island were involved in commerce, as boats arrived from Argentina in the port, and people from Santiago traveled through Quellón on their way to Argentina. This meant many of the visible economic activities were concentrated around certain inns and small hotels. But the economically most powerful people on the whole island were the ranchers and farmers, mostly German, Italian, and Spanish immigrants. The Huilliche, the local indigenous group, were the poorest people there and had been almost completely exterminated after contact with Europeans. They generally worked for the immigrants, the majority of whom arrived toward the end of the nineteenth century.

The ranchers and farmers raised cows and sheep, as well as grew potatoes, one of the island's traditional products. Many of the Chilotes were sure that Chiloé was the first place that potatoes were grown in the world. [While potatoes are actually originally from the Andes, the potatoes in southern Chile—which grow during the long summer days there—are the ones that were adopted in Europe.]

Overall, we were a bit disoriented, because the south of Chile is so different from the altiplano. We arrived in the winter, when Chiloé was cold, dark, and rainy. And even though the altiplano is cold, this was a different, bone-piercing cold because it is so damp. Some Bolivians cried that the climate was intolerable. We had to cover our faces when we slept and keep our hands inside the blankets, because otherwise it felt like they would freeze. Chiloé was so far south that it was dark almost the entire day, whereas even in the winter the altiplano days are always sunny and relatively warm.

The isolation made it more difficult for us. We didn't receive any news from home. Some of my *compañeros* became very depressed and worried about their families. Several became so sick from the combination of the bad weather and worry that the UN High Commissioner for Refugees (UNHCR) moved them to Santiago.

Those of us who stayed behind gradually became friends with some of the townspeople. Among these was a schoolteacher, a socialist under Allende, who talked politics with us during the long, dark evenings. Because he was wealthy, he was somewhat protected from the repression. He surreptitiously lent us books on social themes, including work by the Chilean Marxist-Leninist Marta Harnecker and poetry by the famous Chilean poets Pablo Neruda and Gabriela Mistral. Reading and talking about these works gave us strength and encouragement to continue our political work.

People from the church also helped us, particularly four local nuns and two priests who arrived every weekend. They arranged with the police to show us the surrounding islands, so we got to know the area pretty well. But our dream was always to return to Bolivia to carry on the struggle.

Slowly winter faded while we spent our time reading and writing. Rodolfo Siñani wrote a book of poems and another about the legends of the island. As winter disappeared, we realized how beautiful the place is. The freezing climate and the circumstances of our arrival had masked its attractions. Nonetheless, we felt strange, that we had been transported to a place where we didn't belong. For us, this sense of alienation was stronger than the charms of the landscape.

In summer, people on vacation from other parts of Chile visited the islands. They spent hours on the beach walking, swimming, and sunbathing. The climate changes completely in the summertime, and the sun comes up at three or four in the morning and sets almost at midnight. It was a rhythm of life that was totally different from what we were accustomed to. Even work hours shift in the summer, as people often slept in the middle of the day to escape the heat. When tourists headed for the beach, the only thing

Félix and other exiles on a boat in southern Chile. 1976. From the private collection of Félix Muruchi.

they carried with them was a bit of salt, wine, and bread—nothing else. At that time there were hardly any restaurants or snack bars on or close to the beach, but people ate seafood right from the shore. Small bubbles in the sand indicated that a clam or some other shellfish hid below. They dug it up, rinsed it off in the sea, salted it to taste, and popped it in their mouths. Clams or mussels, along with their wine and bread, made a typical lunch. I found it really interesting that people could eat directly from nature without needing anyone to prepare their food. During my time in Chile I learned to eat seafood, something I never even knew existed when I lived at Siglo XX.

Flight

As the months passed, Fausto, Rodo—before he fell ill with an ulcer and was moved to Santiago—and I developed an escape plan. Walter Villagra, the student leader from Oruro exiled on a nearby island, snuck over to help us. We had two options: flee to Argentina or head to Santiago. We decided against Argentina, because we knew neither the road nor anyone there.

And besides, Argentina was in the midst of the dirty war under the military dictatorship of General Jorge Videla, who some said was even worse than either Pinochet or Banzer. It was easier to go to Santiago, because we knew the route, and besides, we were in touch with people who traveled there frequently and could assist us. Also, it wasn't the first time I had been in Chile, as I had come secretly during the Allende period. In general, I found the Chileans a very open, kind, and supportive people. We spoke with many of them about places and routes, and they always shared information. They assumed we were asking out of curiosity.

Soon after Rodolfo was transferred to Santiago, Walter was also moved for health reasons by the UNHCR, which managed to get their status changed so they could go into exile. This left Fausto and me the only Bolivians still on the southern part of the island. Because we remained healthy, we realized that there was no possibility that the UNHCR could directly help us attain political asylum. We also came to the conclusion that it was impossible to return to Bolivia from the islands; it was just too far and much too dangerous. We made up our minds to seek exile to a European country.

Two key people assisted us. Jorge Moya, a comrade from my political party in exile on a nearby island who was also determined to escape, had a Chilean girlfriend who helped us plan every step. She transported contraband goods between Chiloé and Santiago. As she traveled frequently, she could gather information about police checkpoints, how long each stage of the trip took, and the fastest and safest form of transportation for each leg of the journey.

The biggest challenge was passing the numerous police checkpoints. If we were caught, the risk was enormous that they wouldn't just arrest us, but rather simply kill us, a common method of dealing with activists under Pinochet. When we first arrived the police warned us that the army had instructions to shoot fugitives. And, because we were Bolivians, the soldiers hated us even more than they despised Chilean activists, probably because of the War of the Pacific Bolivia fought with Chile, even though the hatred was created by our respective governments. But nonetheless, by attempting to escape, we were risking our lives and honestly felt that we either would succeed or be killed in the effort.

Rodolfo also played a critical role from Santiago. He and Walter Villagra had both been granted exile in Sweden for humanitarian reasons and were finalizing their exit visas.

Fortunately for us, even though we were political prisoners in internal exile, the Chilean government provided us the same identity cards as those used by its citizens. As we possessed no other identification, we presented these at police checkpoints. We had figured out that we looked a lot like Chiloé's indigenous inhabitants, and many people thought we were local native people. Because they were so poor, the Huilliches often migrated for work. So Jorge's girlfriend assured us that all we needed to do at the checkpoints was to show our identity cards from far away and hope that the authorities wouldn't examine them too closely and discover we were Bolivian, not Chilean, nationals.

One difficulty that at times seemed insurmountable was how we were going to pay the trip's costs and cover additional expenses in the case of an emergency. Jorge practically lived with his girlfriend, and she offered to pay all his costs. Fausto had received some money from his brother through one of the nuns. I had less luck. Although I sent a letter to my family through the Church, they had written back to say that they weren't in good enough financial shape to send me any money.

In October, a young, attractive, dark-haired Spanish nun arrived from Santiago. She worked on human rights issues, and through a contact with UNHCR, had initiated an investigation regarding the Bolivian exiles. UNHCR hired her to interview all of us who had been deported to the south of Chile. Originally, she planned to visit for only three days, but she ended up staying an extra week and then announced she'd like to visit an island even farther south. We were getting along really well, so she asked me if I wanted to accompany her. We obtained police authorization because of her association with the Church and headed off.

During the trip, at some point I realized how attracted I was to her, and I started holding her hand. She looked at me quizzically and said, "You know that I'm a nun, right?" As if she was saying that I shouldn't hold her hand.

I replied, feeling quite bold, "I am aware of it, but that doesn't mean we couldn't have an affair."

She beamed and laughed. We hugged and started to fall in love.

When we returned to Quellón she said she would extend her trip for another week if I promised to visit her every day at the parish.

That's when I told her about my escape plan. She was willing to help because she was very supportive of us politically. She also realized that I would most likely be exiled to Europe and that we could possibly meet again there. I asked her to help me with a loan. I said we needed a total of three hundred dollars, each one of us a hundred.

"I don't have that much money, but I can give you one hundred dollars on one condition," she said. "I want to see the plan carried out. I don't want to feel you're taking advantage of me, as I've seen that happen too often to nuns. People think we will turn over money under any pretext."

I promised her, "If everything goes according to plan, you'll see results."

She handed me the money and returned to Santiago a few days later. Her generosity was an act of great solidarity and made our escape possible.

We had lived on the island for six months, and during this entire time, our behavior had been exemplary. We were always on time signing in; we never forgot our appointments, and, in fact, we had become quite friendly with most of the police so that they wouldn't suspect us of planning an escape.

We made our move before Christmas. Our travel plan involved a combination of buses, a boat, and a train. At six in the morning, Fausto and I set off north on the first bus. We didn't get on at the bus stop, but flagged it down on the road just past the police checkpoint. But as the bus pulled up, we were dismayed to spot one of the most unpleasant policemen we knew from Quellón sitting right beside the driver. We were in a panic: we couldn't postpone our plans, because everything was set up for that day and we didn't have any alternative.

We saw no choice but to take the risk. We didn't have a clue if the authorities had discovered our plan or if the policeman's presence was merely a coincidence. Luckily for us, the bus had both front and back doors. We quietly entered the rear door and found an inconspicuous seat. It is likely that because we looked so much like local indigenous people, even if the policeman noticed us, he assumed we were just another pair of local men traveling north in search of work. Fortunately, we were able to pay our fare to the assistant.

When we arrived at the next town, Castro, where Jorge Moya was waiting for us, the policeman got off. It was clear he hadn't recognized us. But we needed to hurry to the next bus, which was the tightest connection of the entire trip, and the policeman was strolling casually in the direction we had to go. We were incredibly lucky, as not only was he completely oblivious to our presence, but he turned when he came to the first corner. We took off sprinting as fast as we could. We leapt on the bus seconds before it pulled out and headed for the ferry that crossed the Chacao Canal to the mainland. This was our only opportunity to catch the ferry, because it ran precisely on schedule.

Six policemen, three on each side of the walkway, were checking luggage and the documents of people boarding the boat. But because our bags were the same as those used by the locals, the police assumed we were migrants and didn't pay us much attention. We showed them our identity cards from a distance. They barely looked at them, and then they waved us through, "Go on. Go on." But just past the checkpoint one of them suddenly turned toward us, and we began to shake with fear. But he only asked, "Where are you heading?"

We answered, "Santiago."

"Okay," he replied. "Good luck. I hope things go well for you there."

Once the boat was crossing the canal, we were enormously relieved, because we had overcome the first big hurdle without a hitch and were right on schedule.

When the boat docked, we found ourselves confronting an even stricter checkpoint, which turned out to be the worst of the whole trip. Policemen were everywhere, but once again, seeing our Indian faces and our meager bags, they tended to ignore us. Some people were pulled out of line to have their documents, bodies, and suitcases checked for contraband coming from Argentina, but as we looked poor, they decided we couldn't possibly have anything of value. Once we passed the control, our immediate tension eased, and Jorge's girlfriend was waiting as she had promised. She hailed a taxi that took us to the bus station, where again we arrived with just enough time to board the bus clutching the tickets she had purchased for us.

She traveled with us several hours north until we boarded an express train that only stopped in Concepción before arriving in Santiago. She had figured out this was not only quicker, but would allow us to avoid the multiple police checkpoints that dotted the road. In Concepción, a lot of people got off and on the train. Conductors, but not police, walked through and checked our tickets. Seven hours later we arrived in Santiago.

Rodolfo Siñani and Walter Villagra were anxiously waiting for us. They were lodged in a small hotel under UNHCR protection. They took us to a hostel they figured could serve as a safe house, and once settled in we discussed the next step. By then news of our escape was being broadcast all over the radio and newspapers, warning the public to be on the lookout for three Bolivians—Jorge Moya, Fausto Arce, and Félix Muruchi—who had escaped from Chiloé. According to the announcements, all trains and highways to Santiago from the south were under strict surveillance. As well, authorities had blockaded the routes to the border with Argentina. We realized how incredibly lucky we were that we had made all our connections. While they thought they had us surrounded, we had escaped their dragnet and were already in Santiago.

We decided our best option was to contact UNHCR. Fortunately, Ms. Herrera, who had visited us in Chiloé, was still in Santiago. Early the next morning we appeared at her office, and when she saw us she nearly fainted. Visibly upset, she demanded, "What have you done? And why? They are going to put all kinds of pressure on me because of this. The Chilean police are looking everywhere for you."

One of us, I don't remember who, told her, "We fled because we couldn't stand it there any longer. It's been six months, and there's no indication that we would ever get off the island. We want to leave the country. So, what do we do now?"

It was clear that she didn't have a clue how to proceed, but we were insistent. As our other *compañeros* were waiting for exile in Sweden, we suggested, "Why don't you phone the Swedish ambassador immediately and request an appointment? We'll ask him for political asylum."

She called the ambassador but didn't tell him what we wanted. He responded that he couldn't meet with us for at least a couple of days. We were well aware that we had very little time, so we requested she call another embassy.

She suggested the Dutch. She phoned the ambassador for an appointment to visit with three Bolivians to talk about international issues. He agreed to meet us in the afternoon. With Ms. Herrera at our side, we were ushered into the ambassador's office. I remember he was very tall and dressed in a suit, which intimidated us a bit. But we wasted no time. "We are political prisoners pursued by the Chilean police," we informed him. "We want to apply for asylum in Holland."

The ambassador's immediate response was genuine fear, and he almost shouted, "How could you do this to me? Why did you come to this embassy? I am just a simple representative of my government, I can't just do what I want—I must consult with my government first." He paused, calmed himself down, and then continued in a professional tone, "What I can do is see if my government is prepared to receive you as political exiles."

We insisted that we would not leave the embassy, and if they rejected our appeal for asylum, we would just have to stay there. The ambassador got flustered again and called Holland immediately. His counterpart obviously couldn't give him a reply right away, and he told us, "Just wait here until we get some word from Holland."

Right before three o'clock, we found out that our request had been accepted. We were overjoyed. The ambassador then asked, "How many more Bolivians are there exiled in the south of Chile? My government wants to know, because it is willing to help them as well." This was overwhelming news for us. Not only had we managed to escape, but it looked as if our efforts could win asylum for our *compañeros* still stuck in the south as well.

The next obstacle, the Chilean government, was huge. The ambassador was worried that if he revealed where we were, we risked arrest, but he could see absolutely no way around it. He explained, "You are under Dutch protection, and we guarantee your personal safety. But because we are in Chilean territory, they have to provide exit visas, and, therefore, we must inform them that you are here." He and Ms. Herrera had intense discussions trying to figure out how best to resolve this conundrum.

A little later, the ambassador told us, "We have gotten in touch with the Chilean government. Before they will grant you exit visas, we must hand you over to them so they can record your statements. Otherwise they'll never let you depart the country. We don't see that we have any choice." He tried to reassure us, "I will take you personally to the Ministry of the Interior to guarantee your safety. They have also promised me that they won't torture you."

He asked us if we agreed to this plan. We talked about it a few minutes and replied, "Yes, we don't see that we have any other choice."

The appointment was set for ten or eleven the next morning. In the meantime, the ambassador moved us in his official car to a safe house that belonged to a Chilean journalist. The next morning we were picked up by the same vehicle. With the ambassador at our side, we cautiously entered the Ministry of the Interior.

The secretary said, "Mr. Ambassador, the minister would like to see you in his office for a few minutes." When we tried to accompany him, we were stopped short by the secretary, "No, not all of you, just the ambassador." Looking a bit confused, the ambassador was ushered into the office, while we remained in the waiting room.

Suddenly two or three different doors burst open and armed guards rushed in. They grabbed us and pulled us out of the office, roughly shoving us. We couldn't believe this was happening and kept shouting, "What are you doing? Where are we going?" They replied that they were simply taking us to record our statements. The three of us were separated, and they hauled me down a long corridor.

I was stuck in a bare office that had only a desk, a manual typewriter, three chairs arranged behind the desk, and one in front where they forced me to sit. Three civilians interrogated me. They utilized the same methods as those in Bolivia: the good cop, bad cop, and the reporter.

The good cop started, "Tell us the truth about this escape from Chiloé to Santiago. We are counting on you."

Another man, standing up and half-leaning on the desk, warned me, "If you don't tell us the truth, just wait and see what we'll do to you. You can count on me for that."

They demanded, "What time and day did you leave Chiloé?" As interrogation was nothing new for any of us, we had discussed long and hard about how critical it was for our stories to match. The best approach was to tell the truth. But as we couldn't betray any of the people who helped us, we had to be sure not to tell them the whole truth.

"Who did you come with?"

I explained we had come on the same bus as Sergeant Carcomo, the Puerto Quellón policeman who had walked so slowly in Castro. We had decided to reveal his name to the authorities if we were captured because he had always treated us so poorly.

The seated man stood up, and the three of them left the room, leaving me on my own. About an hour later, they returned and demanded, "What arrangement did you have with this policeman?"

"We didn't have any arrangement," I answered.

The interrogator continued, "What Chilean helped guide you to Santiago?"

I responded, "We came on our own, using public transportation."

The one playing the bad cop thrust his face into mine, "That's a complete lie. I warned you: speak the truth." He hit me on the back. Then he threw me off the chair and beat me until I was about to faint. They really frightened me, because I was convinced they might kill me. We knew what they had done during the coup, and that they had murdered many more people than the Bolivian military ever had.

They demanded to know how we had crossed the Chacao Canal and who transported us in their boat. When I answered that we had traveled on the public ferry, they didn't believe me and I was beaten again.

Because at that point I was an old hand at being tortured, I knew exactly what they would do and precisely what they wanted. We had carefully prepared ourselves to make sure that we would all reveal the same thing about several key points—the time we left, the specifics of each stage of the trip, how we developed our plan by talking to tourists, that we worked it out together and decided everything collectively. I assumed that the others were being questioned just like me, and even though I didn't know exactly where my friends were, I was sure they were close by. Every time they extracted information on one stage of the trip, they left the room to verify that it matched the statements of the others. Anytime they discovered what they thought were contradictions, they assumed we were lying and started beating us again.

This went on all afternoon, until about six or seven at night, when they hauled us back to the waiting room, totally bruised but not seriously hurt. The ambassador was sitting there, and I assumed that he had just arrived back at the ministry to pick us up.

The Chileans blurted rudely, "Here are your three Bolivians. We honored our promise." The ambassador jumped up, and we raced out of the ministry as fast as we could. From the moment we were kidnapped, the ambassador told us, he had not budged from the minister's office. The only thing that he was willing to discuss with the minister was our prompt return and our exit visas. They went around and around until the minister finally agreed to provide the necessary paperwork. He then informed the ambassador that we had to be out of the country within three days. This proved to be a very important condition, because otherwise we would have had to remain in the embassy indefinitely.

We were thrilled with this news, and at the ambassador's office, he offered us some soft drinks to celebrate. We explained everything that had happened to us at the ministry, and he was furious that the Chileans had broken their promise not to torture us. To reassure him, we said, "Well, they didn't torture us much, but they did give us a sound beating."

The next day the driver picked us up early to begin the paperwork for our passports and exit visas. Suddenly another obstacle arose. The only direct flight within three days from Santiago to Europe was a Lufthansa plane that stopped in La Paz. If we were captured again, who knew what they would do to us. As it was clear we couldn't return to Bolivia, the ambassador spoke to the airline and then directly with the pilot. On the following day, December 28, 1976, with our exit visas about to expire, we nervously headed to the airport still unsure if we could travel. The pilots had agreed to hide us from the Bolivian authorities. With this promise, we climbed aboard the plane.

When we landed in La Paz, the pilot said, "Just stay here" and stuck us in the cargo section behind a curtain. In the meantime, the people who cleaned the plane climbed aboard. We were really worried that Chilean agents had informed Banzer's Ministry of the Interior that we were on the plane. We feared they would kidnap us again and we would be worse off than when we started. But our luck held, and as the plane rose into the sky, a sense of relief and joy swept over us, as we were safe.

At the same time, just to be in Bolivia again, even for a little while, even though I couldn't get off the plane, saddened me deeply. As I peered through the plane's windows I saw the city of La Paz and realized I was an exile without the right to enter my own country. I was bound, against my will, to begin a new life in a new land.

Chapter 8

Exile in Holland

EXILE

Physically forcing political foes into exile has been a tactic utilized so frequently throughout Latin American history that it has profoundly affected the evolution of the region's politics. The very term "Latin America" was coined by exiles in Paris during the mid-nineteenth century, highlighting the crucial role that exiles have played in developing regional identity.

Latin America's brutal dictatorships in the 1970s created a flood of exiles from countries as disparate as Chile, Argentina, Brazil, Uruguay, Bolivia, Peru, El Salvador, and Nicaragua. They often escaped not only by fleeing to other countries in the region or to the United States, but also to Canada and Europe. From the 1960s to the 1980s, their principal European havens were Sweden, Norway, Denmark, Switzerland, France, Germany, Holland, Great Britain, Spain, and Portugal. Most were political refugees; inevitably some took advantage of the political persecution to seek better economic opportunities elsewhere, although the dividing line between political and economic causes for migration is virtually impossible to determine. For those of European origin, they were often returning to places their grandparents or great-grandparents had emigrated from generations before.

Many Southern Cone refugees were highly educated, were fluent in a second European language, and had previously traveled abroad. These individuals had a far easier time finding suitable work and living situations than exiles from poorer, less Westernized countries. Some refugees were like Félix: working class and poor, with few job, language, or cultural skills appropriate for their new homes.

Their varied experiences in exile were shaped in no small part by a combination of factors: the country that expelled them; the dynamics of the country that received them; and their ethnicity, gender, and economic class. In some countries, like Félix's experience in Holland shows, they received considerable support from a government willing to facilitate their adaptation. But in other countries, like the

United States, with fewer social and support services, they often faced poverty and exclusion, although they frequently had the advantage that they could incorporate themselves into larger existing Latino communities.

Many suffered what is now recognized as post-traumatic stress disorder (PTSD) from their experiences of torture and fleeing for their lives, often leaving families and friends to a horrendous fate at the hands of the dictators. Exile meant the loss of their roots on the one hand and new possibilities for education and social advancement on the other. Many struggled with the loss or alteration of their sense of identity and purpose, as well as isolation and a profound guilt at their inability to adapt successfully to the country that often had saved their lives.

Others struggled to overcome a sense of feeling like victims in their host society. Some felt tremendous relief at their escape from dictatorship; but for many, exile was an insurmountable tragedy. In a strange land, some discovered a sense of strong national identity for the first time, as well as a shared identity with other exiles. Exiles are often cast into the role of representing their country in their new home, but inevitably they are also shaped by the society they find themselves in. New challenges arise when their children grow up as French or Canadian, rather than as Brazilians or Salvadorans.

Félix's experience in Holland touches on many aspects of the realities of Latin American political refugees from the 1960s to the 1980s: the often complicated relationships among communities of exiles from different countries and of varying political tendencies; the importance of continued political activism in conjunction with local solidarity and political activists; the often profound differences between exiles of different backgrounds; the importance of support and personal determination; and for those who returned home, their reintegration and often important role in democratization (Hite 2000; Roniger and Green 2007).

The political issues current in their host societies also affected their perspectives: many returned home from North America or Europe with different views on gender, sexuality, and race; the importance of protecting the natural environment; and the role of left political parties and the various strains of Marxism, as is clearly seen by Félix's transformation. They brought these changes in viewpoint back as they engaged as political activists in their countries once again.

We landed at Frankfurt's enormous airport after a long, tiring flight. I had never seen anything so large and modern in my life and was tremendously impressed. A Dutch government representative was waiting for us at the gate. As we had to change airlines, the representative escorted us. He gave us a voucher for lunch, and, after showing us where we could eat, headed off to attend his other responsibilities. In the restaurant, we had our first encounter that hinted at the huge adaptation that lay ahead. No one spoke a word of Spanish. We asked for chicken by pointing to it on the menu and managed to ask for "orange" to drink. The waiter offered us wine as an aperitif, and we had no idea how to respond when he asked us, "Red or white?" When we didn't answer, the waiter pointed first to his dark red jacket and then to the white linen tablecloth to indicate the choices. It was the first of the many culture shocks we would face in Europe.

When we landed in Amsterdam, a crowd of Bolivians, Chileans, and Dutch greeted us at the airport. They applauded enthusiastically as we got off the plane. I was a bit startled because I didn't know anyone in the crowd, but I figured that many of them must be exiles who had heard about our case. It was a great relief to know that there were people concerned about our well-being.

After dinner at the hotel where they put us up, a Chilean *compañero* offered to give us a tour of Amsterdam. The first place he showed us was the red-light district, which was right behind our hotel. Seeing women exhibiting themselves completely nude in windows that faced directly onto the street was my second cultural shock. Such open commercial sex upset me profoundly, leaving behind a confusion that lasted for months. We had arrived in an advanced country and lacked any context to understand what we were seeing. Was the whole country, and the rest of Europe for that matter, like this? Why did our friend think this was the first thing we should see? Honestly, it made me want to run away. For a long time afterwards, whenever I visited somewhere new, I wondered what relationship this new place or experience had with that world of naked women displaying their bodies in windows.

The next day we made an appointment with the Dutch National Workers' Federation, and we met with the leader, Wim Kok, a socialist who later became prime minister of Holland. He welcomed us warmly. A representative of the Dutch Workers' Federation accompanied us, and we had the opportunity to explain in some detail the situation that Bolivian miners were facing.

Finding a Place to Live

A refugee assistance organization helped us get settled and integrated into Dutch society, covering our costs for food and lodging. We stayed for about a month in a hotel full of refugees, mostly political exiles from Chile, Argentina, and Uruguay.

Henk Pelgrom, a Dutch man who had been in touch with several Bolivian refugees in Sweden, including Rodolfo Siñani, came to visit us. Although he didn't speak any Spanish, he was determined to communicate and arrived with a Dutch-Spanish dictionary in hand so that we could understand each other a bit. He also brought us a message from Rodolfo.

Henk invited us to visit his house, where we met his friend Mr. Lucas Vis, who had worked as the national director of the symphony orchestra. Henk and Lucas had been schoolmates, and the two of them became our first Dutch friends. They asked us where we were staying, and we told them about the hotel. As Lucas had recently separated from his wife, the next day when we visited his house he suggested, "Look, why don't you live here with Henk and me? Just put in your share of the rent, the electricity, and the other costs." The invitation to stay in their house was a real demonstration of solidarity, and through these two men we began to make new Dutch friends who made our adaptation much easier.

At the immigration agency we filled out the paperwork that allowed us to move into Lucas's house. Once we had settled in, we were much more relaxed, because aside from being in a real house, we felt much safer. We were still terrified of persecution and thought that if Operation Condor came after us, we would be much harder to locate in a private house than in a hotel.

Fausto, Jorge, and I tried to network with political parties in Holland, but Dutch party representatives were explicit that they were already in touch with the national level of Bolivian parties, and all contact needed to be channeled through them. As we were not authorized by the national PCML to establish contacts, these relationships didn't go anywhere. We did have good results, however, with the very active solidarity movements led by social, labor, and educational groups working against nuclear energy.

The refugee program administrators were impressed because many Latin American refugees had problems finding places to live and integrating into Dutch society. Our rapid transition was unusual, as we resolved the key problem of housing early on. I learned Dutch in the university, and decided to apply to the economics program because I thought it would be easier to get into than engineering. Several friends studying there encouraged me to enter economics as well. After some time my *compañeros* set off to attend university in other cities: Jorge to Rotterdam and Fausto to Wageningen, both to study engineering.

I stayed in Amsterdam with Lucas and Henk, who both had socialist tendencies. Henk had strong contacts with the left and was an adventurous sort who worked at the post office for a while and also translated communist literature from Dutch into Swedish. Both he and Lucas expressed interest in learning about Bolivia in general, as well as about my experiences as a miner. We talked for hours about what I wanted for both myself and my country, why I had joined the PCML, why I had been imprisoned and later exiled. At that point, socialism was very much in vogue, but Bolivia was not. As a result, the only thing they knew about Bolivia was that it was where Che Guevara had died.

I was really shocked when I figured out that most people saw me as an indigenous person. Bolivia, even today, continues to be a deeply racist society, and in the 1970s negative feelings towards indigenous people were shared openly among my mining *compañeros,* even though almost all of us had indigenous roots. I viewed myself as a miner—I never would have self-identified as indigenous, even though my parents are Quechua and Aymara campesinos, and these were my first two languages. As well, I lived in an indigenous community for the first part of my life. But in Holland, I wasn't a miner anymore, but I was still indigenous, and it was there that I realized I would be indigenous all my life. The process of learning how others saw me helped me develop a clearer and more positive understanding of what it meant to be an indigenous person.

The Spanish nun whom I had been involved with in Chiloé visited me once in Holland. Without her help, I would never have escaped, and I was extremely grateful to her. We had been in touch by mail, and while we weren't passionately in love, I was really pleased to see someone who shared some piece of my past. We enjoyed our days together in Holland, and she asked me to visit her in Barcelona, but I never arranged a visit. I realized that there was no future in a relationship with someone so deeply committed to the Church.

Sometimes the relationships between Bolivians and other Latin Americans in Holland were very conflictive. Even though we were exiles for the same fundamental reasons, party, political, and ideological differences, not to mention those of class and nationality, were always present. These tensions were exacerbated, as the Bolivians had different levels of social integration into Dutch culture. Those who had brought their families with them, for example, had real problems adjusting, in part because their children adapted more rapidly and the parents could neither control nor help in the new context. They spoke Spanish at home, so learning the language was far more complicated for the parents. As a result, they were often resentful toward those of us who adapted quickly. I think that I was very lucky with the people I met just after I arrived. Because I was single, I was compelled to find friends and contacts beyond the small group of Bolivians. I also think my natural curiosity served me well—it was something I had since I was a child—and I always enjoyed exploring other places and realities. This motivated me to make the effort to learn the language and develop friendships with Dutch people.

Visit to the German Democratic Republic

In May 1977, I had the opportunity to visit the German Democratic Republic [East Germany], which, at that time, was ideologically inclined toward the Soviet Union. My visit was possible because my younger brother Germán was still in exile there, studying economics, after being expelled from Chile. I was keen to visit East Germany because it was a socialist country, and one of the principal ideological goals of both the miners' union and my party was to build socialism. I was curious to know what life was like there, even though I didn't believe that East Germany represented true socialism, because it was affiliated with the Soviet bloc. According to my ideological training, a country had to carry out its own revolution to construct a true socialist society. That hadn't been the case in East Germany, because Russia had imposed socialism after World War II. But even though I considered it an immature revolutionary society, I still wanted a glimpse of a possible future. I assembled my papers for the visa carefully, because it was difficult to visit the Soviet bloc if you didn't belong to the Communist party. Fortunately, East German officials granted me authorization.

The visit made a huge impression on me. Mostly the experience left me disillusioned, although not everything was negative. The communist system obviously achieved many positive things—for example, unemployment was essentially nonexistent, and thanks to the government, everyone had medical care, adequate housing, and access to education.

But I felt that people lacked the consciousness necessary to deepen and continue the process of constructing socialism. I had the impression that the working class was isolated from its historic aspirations and dominated by a bureaucracy that controlled the country. You saw this even in the public monuments honoring workers: instead of them carrying a hammer—the symbol of the revolutionary worker—or like in Bolivia, a gun, to show that they were agents in revolutionary processes, they carried simple work tools. It showed the workers as passive subjects rather than active agents of historical change.

To maintain its control, the dominant bureaucratic class cut off certain fundamental liberties. The Germans in the east could not enter and leave their country freely, a situation that led many people to despair. The state also prohibited people from expressing their own initiatives in handicraft or commercial activities. When they discovered that I had just arrived from Holland, many people were anxious to meet me. Just by living on the other side of the wall I embodied a kind of freedom, and just being in my presence allowed them to experience my freedom vicariously.

As the Bolivians I knew studying there were all young, they introduced me to other young people, including women keen to get involved with me in hopes that I might provide them an escape through marriage. I had a leather jacket, and some people touched it frequently, saying, "This is from a free country." More than one person offered to buy it, not because of its quality, but because it embodied some essence of freedom. I was profoundly struck by these actions, which felt pretty strange, but I understood them as an indication of political and social oppression. It struck me that socialism in East Germany was incapable of attending to more than just the basic necessities, falling short in terms of fulfilling spiritual, social, or psychological needs. The reality was that the working class labored as it always did and was not in charge of anything.

It appeared the government lacked development policies in both science and technology to improve people's daily lives. Instead, the tremendous bureaucracy blocked advances. For me it was tremendously hard; my hopes for socialism were crushed, but I still maintained faith that there were better socialist countries, like China, Albania, or Cuba.

I returned to Holland after two weeks, and, on reflecting on my experience, I, of course, compared it to life under democratic and military rule. I began to ask myself some fundamental political questions. I recognized clearly that the capitalist social democratic system in Holland provided far better for the majority of the population in material terms than the democratic-centralist socialist system in East Germany. In Holland, people could find work that satisfied them. Also, they were able to travel freely and had access to consumer goods unavailable to most East Germans. And even though it was a capitalist country, no beggars roamed the streets, like in Bolivia and Chile, the two other capitalist countries I had known. This reflection led me to begin to seriously question the political party line I had always accepted as the truth. My trip to East Germany had opened me up and made me much more critical.

Two other factors contributed to this change. For the first time I had access to literature about ways of understanding the world that were more varied and extensive than the communist materials I primarily read in Bolivia. Also, through travel I experienced other cultures and social processes. When I compared East Germany to Holland, Dutch people not only lived better but appeared happier. Clearly, something was missing in East Germany. I became increasingly disenchanted with the socialist paradise that I so fervently believed was possible.

Nonetheless, I still believed socialism would make an important difference in Bolivia and spent many hours reflecting on how we could advance the process. I came from a country where more than half of the population lived in preindustrial conditions, almost as people lived in the Middle Ages, in spite of the rich natural resources we possess. Bolivia has tremendous economic potential because of our gold, tin, and other mineral reserves, not to mention tropical forests, coca leaf, and oil and gas. We commonly say that we are beggars sitting on a throne of gold. At this time, the great majority of Bolivians were poor, and a privileged group ran the country. They lived extremely well and profited from our natural and human resources, but none of the wealth benefited the majority. In addition, Banzer's military government, a group of corrupt civilians and military assassins, controlled the country by terror and had forced me and others like me into exile.

We Bolivians have always realized that we could change the miserable and unjust situation we live in. The history of humanity indicates that everything is in a permanent state of flux, which I learned when I read about the French and the Cuban revolutions. These stories show us that triumph is possible. We know that a repressive government will someday crumble, and that knowledge keeps alive the hope that we are capable of creating a new government more favorable to the population as a whole. At that time, in our country we were in the throes of a difficult fight to restore democracy. Even though we were far away in exile, we were moved by our people's continued struggles.

While I was living in Holland a famous hotelier, Mr. Carranza, was kidnapped. One morning I started chatting with a Dutch woman at the tram station when she said, "I am really concerned that if someone kidnapped Carranza, this country really is not safe. I'm worried that if rich people get treated like this, they'll all leave. What are we poor people going to do all alone? Who will give us work?"

I asked, "What do you do?"

"I'm a waitress."

Her comments made a real impression on me, because it never occurred to me that some Dutch people thought that they couldn't live without the rich. I thought differently: that the rich were the fundamental problem because they try to keep everything for themselves.

The ongoing struggle of the Bolivian people to regain democracy came to a head at the end of 1977 and the beginning of 1978 with a hunger strike started by four women from the Housewives Committee from the Siglo XX mine, including Domitila Chungara. This group quickly expanded when the families of political prisoners and clandestine union organizations joined in. In a strike that lasted over a month, they demanded the freedom of all political prisoners and the return of those who had been deported and exiled. I found out that my eighteen-year-old sister Margarita, who lived in the mines with my parents, had joined the hunger strike early on in La Paz. The movement ended in triumph when the government announced an amnesty for political prisoners and exiles. My elation was short-lived, as my name was on the list of 380 people whom the government wouldn't allow to return. I felt angry and impotent. I had had very little contact with my family since I got to Holland, and I missed them terribly. I must have received only two letters during this period, largely because it wasn't part of our culture and experience to write letters, as everyone usually lived nearby each other. Besides, both my parents were illiterate, so someone else had to write letters for them.

At the beginning of 1978, Rodolfo Siñani called me by phone, "We are off to Paris because better possibilities exist there for carrying out actions in favor of Bolivia than in Sweden. Come with me; I'll find you a place to stay with other comrades." When I arrived in Paris, Rodo was there with Raúl Nava, another party comrade. They picked me up in Raúl's car and took us to his house.

The next day we got on the metro, and I was really impressed by the huge number of people in the crowd. I thought to myself, "With all these people here, what are the chances I could run into someone I know? Just about nil." In one of life's strange coincidences, at just that moment a young woman with a distinctive, brightly colored scarf from the north of Potosí wound around her neck entered the metro car. The scarf immediately drew my attention, because the vivid lime-green and red were part of my identity and commonly used in the area I come from. I looked at the girl carefully and realized that it was Marta Laguna, who had lent me the money to buy a gun. We were so happy to see each other again!

We hugged each other. "I knew I would see you," she said, "because I heard that the military had banished you to Chile and later you had escaped to Europe." She also knew Raúl Nava. She had great contacts with the press and spoke perfect French.

The next day she took us to see people in the press and union organizations. They published interviews with us, along with news about the Bolivian situation, all over France, as it became increasingly clear that Banzer's government was about to fall.

Banzer's Fall

I returned to Holland. Meanwhile, in Bolivia, the hunger strike grew, Banzer was forced to capitulate, and we won unrestricted amnesty for the remaining exiles. I was exuberant!

In April 1978, I received a letter from Colonel Vargas, the minister of work, granting me permission to return to my job in the mine. I felt a sense of triumph, as I considered that letter validated my actions, and in allowing people to return home, the government acknowledged it had been wrong. I interpreted the letter not only as a formal recognition of my citizenship rights, but also an invitation to rejoin the struggle.

Suddenly all the exiled Bolivians were forced to make a decision. During their time away, many had become well established, had their wives and children with them thanks to special reunification plans set up by the UN High Commissioner for Refugees (UNHCR), and no longer were anxious to return. My *compañero* from Quellón, Fausto, had married a Dutch woman and elected to stay, as did Jorge, who wanted to continue his studies in engineering. In my case, although I spoke Dutch pretty well, had applied to study economics, and really appreciated everything the Dutch had done for me, I wanted nothing more than to go home.

As I was a Maoist party militant, the party's first secretary sent someone to propose I visit China before heading home to Bolivia. For me it was a difficult decision. Traveling to China implied increasing my commitment to the party and would also delay my return. Also, I was convinced that they wanted to send me, not so much to strengthen my skills as a leader, but to make me more obligated to the existing leadership and integrate me further into the party apparatus. My experiences in Europe led me to question profoundly what I had learned in the party, and I no longer trusted everything it said and did. I decided to return directly to Bolivia. Not only was I determined to get home as fast as I could to see my family and country, but also I wanted to get back to work and the political struggle.

I was about to leave Holland, with all its development and comforts, to go back to the mining settlements, where everyday life is full of suffering. But the thought of returning gave me enormous satisfaction, because I would reinitiate my participation in the struggle, which was an important part of my personal identity, as well as the fulfillment of my commitments to the brothers and sisters of my class.

CRISIS AND TRANSITION

The period between 1978 and 1980 was a tumultuous one in Bolivia. Plunging prices for commodities and fragile alliances among right-wing business groups created an opening that popular movements seized to end Hugo Banzer's military dictatorship. Business elites were tiring of rapidly expanding state enterprises designed to fulfill the dictatorship's political patronage obligations, as they were convinced these curbed their own business opportunities. As Banzer promoted clientelistic relationships with individuals, he increasingly alienated many members of the business sector that constituted the core of his support. Rampant corruption imposed unforeseen costs and delays that hampered the efficient operation of business. This contradictory position—simultaneously benefiting from the dictatorship while exerting little influence over policy—convinced Bolivian elites, like their counterparts throughout Latin America, that military government was not conducive to a stable business climate. As their conviction that the military should leave politics grew, their cohesion increased (Malloy and Gamarra 1988).

U.S. president Jimmy Carter's focus on human rights also brought new pressure to bear on the Banzer regime. Just as the withdrawal of U.S. support for the Somoza administration in Nicaragua facilitated the dictator's 1979 overthrow, U.S. pressure on Banzer was critical in compelling him to call for elections in 1978. The regime was so fragile that the hunger strike initiated by four women and their children from the Comité de Amas de Casa de Siglo XX (Housewives Committee of Siglo XX) spread like wildfire under the leadership of the COB. The government had no choice but to free political prisoners and undertake a democratic transition.

General Juan Pereda, Banzer's handpicked successor, lost the 1978 election, but seized power anyway. This marked the beginning of four years of political chaos that saw eight different governments, including two brief periods of civilian rule. By consistently demanding that election results be respected, the COB emerged as democracy's champion.

As the economic crisis worsened, both state-controlled mining and hydrocarbons production plummeted. Governments were increasingly corrupt, particularly the brutal one-year rule of Luis García Meza, whose regime was built on illegally marketing cocaine, land, and precious stones. By the time it ended, pressure to end military rule came not only from students, labor, and business, but from segments of the military itself.

Chapter 9

Return Home

I requested that the UNHCR authorize my trip home, and it agreed to pay my airfare. I arrived in La Paz on May 1, 1978, International Workers' Day. In Bolivia we celebrate every year with a huge march to commemorate international worker solidarity and the Haymarket martyrs killed in Chicago in 1886. Usually about half a million people participate, but 1978 was a special year because the march commemorated the people's historic victory over the dictatorship. I would have so much liked to march but I arrived two hours after the demonstration ended, and the only thing left were the fliers and pamphlets scattered about on the streets. Right away, I headed to the offices of the Bolivian Workers Central (COB) and the Miners' Federation (FSTMB), which were on La Paz's main street, the Prado. All the politicians usually gathered there, but I found the building deserted for the holiday.

The next day I had better luck and met with the executives of the FSTMB and the COB. We embraced and were overjoyed to see each other still alive. I showed the letter authorizing my reincorporation into the mines and asked them to initiate the formal arrangements for my return to work. Then we went to eat *salteñas*, a Bolivian meat pastry, as a way of celebrating. I waited a full week for the paperwork to come through. Approval required an appointment with the president of COMIBOL.

During one visit that week to the Miners' Federation, I ran into Emilse Escobar. I had known her by sight since childhood when we were in the same school. Who didn't know the daughters of Federico Escobar? He was a famous public figure, and part of that trickled down to his daughters as well: even when they were little everyone knew who they were, but in those days, we weren't friends.

We spent more time together when I joined the party in 1966. I participated in an event in La Paz and saw Emilse there, but we didn't get to know each other much because she was not living at Siglo XX then.

But later she went to work for the Catavi mining company and started to participate in the Siglo XX youth activities. She lived in the center of town, and the group often gathered at her house.

After Federico's death, Emilse, her sister, and her brother received scholarships to study in Albania, due to that government's solidarity with the Maoist-oriented PCML. When she returned five years later, we often saw each other when she visited Siglo XX, and we always talked about politics. When I was imprisoned in the San Pedro jail before I was banished to Chile, she came to visit me.

I was having coffee with Gabino Limachi in the café called "Lechíngrad"—a play on the city name of Leningrad and that of COB leader Juan Lechín. The place, on the first floor of the Miners' Federation building, was filled with political types. Emilse and I spotted each other and had a very emotional reunion because we hadn't seen each other in over three years. Gabino, who was a student leader *compañero*, had just recently returned from Argentina. Emilse invited us both to have lunch at her house, which the miners of Siglo XX gave to the family in recognition of Federico's service.

The house was up in Alto San Pedro, about 500 feet above the Prado, a climb of about a thousand steps. Because I had been away from Bolivia so long, I was suffering from altitude sickness at 12,000 feet above sea level, as my lungs had become accustomed to the oxygen-rich air in Holland. I couldn't keep up with Emilse and Gabino as they strode up the hill. I found myself gasping for air, and only arrived in time for dessert. Emilse helped me to get around for a few days until my body adjusted to the altitude once more. She also helped me find a place to stay.

Emilse was working as a pharmacist in Uyuni, a mining center in the southern part of Potosí department, which had been the most important train stop in Bolivia during the nineteenth century, as it was close to several mines. Emilse was in La Paz on business for a week, and we began to fall in love. We traveled together to Siglo XX, and later Emilse returned to Uyuni. We saw each other every couple of months when she came back to Siglo XX to visit her mother.

During this period, I was also briefly involved with a neighbor in Siglo XX, Lucy Martínez, who was a student and the daughter of the director of the Miners' Voice radio station. A little later, Lucy disappeared from Siglo XX, and I was told that she had gone off to study. I later found out she was pregnant; I helped her out economically until she gave birth to our daughter Maya Yesbel. I have never had much contact with my eldest daughter, Maya. The last time I saw her was in 2000 in Cochabamba. But throughout her childhood I always assisted with her education and expenses. Sometime later Lucy became involved with my younger brother Máximo, and they moved to Cochabamba, where he worked as a driver for a nongovernmental organization (NGO) called INEDER. After having a child together they separated. Maya graduated from both high school and a professional course in marketing, and went to work at the local telephone company, COMTECO, before moving to Italy, where she married and now has a daughter, my granddaughter.

Emilse and I continued to see each other, and when our relationship deepened, we decided to marry. We had a close friendship and a lot of common interests. I realized that my life had been very chaotic and not particularly stable. A *compañera* who was psychologically prepared for anything would be an enormous asset, as I knew that I always would be politically active. I really wanted a partner who understood what the type of life I had chosen would entail, because at times I had been hunted and I knew I could be again. Emilse had experienced this growing up. Federico's life centered on his political work, and this had taken a huge toll on his family, as he was imprisoned various times, exiled, deported, and died quite young under highly questionable circumstances. I was pretty sure that Emilse, as well as the other members of her family, knew how to make the adjustments necessary to an activist's life.

An understanding of these challenges was crucial in the formation of a political couple. I knew several comrades in my party and some other revolutionaries who had serious difficulties with their *compañeras*. Sometimes completely innocently, a wife led state agents to her husband. At other times, if a relationship was problematic, she did so expressly for revenge. And sometimes it wasn't the wife, but a relative or someone else, who betrayed an activist either out of jealousy or for money. So I had to find a brave *compañera* willing to share the potentially hard life of an activist. I saw in Emilse a strong woman, determined and committed to permanent political struggle.

MARRIAGE AND FAMILY

Félix was among the many political exiles who returned to Bolivia after Banzer's downfall, hoping that with the return to democracy they could restart their lives. But he was no longer the young radical student he was when he left. Rather, he was ready to settle down in a family despite the difficulties he faced as a committed political activist.

Marriage and children are central to mining families' lives. But these families differ from rural indigenous ones, as the often disruptive move to the mining camps occasioned a shift to a more nuclear family structure. This migration granted men greater autonomy from family and community kinship obligations: in the mines, they found greater freedom to choose their own partners, residences, and spending habits (Nash 1993). This liberty came at the expense of women, who were more dependent on men in the mining camps than they had been in rural life.

In the 1940s, mine owners gradually realized that having families close by benefited them, as it created a more stable workforce, and that an emphasis on family life could compete with radical union activities, drawing both men and women to the private rather than public sphere (Nash 1993). The result was increased construction of family housing, significantly improving living conditions for miners.

Contraception in the mining settlements was virtually nonexistent and, where available, very expensive, in part because of the Catholic Church's opposition to birth control. A general fatalism prevailed: the number of children was determined by God, and women who attempted to limit their family size mostly did so through abstention rather than prevention. The resulting large families meant that wages were insufficient for a man to support his family, so both women and children often worked as well. Family stability was built on a shaky foundation: at any moment it could disappear due to a mine-related accident or illness.

To compensate for the geographical separation from their rural support structures, the miners' short life span, and the increasing reliance on the nuclear family, fictive kin, or *compadrazgo*, assumed greater significance. Godparents (*padrinos*) were chosen for all the principal passages in life, the most important being a wedding, a baptism, and a child's first haircut (*rutusqa*), followed by religious confirmation. But a *padrino* or *madrina* could be solicited for any event, from community parties and school graduations to a girl's fifteenth birthday, although baptism is the most significant. Your child's *padrino* or *madrina* became your *compadre* or *comadre*.

Asking a person to serve as a godparent (thereby becoming a *compadre*) creates a relationship of mutual, although asymmetrical, obligations. Godparents are expected to help support families in times of crisis or help children locate jobs or gain access to schools. In some cases, people seek out *padrinos* of higher social standing in an effort to improve their status or to broaden their social safety net. *Padrinos* are consulted for advice, much as someone in Western society might seek out a therapist. Godparents also can make demands on their godchildren. In rural areas the *compadrazgo* relationship serves to provide godparents preferential access to labor resources, allowing them to command help with the planting or harvest. These relationships, however, are not cast in stone: if there is irreconcilable conflict, the *compadrazgo* can be terminated, usually with the return of all the gifts.

Mining family structure tends to be authoritarian, with men in charge, boys preferred over girls, and sibling rivalry over scarce family resources often fierce. Women are expected to defer to their husbands in arguments so as to preserve the marriage. In terms of courtship, the man chooses and the woman yields, although many young women are in no hurry to enter into relationships with men, largely because they are well aware of the costs—constant pregnancy and childbirth, as well as early widowhood. While miners are seen as adventurous in their romantic relationships with women, most women lack the money, the independence, and the opportunity to initiate romance either before or after marriage (Nash 1993).

When couples decide to marry, many begin with the traditional formal betrothal, *makemanaku*. But in contrast to its rural variant, this engagement is now typically initiated by the couple rather than their parents. Some couples forgo a wedding because of the cost.

When formal marriage occurs, it can stretch the limit of the couple's resources, usually costing the equivalent of two to three months of salary. Even with *padrinos* to pay for various parts of the ceremony such as the rings, the cake, or the beer, couples acquire financial and social obligations that can take years to repay. While not as extensive as in rural areas, wedding celebrations in the mines often last for three days. Friends of the couple and their parents compose about half the guests, rather than the entire community, which is the rural norm. Guests typically bring gifts such as glasses, dinnerware, and flatware.

For most miners, the family provides the object and motivation for living and work. With early death or desertion by the husband almost guaranteed, women are the foundations of family continuity. The mother-child bond is seen as life's most important, and there is a deep belief that most of one's blood comes from the mother. This blends with the reverence in indigenous culture for the Pachamama, the earth mother. Reinforcing this conception is the way self-sacrificing motherhood is sentimentalized in mestizo and criollo Bolivian culture beyond the mines.

One evening I told my parents I was going to marry Macho Moreno's daughter. My father was relieved, because he considered me wild and out of control. Since my return from exile he had insisted repeatedly, "They have arrested and deported you, beaten you, police have come to the house searching for you. I ask myself, 'What can we do?' You know, son, I think it would be best if you married a good woman and settled down."

My mother replied, "Let him decide. Why do you have to get involved? You're not going to be responsible for what happens in his marriage."

But when I announced my decision to marry, there was no bickering. Instead they quickly responded, "Let's go and ask for her hand from her mother."

I retorted, "I've already done it."

They were surprised, "How could you have done this on your own?"

I explained, "But there was no need for anything more. Anyway, we have decided to get married only in a civil ceremony, not a religious one. We've set the date for three days from now. It's not going to be a big party; we'll just invite close relatives."

They got really angry, and my father complained, "What are we going to do? I don't understand. What are we going to tell the family? Everyone will want to come to the wedding."

My mother suggested, "We'll tell them that they'll do the religious ceremony later and that they'll be invited to that." She thought that the promise of a future celebration would satisfy the family, and then we could just postpone it indefinitely.

On December 22, 1978, we had a civil marriage. We didn't want a traditional Bolivian wedding, both because of our political vision and our international experiences. Not only did we not first consult my parents and then ask for permission from Emilse's family, we rejected the custom of naming *padrinos* for the service, the ring, and even the cake. We wanted a small wedding limited to our immediate family, but that was still a big group, as I had seven brothers and sisters and Emilse had eight.

But it didn't quite work out the way we planned. Mining camps are like small towns, so there was no way to keep the wedding a secret. Word quickly spread to friends, relatives, and party comrades, and the celebration mushroomed, lasting two full days. We held the party at Emilse's mother's house, and about a hundred adults and dozens of children showed up. As we hadn't arranged for *padrinos* to help cover the expenses, it ended up costing our families quite a bit. People partied late into the night and then were back at it again the next day. Even with the considerable expense, my parents were happy, because they had really wanted a big wedding. This was typical of the compromises we agreed to, as we sought to escape from traditional customs, due to our political commitments and experiences in modern Europe, while simultaneously being embedded within a traditional society. We wanted to be bridges for change in our society and not just parrot what always had been done for tradition's sake alone.

Return to the Mine

The reception when I returned to the Siglo XX mine in May 1978 was interesting. My friends were glad to see me; there were even acts honoring me. My father was still working in the mine, and only my brothers and sister, Máximo, Willy, and Margarita, remained at home, all of them still in school. None of the younger ones was working in the mine. All the older ones, except for Cursina, who lived with her husband, a railroad worker, had already left for other places.

My father was convinced that I had become a political activist because I had attended school; therefore, he refused to encourage my younger brothers and sister to study. My sister complained to me, "Wilfredo is not finishing his homework, and when I told Dad, he said, 'It's not a problem because when children are encouraged to study, they turn out politically persecuted and imprisoned like your brother Félix.'"

Many of my workmates were sure I had been killed. Some seemed envious, "Look at you, you still appear young, and we all look so much older. While we were sweating in the mine you were in a golden exile." It was said as a joke, but underneath there was a kernel of truth. They simply couldn't understand why I had come back to this poor and desolate place, and more than one insisted I was stupid for doing so.

Nonetheless, it was great to be home, although I found it quite difficult to adjust. I arrived full of enthusiasm, but when I saw material conditions that were far worse than I remembered, I sometimes wondered if I had indeed made a mistake. But for the most part the lack of potable water, heat, and other basic services was compensated for by the warmth and friendship of my family and *compañeros*. This contrasted markedly with Europe, where the material conditions were excellent, but it seemed these were obtained at the cost of close-knit human relations.

I worked in the mineral preconcentration plant, where I was reelected, first as a delegate of my section, and later, at the invitation of Artemio Camargo, general secretary of the Siglo XX Miners' Federation, as a union leader of the national federation, or FSTMB. This support encouraged me and reinforced my commitment to the struggle. We managed to strengthen our organization within the mine, incorporating other workers who had come back after being imprisoned, exiled, or deported. We reorganized at the political level as well.

Once we had recovered democracy, we participated in the presidential elections, and I was a candidate for deputy in the north of Potosí, representing the miners. But the electoral process divided us. I was aligned with the Left Revolutionary Front (Frente Revolucionario de la Izquierda, or FRI), which included the PCML, the Trotskyist Workers Vanguard (Vanguardia Obrera), and the Revolutionary Party of the Nationalist Left (Partido Revolucionario de la Izquierda Nacional, or PRIN), among others. Our political front did not win very many deputies. The Democratic and Popular Unity (Unidad Democrática y Popular, or UDP), which incorporated the traditional parties like the MNR and others that were more radical, like the

Left Revolutionary Movement (Movimiento de Izquierda Revolucionaria, or MIR) and the Bolivian Communist Party (Partido Comunista de Bolivia, or PCB), managed to win the majority of the seats. Although I didn't get a seat, we continued to fight, but this time within a democratic context. The political objectives had changed to focus on the defense and the deepening of democracy for the country's poor majority.

In 1978, Hernán Siles Zuazo, who had been president from 1956 to 1960 as part of the MNR government, won the presidential elections. But he didn't assume office, as the country plunged into a political crisis because Banzer's handpicked successor, General Juan Pereda Asbún, refused to respect the democratic process and instigated a coup in July. His government didn't last long, and he was ousted by General David Padilla in November. Elections for Congress were held in July 1979, and because no party won a clear majority, Congress selected Walter Guevara Arce to serve as interim president for a year. He survived until October 1979, when General Natusch Bush launched yet another military coup, although his coalition only lasted two weeks. Congress then elected Lydia Gueiler Tejada, who was a MNR militant during the 1952 revolution and who was a member of the FRI coalition, to be the first woman president of Bolivia.

Politics in the Mines

While the country lurched from coup to coup, life in the mines remained much the same. The miners rejected all de facto governments, denouncing the military, but luckily we avoided the type of confrontations with the armed forces we suffered during the Barrientos and Banzer regimes. At Siglo XX, faced with corrupt governments, whether civilian or military, we sometimes declared ourselves an independent republic as we had done under the MNR during the 1960s. We maintained this position during the subsequent military dictatorships, keeping our union organizations alive despite the prohibition against them.

More than five thousand workers labored in Siglo XX at the time, and it had the reputation as the most combative mining settlement in all of Latin America. It also served as a major center for the left-wing political parties, and, of course, the government never ceased in its efforts to corrupt union leaders. Honesty in leaders was paramount, and in practice it was not so easy to corrupt union leaders in the mines because of the strong degree of social control. Any leader suspected of being compromised immediately lost all grassroots support.

While we could regulate the leaders in the district, at the national level some COB leaders manipulated and pulled strings that enabled them to dominate the workers' movement. Juan Lechín, chief executive of the COB for three decades, for example, always made pacts with the governments in office, playing politics with a double-edged sword. On the one hand, he would negotiate labor demands in an effort to maintain peace. On the other, he utilized government resources to buy off leaders not only in the small mines but also in other member unions of the COB, so that he could retain his position and power.

National leaders were politically sophisticated, but they were always nervous about finding themselves in a confrontation with Siglo XX workers. We constantly invited them to participate in our assemblies to lay out their political positions, as well as their stance on labor issues. But they were often too scared to show up and instead sent subordinates, who often appeared only reluctantly. If they couldn't get anywhere by persuasion, in the last resort, Lechín showed up, and usually reacted defensively to the inevitable criticisms.

Once he attended a meeting with over three hundred miners and local leaders. He tried to justify a journey to Europe at a time when the country was facing a serious threat of a coup. He argued that he traveled to strengthen international contacts in order to protect the country's labor movement.

I retorted from the floor, "The most important thing for the workers' movement at times like this is to prepare and organize the resistance, not travel abroad, leaving the troops abandoned."

He looked straight at me, "First, the *compañero* is right, but it is also important to have international contacts. Clearly the *compañero* lacks international experience." I had more international experience than Lechín, but he didn't give me a chance to respond. In this case, as he did so often, he utilized his power as chair of the meeting to impede frank discussion.

I'm pretty sure that Siglo XX was the only place where Lechín was subject to these kinds of criticisms, because no one in the other mines and unions stood up to him. As a consequence, the established leadership of the COB worked to prevent us from getting elected to the leadership of the FSTMB. Instead, they tried to install leaders from other mining districts, whom they could count on to follow orders. It was clear that power for union and government leaders was bought for cash and maintained with obedience. As for Lechín, I feel he stymied the revolutionary movement and any advances in creating true popular power from his position as the head of the labor movement.

The extreme polarization in the unions had several negative effects. For example, in some cases leaders elected by the workers weren't able to assume their posts. This happened to my party in spite of the fact that we demonstrated that we were capable and had won union elections democratically. These internal political struggles, due to ideological differences among different factions, however, helped me clarify my own analysis. But just as often the infighting was counterproductive, because some political parties and individual leaders assumed extreme and intransigent positions only to strengthen their own interests instead of serving the movement's broader interests.

The PCML twice won union elections in Siglo XX, but opposition political parties prevented us from taking office by questioning the results, arguing that we had won through lies and manipulation. Unfortunately, this happens all too often in Bolivia in both union organizations and left political parties. This was very destructive, because sometimes the rancor created meant we were unable to unite to resist the dictatorships. In reality, if the COB and the FSTMB were functioning well, it was because they were following the analysis coming from the Siglo XX miners. In this sense we had a tremendous influence on national political movements and could organize strikes and large mobilizations. Several times large groups of miners would converge on La Paz to move democracy directly into the streets.

In 1979, my party formed an alliance with the MNR, the center-right party of Paz Estenssoro and Siles Zuazo, to join the government led by President Lydia Gueiler. This created an enormous internal conflict that seriously damaged the prestige we had built up over the years and jeopardized party unity. To resolve the conflict, the party held a national congress in Cochabamba in May 1980 that was charged with two tasks: first, to define the party position regarding the pact with the MNR and, second, to elect the party's leader. Due to manipulations by the existing national leadership, participation in the coalition government was ratified. Then three people were proposed as the new party leader: Oscar Zamora Medinacelli, the outgoing first secretary and a lawyer, Raúl Ruiz, who was a university professor, and I. In the final vote on the floor, I won. I was very surprised and immediately anxious, because it was a huge responsibility and I never expected to win.

To me, it demonstrated that the party members wanted a miner as leader. In other words, I won the election, not because I was Félix Muruchi, an individual, but because I was from the mines and would represent the miners. But the results were challenged by the standing directorate, who argued that they alone should determine who led the party. They chose Oscar Zamora. That's how democratic centralism works. For me, it added one more level of disillusionment about how the party functioned, as well as a lesson on the limitations inherent in democratic centralism.

This power play frustrated many party militants, and affected me considerably, not so much because I was determined to serve as the first secretary, but because I strenuously opposed forming an alliance with the MNR. I was convinced that a FRI-MNR coalition government signaled the failure of our political project and would cost us all our hard-earned political legitimacy. We should have maintained our distance from the government to save the party, but our first secretary clung to the alliance with the MNR. This was the situation when Luis García Meza staged his brutal coup in July 1980.

Afterward, I left the party, because I saw no future in continuing the struggle through the PCML. Not only did I no longer believe that the party could address the demands of the Bolivian people, I did not consider it a Leninist party, because it was increasingly following an electoral and not revolutionary strategy. For me, Marxism-Leninism was a philosophy that could help interpret the current reality in important ways. I learned from Lenin the necessity of conducting an objective analysis and basing action on the results. However, I felt that Leninism was limited, as it failed to allow leaders to respond to the felt necessities of the people, even if they didn't agree with them. For example, if the people asked for more churches, I felt that it was the obligation of a leader to commit to help build them.

I became more and more aware of the problems caused by the political parties themselves. Their great limitation is that at any given moment their interests as a party become more important than the liberation project or the defense of an oppressed group. In the case of the PCML, Oscar Zamora Medinacelli pursued personal power and ended up destroying the party. Ironically enough, he ended up using the FRI as a platform to put himself forward as vice presidential candidate in General Banzer's bid for the presidency in 1989.

I learned that to find meaning in life, you can't separate yourself from serving people and giving your life to them. This is what great leaders like Che Guevara, Túpaj Katari, Bartolina Sisa, Luis Espinal, and Marcelo Quiroga de Santa Cruz in Bolivia, and at an international level, people like Nelson Mandela, Martin Luther King, and Mahatma Gandhi, have always done.

Chapter 10

García Meza Coup

BACK TO HOLLAND

In early 1980, Valeria, Emilse's and my first daughter, was born at the COMIBOL hospital in Catavi. In Holland I had learned about the importance of physical exercise during childbirth, so we walked to the hospital by foot, a little over one-half mile. I would have liked to have been present during the birth, but such practices were not accepted in Bolivia and the doctors threw me out of the delivery room.

I was deeply moved by the birth of my daughter, and it cemented a firm commitment to our family. Life became very busy for us after she was born, because I had to balance helping to take care of her with my political activities. Three months after she was born my time with her was cut short, because the García Meza coup turned the country, and my life, upside down once again.

When the coup was imminent, *compañero* Artemio Camargo, the general secretary of the Siglo XX Miners' Federation, approached me to join him as secretary of conflicts and help strengthen the union. He encouraged me, "With the dangerous political situation the country is facing, we need your advice as an experienced activist. Please join the union's leadership."

I accepted to help unify the movement. Almost at that exact moment, García Meza launched his coup and completely devastated us. Later, after I had fled into hiding and exile, Artemio was assassinated with a group of his *compañeros* from the MIR party in a house on Harrington Street in La Paz.

With this new coup, once again the miners led the effort to defend democracy, and we offered more resistance at Siglo XX than anywhere else in the country. For almost two weeks the district was a war zone, with the military pouring out of the barracks at Uncía to attack the civilian population. Soldiers attacked day and night, lighting their assaults with flares shot from airplanes. They raided repeatedly, firing at anything that moved, killing whatever human or animal crossed their path. Because they couldn't muster sufficient strength to occupy the entire settlement, their aim was not so much to conquer the place as to terrify the population. Clearly they were biding their time, waiting for reinforcements from other parts of the country to consolidate their occupation.

We attempted to fortify the mining camps and block all road access. On the second night, I snuck out with workers from the "sink and float" plant and from "block caving" to close the road into Llallagua from Oruro. About fifty of us placed explosives on the surrounding cliffs and blasted tons of rock onto the road, effectively cutting it off. We were pleased because we had carried this off without directly confronting the military.

On the third day, while I was guarding the urban perimeter of the settlements, other miners assaulted a military post in Catavi to steal arms so that we could continue the resistance. We were joined by the campesinos who lived around Siglo XX, because in 1979, the Confederation of Campesino Workers' Unions of Bolivia (Confederación Sindical Única de Trabajadores Campesinos de Bolivia, or CSUTCB) had affiliated with the COB. With this newfound unity, the COB provided the leadership for the national resistance.

GARCÍA MEZA

The García Meza coup was arguably the worst Bolivia has ever suffered. On July 17, 1980, the ultraconservative Luis García Meza Tejada, a career military officer from La Paz, seized power in what was often called the "Cocaine Coup" because of its strong links to drug trafficking. He outlawed all political parties, exiled opposition leaders, shut down unions, and silenced the press. During his thirteen-month dictatorship about a thousand people were murdered, often after being tortured (Dunkerley 1984).

García Meza did not act without help: he received strategic assistance through Operation Condor from a secret Argentinean army intelligence unit. The "Butcher of Lyons," Klaus Barbie, a Nazi officer known for his brutality against French resistance during World War II, had found haven in Bolivia and was one of García Meza's key advisors. But unlike in the past, this coup had no U.S. backing, as President Jimmy Carter's commitment to human rights led him to denounce the regime almost immediately.

Marcelo Quiroga de Santa Cruz, congressman, writer, university professor, and outspoken socialist leader, who had publicly denounced military dictatorships since the time of Barrientos, is perhaps the best known of García Meza's victims. Quiroga de Santa Cruz was actively demanding that General Banzer be brought to trial for human rights violations and economic mismanagement when he was seized and murdered on July 17, 1980.

García Meza's main ally was the much-feared minister of the interior, Colonel Luis Arce Gómez, who was later extradited to the United States, where he served much of a thirty-year sentence for drug trafficking before being returned to Bolivia in July 2009 to face additional charges. While the cocaine trade had originally spread throughout the lowlands under Banzer in response to burgeoning northern demand, under García Meza, production skyrocketed. Drug mafia involvement in the regime made it an international pariah, weakening García Meza and thwarting his plans for Pinochet-style rule in Bolivia.

Escape to Peru

Although we prevented military occupation over the short term, García Meza rapidly consolidated the coup nationally. This isolated the miners of Siglo XX, and we saw no alternative but to surrender. Information smuggled to us indicated that García Meza planned to kill five hundred leaders and activists on his blacklist, and unfortunately my name appeared on the list. I had to flee Siglo XX to avoid what I assumed would be certain execution. But how would I leave the country again?

Due to a fortuitous circumstance, Emilse was at a meeting in Lima, where she contacted the Dutch embassy and explained my situation. The embassy couldn't provide any support from Peru, but said if I could find my way there it would grant me refugee status in Holland again.

By then I was in hiding in La Paz. One day I had the bad luck to be recognized near the FSTMB office by a paramilitary from Siglo XX. He followed me and figured out that I was staying at Emilse's mother's house in San Pedro. Shortly afterward the house was surrounded. But my luck was not all bad. I had gone out, and as I approached the house I realized it was under surveillance. I turned on the spot and fled to El Alto, where my younger sister Carmen lived with her husband, a truck driver. With them, I frantically began preparing my escape, because I knew the military wasn't far behind.

The challenge was to find a truck that could cross the border into Peru without inspection. My brother-in-law identified a truck carrying coffee, and the driver, without realizing that I was being sought by the Ministry of the Interior, helped me after I paid him for the passage. Ironically, the truck was part of a six-truck caravan owned by the widow of Joaquín Zenteno Anaya, the commander who captured and assassinated Che Guevara. Zenteno had later been assassinated when he was Bolivia's ambassador to France in 1976, presumably by an agent of the Banzer government. That's just how small the country is.

The truck driver, accompanied by his helper, picked me up midmorning, and we pulled up to the Bolivian border control in Desaguadero at eight that night. During the trip to the border the driver stopped for a *cholita* to climb aboard. She also had no passport or other identity papers, and they hid us both in the sleeper berth in the cab. This made me very nervous, and, although I considered it very irresponsible of the driver to pick up another illegal migrant, I was in no position to complain.

Because it always took hours to cross the border, the driver began to drink beer with a group of his trucker friends. I joined in. I felt comfortable with them, and they quickly accepted me into the group. I made an effort to be friendly with some of the other drivers so that I could change trucks after the border if necessary. As we were downing our beers, a driver told us that our truck's window had been smashed. When we rushed outside to see what had happened, the *cholita* whom we had left behind in the cab was shaking with fury and threatened to hit the driver for leaving her there alone. He got her to calm down enough to talk, "Why are you so angry? What happened to the window?"

The *cholita* answered, "Your helper tried to rape me, and to save myself I had to break the window."

The helper, knowing his boss would be furious—more because of the broken window than the assault on the girl—had run off.

This turned out to be extremely lucky for me, because when we finally pulled up to the border inspection station, the driver handed me the helper's identity card, and with the *cholita* hidden in the berth, we passed through the Bolivian control. On the Peruvian side, I continued to play the role of helper and presented, for review, the documentation on the cargo along with the driver's and his identification cards. The driver handed me a carton of Derby cigarettes, and I rewarded each customs stamp with a pack of cigarettes. We repeated this exercise at every checkpoint until we got to Arequipa, where we parted ways.

I then hopped a bus to Lima and headed for the Dutch embassy, where I waited for over a month for the official authorization for my exile. During this time, the UN High Commissioner for Refugees (UNHCR) helped with my expenses. Fortunately, Peru had a democratic government at the time, and I had no problems.

Through my political party connections, I contacted several left-wing parliamentary deputies, who put me up in the house of the Peruvian ex-chancellor Bedoya for a week. And of course, I sought out other exiled Bolivians as well. One worked in an architecture firm, and he, too, was searching for a place to live. He found out about a house through a colleague, who offered it to us but explained, "There is a bit of a complication, but

I don't think it will bother you. Come over tomorrow afternoon. I'll introduce you to my mother, and she'll give you the key."

The next day when we met his mother she said, "I have to tell you something important. The house is haunted and is being cleansed. You must be very, very careful."

She didn't charge us rent, because she mostly just wanted caretakers. She just requested that we allow a shaman in one afternoon a week to purify the house, a huge and luxurious place in San Isidro, a very exclusive neighborhood. It sat empty because it was supposedly haunted, and, as it was filthy, we began cleaning.

Just as the newly mopped floors finished drying, the shaman appeared at the door. He hauled out a container with about three gallons of mashed-up herbs stored in a closet. Fortunately, we hadn't thrown it out, because it was too heavy to move easily. The healer spread the contents of the container everywhere. To end the session he formed herb crosses on our chests so that we wouldn't be contaminated by witchcraft. He requested that we leave the liquid on the floor for three days. He explained that as a consequence of the house's possession by evil spirits, the architect's mother had fallen very sick. I assume the healer's treatment was effective, because we never got ill. Actually, I thought it was all nonsense, and nothing more than a show, although it suited us to maintain the facade so that we could continue to live there comfortably and safely for free.

During my time in Lima, I was involved in solidarity work, particularly assisting delegations from Europe who were heading to the Bolivian mines to check on the human rights situation and publicize violations under the García Meza dictatorship.

Given the active political repression, I had to leave my family behind, which was painful for me. They stayed at Siglo XX for months until I could arrange the paperwork to reunite us through a refugee assistance center in Holland. It was a very difficult time for us all, and Emilse was mostly alone in Siglo XX with a small baby. Also, only a few months after Valeria's birth, she got pregnant with our second child, which, of course, made everything that much more complicated.

My Second Exile

When I arrived in Amsterdam this time, two people from the Dutch Foundation for Exiles were waiting for me at the airport. They took me to a welcome center in the city of Bergen, where there were refugees from all over the world. The next day I got in touch with Henk, who was not at all surprised to hear from me because he had been following the political events in Bolivia. He was relieved that I had managed to escape and came to pick me up. From that point on, I lived with him in Amsterdam, even though I was registered as living in the welcome center and had to return there almost daily to process my application for family reunification.

Getting established in Holland this time was easy, because I already had friends and could speak some of the language. Because of my friendship with Henk, I had a place to stay, which was very lucky because at that time, even for the Dutch, finding decent housing had become problematic.

I started taking language classes five days a week, one hour a day with another hour dedicated to homework. I studied with a dozen other students, all of them refugees or immigrants: Americans, Africans, Arabs, and Asians—mostly from Vietnam—as well as political refugees from Indonesia and China. Some of the students worked in embassies in Holland, and others had married Dutch citizens. I also met people from Iraq and Iran, because of the war between those countries at the beginning of the 1980s. The African refugees, mostly from Eritrea, fled their homes because of civil war and drought.

While we shared refugee status, it was a real challenge to communicate, as we had such different cultural and linguistic backgrounds. Of course, we could understand each other a bit by communicating with our hands, feet, and heads. In general, most of the Arabs were religious Muslim fundamentalists. The first thing they wanted to know before becoming friendly was your religion. They were very conservative and generally not interested in getting to know non-Muslims. The Africans, in my experience, were also pretty closed and shy. It was difficult to talk to them and even harder to form friendships. The Asians were more open, but their Dutch pronunciation was hard for me to understand.

The Latinos mostly originated from Chile, Argentina, and Uruguay, and they clearly differentiated themselves by class. Most of the middle-class refugees were able to adjust rapidly, because they had advanced education and knew how to study a language. The government provided professionals training in their respective fields so that they could join the labor force. The working-class exiles had the most difficulty. They didn't have the experience of studying either a technical field or a language, and they had to make a real effort to adjust to the context.

Even among the working-class Latinos, relationships were often conflictive. As these were largely political refugees, people remained committed to their political parties, even though they were far from a setting where those parties held sway. This sometimes led to ugly scenes and even fights at alcohol-fueled Dutch-sponsored solidarity events for Latin America. I remember an awful night when a commemorative event for Chile was ruined when fistfights broke out between refugees from different political parties.

Tensions also surfaced between Latin Americans from different countries. Most of them, especially those from Argentina, Chile, and Uruguay, discriminated against the Bolivians and Peruvians because they perceived us as backward Indians. I remember one night a Bolivian coming out of a bar was jumped by several Chileans and beaten so badly that he was hospitalized for some time, all because of some silly argument. But the hostility wasn't only directed at Bolivians, and I repeatedly saw conflicts grow out of the nationalist prejudice of many exiles.

Apart from learning Dutch, my principal activities were filing the necessary paperwork to bring my family to Holland and applying to educational institutions. The process of reuniting the family was delayed for months, mainly because of the relationship among Holland, the UNHCR, and Bolivia. The García Meza regime made it almost impossible to arrange my family's departure. During this time I felt alone, and I was afraid that they would reject the exit visa request. After several more difficult months our persistence prevailed, and Emilse was issued the paperwork that allowed us to be reunited.

At the same time, I was active in solidarity work with Bolivia and in educating Dutch people interested in the problems of Third World countries. We put together an information bulletin with the name *Wayra,* which means "wind" in Quechua and Aymara, with the help of Jorge and Fausto among the Bolivians, together with Dutch friends Marianne, Jeanny Kers, Aik Meusse, and two university students. In the *Wayra* bulletin, we published all the latest news about Bolivia in Dutch. We distributed it at solidarity events in Holland, as well as to interested people in Belgium. At that time, about twenty Bolivians lived in exile in Holland.

The situation in Holland had changed somewhat since my previous exile, because globalization had begun to bring new social policies. Even as a casual observer I could see that social problems had worsened, as there were beggars and drug addicts in the streets, a dramatic change from my previous experience in Amsterdam. The labor market had changed too. When I was first in Holland, for example, I noticed that the Dutch engaged in certain occupations, which permitted economic immigrants from other countries to fill relatively low-status jobs. With the growth in unemployment and the burgeoning numbers of immigrants, some Dutch people were starting to hate foreigners and blame them for stealing their jobs. As a result, racism had grown. In some cases the Dutch attacked immigrants. Sometimes when I got on the tram, even though there was room to sit beside me, a Dutch person preferred to travel standing up.

Félix with his daughters, Khantuta, left, and Valeria, right, in Amsterdam, 1984. From the private collection of Félix Muruchi.

When Emilse, her brother Fidel, and Valeria arrived a few months later, we all lived together at Henk's for some time. Fidel, who had just graduated high school in La Paz, came because he had become an important support to Emilse with Valeria. He studied economics in Holland and settled there permanently.

Emilse was in her eighth month of pregnancy when she finally arrived, and we immediately began preparations for the birth—which of course involved completing more paperwork to arrange for health care and social benefits. Khantuta, our second daughter, was born in Amsterdam. I was happy that Emilse had made it to Holland, as she received excellent medical attention, and we all had civil rights and social benefits. I was also allowed to attend the birth. This was an incredible experience for me, and really made me feel like a father. It is an amazing experience to see with your own eyes the creation of human life. But at the same time I felt powerless to help much in the face of the powerful contractions and pain that Emilse was undergoing.

As we settled in we began to plan our future, as up to that point, my life, as well as our life together, had been very chaotic. With two children it became important to develop some degree of stability. Emilse and I realized that we would likely have to live outside of Bolivia for a long time, although we both wanted to return home as soon as possible. Even though the Dutch government and people had been incredibly generous with us, it was just not our destiny to stay there as immigrants. We differed significantly from economic immigrants: we hadn't chosen to move there, but were forced to, and, as a result, we always dreamed of returning home.

Given the options, I decided to study a technical field, which would facilitate getting a job more quickly than if I studied economics. I chose to enroll in a three-year training program for machinists. As Holland is a social democratic state, we received a family stipend that covered our housing and basic needs, including health insurance. I was really impressed that the Dutch state invested so much to train workers, transforming unemployed people into technical professionals, who could then make a positive contribution to the country's economic development. This social democratic philosophy recognized the state's responsibility to guarantee citizens' social rights so that they could live a dignified life, and also to provide new ways to allow citizens to help develop the country. This type of social contract has never existed in Bolivia.

During this period, I received the awful news that my father had died of black lung contracted during his long years of toiling in the mines. I felt completely impotent, because I could neither get in touch, nor travel, nor really do anything. I cried a lot, but fortunately my brother Germán was visiting us in Holland with the permission of the East German government. We shared our memories and our grief. It upset us enormously that we couldn't attend his funeral, and it enraged us that we were not permitted to enter our country.

To this day, when I call my mother by phone in Cochabamba, where she lives now, she always scolds me, "When are you going to come? Because you didn't even come to the burial of your father, surely you won't show up at mine either."

During our first year in Holland, Emilse studied Dutch and began to carry out solidarity work with development institutions. In 1982, once again the Bolivian people poured into the streets to force the military to surrender power, and suddenly and rather unexpectedly, we had the opportunity to return home. Dr. Hernán Siles Zuazo, who had twice won elections, was finally permitted to assume office.

Return to Civilian Rule: The Democratic and Popular Unity

After he was forced to resign in August 1981, García Meza fled the country, and in 1993 he was tried in absentia for human rights violations, despite death threats against the Supreme Court judges responsible for the case. Eventually he was discovered in Brazil and extradited in 1994 to Bolivia, where he is currently serving a thirty-year sentence, only the second South American dictator forced back to his country to face trial. His replacement, Celso Torrelio, whom the military believed capable of extending their reign, lasted a little less than a year. By that time pressures to turn the country over to civilian rule were so strong that the next general, Guido Vildoso, had the explicit charge of orchestrating a return to democracy. In mid-1982, Vildoso's transitional government was recognized by the British and then by the United States.

Finally, on October 10, 1982, Hernán Siles Zuazo, who had won the popular vote in both 1978 and 1980, was sworn into office as president at the head of the UDP, a coalition of some twenty groups, including the majority of left parties. The UDP's stated goal was to revive the nationalist economic and political project begun in 1952. The new government heralded the beginning of twenty-five years of civilian rule, the longest period since the country became a republic. Ever since Vildoso's 1982 departure, Bolivia's military has shown little inclination to seize power.

At the beginning of the 1980s, widely known as Latin America's lost decade, Bolivia suffered from an inflationary spiral, crippling debt, out-of-control government spending to support patronage, and growing capital flight. The UDP's

165

electoral victories made it the only coalition with any political legitimacy, and while the government was able to restore civil and political rights, the economic crisis that swept throughout Latin America meant that expanding social rights to guarantee a decent standard of living was close to inconceivable. The broad-based nature of the UDP coalition made effective governance impossible thanks to perpetual political infighting. This was exacerbated by a lack of financial resources, and pressure from international financial institutions to repay a crippling foreign debt by cutting government services.

By 1984–1985, inflation raged as high as 20,000 percent, one of the highest rates the world has ever seen. As the currency collapsed, the government realized that its debt interest to private banks exceeded the country's export income, so it decided to limit payments. Afraid of the precedent that Bolivia might set for other heavily indebted Latin American countries, international banks immediately threatened to freeze Bolivia's assets abroad, leaving Siles Zuazo's administration little option but to resume paying the debt.

Initially, the Siles Zuazo government benefited from the full support of the COB, which insisted that its critical role in returning the country to civilian rule granted it the right to cogovern. Unlike 1952, when the COB was willing to accept a minority role, this time it demanded an equal partnership with 50 percent control. When the issue couldn't be resolved, the COB/UDP alliance ruptured. The reinvigorated and increasingly cohesive Confederation of Bolivian Private Businessmen (Confederación de Empresarios Privados de Bolivia, or CEPB) pushed the UDP hard from the right, demanding the state relinquish control over significant sectors of the economy.

While Siles Zuazo spent almost three years bouncing ineffectually between these irreconcilable demands, Bolivia was racked by over 3,500 strikes and work stoppages. Siles Zuazo was reluctant to unleash repression on the popular sectors, while the incessant unrest cost the COB a great deal of its political capital as the "defender of democracy" (Kohl and Farthing 2006).

Emilse had begun working on a project she developed in 1982 to support women in Llallagua. She twice traveled to Bolivia with Khantuta for extended periods, leaving me in Amsterdam with Valeria, before our definitive return in 1985. We decided that I should stay in Holland to finish my machinist course and then get a job to raise the money we would need to reestablish ourselves in Bolivia. We thought it was wise to buy a house in La Paz, because even at that time it looked like the government would close the mines, as they were perpetually racking up huge losses.

In September 1985, toward the end of my third year of study, I was invited with my schoolmates to visit several large Dutch factories and apply for jobs there. One of these companies was the transnational firm Euro Metal, which made all kinds of machines and tools but principally manufactured arms. Demand for skilled labor was high, because the company was manufacturing munitions and arms for the war between Iraq and Iran. In its factory, production was highly automated, and most tasks related to maintaining quality control. I was not favorably impressed—my aspirations did not include manufacturing arms used to kill people, and, more often than not, poor people. I rejected the job offer, arguing that I was a political exile who opposed war. In any case, by this time I was in the process of returning home, so I was particularly looking for experience I could directly replicate in Bolivia.

As part of my solidarity work, I was invited to give a talk in the city of Antwerp in Belgium. When a student organizing my presentation picked me up, he warned me, "We have arranged for you to spend the night with my family. But I should tell you that in our house we have never had an Indian or a socialist as a guest. In Belgium, most union leaders are socialists, and we assume it is the same in Latin America. I beg you that if anything makes you uncomfortable that you won't let it bother you."

I responded, "Don't worry. I am used to meeting new people in Europe." His father, the fifth generation in a line of dentists, received me very warmly, as did the rest of the family. His father really wanted to talk to me and find out what I thought, but given the student's warning that he was conservative, I avoiding talking about socialism or politics.

After dinner, we headed to the presentation, and the auditorium was packed. The talk and subsequent discussion were fruitful, and I spoke at length about Bolivia's social organizations and miners' unions. Everyone had come to see and hear the Indian, which really surprised me because this was not my identity—I still thought of myself as a miner—and I wasn't really prepared to talk much about it.

Afterwards I met with several students, and we headed to a café. We drank a few beers, and one of them asked, "I thought that Indians wore feathers and painted their faces. Why don't you have feathers, and how come your face isn't painted?"

At that moment, I remembered a song by the Bolivian singer and author Alfredo Domínguez, about the European perception of Indians, and a situation all too similar to this one. I responded jokingly, "Obviously I wear my feathers and normally paint my face, but you know that Belgium is an ordered and law-abiding country. When I crossed the border, the police and customs demanded that I pay duty on my feathers and paints. As I don't have a lot of money, I preferred to leave them there." I assumed this story would start them laughing, but in fact, the response was just the opposite: all of them began to protest against their government and country.

When I saw that they took me seriously, I quickly clarified, "Look, I'm pulling your leg." I explained the difference between highland and lowland indigenous people, and I pointed out that in the highlands we only use paint and feathers in celebrations when we are dressing like "Indians." I also told them how the influence of Western culture and colonization led to the loss of many of our traditional customs of dress. I showed them my leather jacket and explained that it was "typical" dress among mining union leaders.

Return to Bolivia

At the end of 1985, I found a job with CEBEMO (Centraal Missie Commissariaat), a Roman Catholic institution that provided funds for development projects in poor countries. In Bolivia, its projects were operated through the Roman Catholic Archdiocese. CEBEMO needed a machinist, because it hoped to replicate a German workshop that made prostheses and ortheses (orthopedic braces) for disabled people. CEBEMO had all the equipment installed in a workshop housed in a Church-based program called Faith and Happiness. The big problem the organization faced, however, was that it didn't have skilled workers to run the shop. It had attempted several times to train people in Bolivia by sending them to Argentina and Brazil but had not been successful. It decided it would have to hire European experts and searched for one in Germany and another in Holland. This seemed like a great opportunity for the family, given that Emilse's project in Bolivia was already well under way.

As the organization had me make my own travel arrangements, I chose an itinerary with a stopover in Cuba. This was a terrific opportunity, for I was interested in traveling to any socialist country, and both Emilse and I were especially keen to see Cuba. I had been deeply disappointed with the socialism I saw in East Germany, but I was sure it would be different in Cuba. In addition, when I was a PCML militant, I had never thought to make this type of trip. In almost all political parties, generally people from the upper middle class controlled the leadership. They preferred to send people of their class for exchanges, to participate in courses, or visit socialist countries. It was even less likely that I would be able to visit Cuba, because the PCML was identified with China, whereas Cuba was aligned with the Soviet bloc.

When I asked for the visa, the Cuban consulate received me warmly; the consul even offered me a glass of Cuban rum in the waiting room. After the interview, he said, "You have a free night in a hotel in Havana, because we really want to welcome you to our country." I excitedly returned to the house with the wonderful news that we were traveling to Cuba!

I left Holland very pleased about my opportunity to assist the development process in Bolivia, especially as that would allow us to return home comfortably. Some of my Dutch friends simply couldn't understand my desire to go back. During our good-bye party I was asked, "Why would you go? Here you have a good house, work, and the possibility of a good education for your daughters. There you don't have anything. Bolivia is a poor country, there is no security, and you always have political problems."

It was difficult for me to answer in a way my Dutch friends could understand. On the one hand, they were right; Bolivia was a poor country, and I was sacrificing all the security that Dutch life offered. What my friends didn't understand was that for us, we would always be foreigners in Holland, and, even though it would be easy to ensure material security, we would never completely integrate ourselves or feel personally fulfilled.

Although we had good friends, like Henk, who continues to be like a brother to me, and others like Jeanny, Aik, Mariolyn, Hedda, and Marya, it just wasn't enough. During my time there, I had seen how some people suffered the consequences of living outside their social milieu. Many refugees had problems with depression and were unable to adapt. One of my schoolmates, a man from Chile, was so unhappy that he committed suicide. Another Chilean killed himself by setting himself on fire in Amsterdam's main plaza protesting against the system and against his exile. I knew him, and it was very sad because he just couldn't find his way in Holland.

My feelings were not easy to explain, so I just replied, "Look, I'm from the Andes and Holland is too flat. I'm used to living in the mountains."

The friend who had asked took my words at face value and replied, "Oh, of course. Now I understand."

Reflections on Holland

One of the things that most affected me in Holland was the 1985 Technology Expo Fair. As we were studying metals, our institution sponsored a visit to see the robotic exhibition from the highly industrialized countries in Europe, as well as from Japan and the United States. At the entrance gate, a robot stood with pamphlets and information about the exposition. I thought it was just a stationary exhibit, until I moved to pick up its information and the robot pushed me away with its arm, handing me the pamphlet. It really impressed me, because the robot really functioned like a person. Inside, many robots provided answers and assembled autos. They completed all this work in record time—with such precision that corrections weren't needed. As we left, robots handed each of us a Coca-Cola.

This made me realize that you could replace some four thousand workers with forty robots who never ask for salary increases, or social programs, or a place to live. They would be productive twenty-four hours a day with only the need for occasional repair, which could mostly be done by computers that needed just one technician. This experience twenty years ago made me aware what tremendous unemployment was going to occur in Europe and other industrialized countries. Since then, robotic technology has advanced enormously, and unskilled labor is less and less necessary in many factories.

I was very impressed by the social rights of citizens in Holland. For example, if workers lost their jobs they still had an income, because employers paid taxes to insure they would receive a modest salary. The taxes were utilized to create a pool of unemployment insurance, and while the income was less than wages, it provided the workers enough to survive.

Consumerism was rampant in Europe. For each period of the year, different styles of expensive clothing were marketed. It seemed to me that the biggest consumers came from the working class, because they always wanted to seem fashionable, whereas intellectuals didn't seem to care so much what they wore. For example, several times in Amsterdam I watched people change their living room set or their bedroom and other furniture in order to keep up with fashion, not even selling the old stuff, even though it had only been used a year or two, but rather throwing everything out into the street.

We found our own apartment in a working-class neighborhood that had been built after the Second World War. A Dutch couple with an Old English Sheepdog lived above us, and we often ran into them in the neighborhood park. The woman told me that her dog was in training school, but had failed the beginner's course and had to retake it. It really impressed me that not only did she enroll her dog in a training school, but she was willing to repeat the course! I was struck by how Dutch dogs were treated better than many children in my country.

The visit of Pope John Paul II to Holland was something else that had a big impact on me. Many people went to Schiphol airport to meet him: one group celebrating his arrival and the other protesting it. The opposition was so strong that the pope was unable to make some of the stops on his itinerary. Eventually he had to leave Holland through Belgium.

In comparison with those of Bolivia, which legally identifies itself as Roman Catholic, Dutch Catholics comprise about only 30 percent of the population. But what impressed me the most were the women in the opposition who confronted the pope. At a press conference, they denounced him as a sexist because neither nuns nor other religious women could lead a Mass or be pope. In addition, they attacked his conservative position on abortion. In Holland, Catholic women bore lots of children just like in Bolivian mining families, but because of the women's rights struggle during the 1970s, they were guaranteed the right to a free abortion. Women struggled not only for reproductive rights, but also for sexual freedom, which they also won and, of course, which the Catholics opposed.

The exact opposite occurred in Latin America when the pope visited Peru and Bolivia in 1988. The Vatican and the local Church in both countries spent a huge amount of money on advertising so as to ensure a positive turnout. But there were no signs of visible opposition in either country. About that time I realized that Catholicism is a Western religion based in just one God, whereas our indigenous religions are very distinct, based on the Earth Mother, the Father Sun, and the mountains that possess their own gods. But Spanish colonization drove our own religions underground and replaced them with Catholicism. My birth family was always aware of this, but the transmission of indigenous religious beliefs is oral, and its values are expressed only in practice. Children learn one thing at school but practice something else at home and aren't sure what to believe.

In Peru, the pope's reception was amazing, because thousands of people flocked to the airport, where they started crying and fighting to touch him as if he really were a messenger from God. I realized that in poor countries, with so much illiteracy and ignorance, religion is an important form of emotional discharge and hope: the poor person does not believe that relief will come from his or her government, but rather from God. But it seems that the poor don't understand that the Catholic Church shares much of the responsibility for people's backwardness and poverty.

Our history is distorted, because the schools never taught us that our religion worships the sun and that our Pachamama is the holy land itself. This broader understanding may be taught at university, but primary and secondary schools require students to take Catholic religion classes. As a result, when the pope arrives in a country like Bolivia or Peru, the poor receive him enthusiastically. In contrast, in a highly developed country with a better-educated population, the pope is challenged more frequently, because more people know the history of the papacy and its role in the world.

Cuba

For left-wing radicals all over the world, and particularly in Latin America, Cuba assumed enormous significance after its 1959 revolution, which overthrew a much-hated military dictatorship under Fulgencio Batista. The Caribbean island's efforts to construct socialism in the face of constant pressure and threats from the United States, located only ninety miles away, and its success in resisting the U.S. domination felt so strongly throughout Latin America, have contributed in great measure to the regard many have for it. As a result, it is often romanticized by leftists, who herald its accomplishments—excellent health and education systems—and overlook its problematic record on basic political and civil rights, as well as its relatively slow economic growth until 2005. But others who go out of their way, as Félix did, to visit Cuba hoping to find some kind of socialist paradise, only to discover a more complex reality, often leave confused by its contradictions.

When Cuba lost economic support from the Soviet Union and other Eastern bloc countries in the early 1990s, it was plunged into what Fidel Castro's government called "the special period," where shortages and deprivation forced ordinary Cubans to draw on their deep-seated commitment to independence in order to survive (Brenner 2008). The experience profoundly changed the island, as it was forced by its new circumstances to modify its more radical economic positions and accept foreign investment from Canada and Europe, as well as permit a small but growing private sector.

Despite these significant shifts in the original blueprint for the revolution, Cuba's importance in Latin America has surged again in recent years thanks to the recent "pink tide" of democratically elected left-leaning governments in Brazil, Argentina, Venezuela, Chile, Ecuador, Bolivia, Peru, and Nicaragua. Its impressive economic growth since 2005 has both improved the conditions of its population and granted it greater respect internationally (Linger 2007).

The Road Home: Visit to Cuba

We arrived around eleven o'clock at night in Havana, and as we had a hotel voucher, I presented my ticket with its hotel coupon attached. The immigration agent laughed, "This is good for nothing" and arrogantly ripped it up and tossed it in the garbage.

Then I dug out my letter of invitation from a Swedish journalist friend working in Cuba. After glancing at the letter he said dismissively with the same authoritarian air, "This invitation comes from a foreigner, and in Cuba foreigners can't invite people to visit. You have to be invited by a Cuban."

Rolf Ericsson, an old friend, served as the second secretary of the Swedish embassy in Cuba at the time. So I pulled out his invitation, but it was rejected out of hand too, "He's not a Cuban either. You need to have a reservation at a hotel; without it, you can't enter."

It was almost one in the morning, with the girls asleep on the floor, so we had no option but to stand in line and make a hotel reservation that cost US $50, which was a lot of money for us, before the official finally stamped our entrance visa. Our journalist friend stood outside waiting patiently for us. Once we arrived at the hotel, the desk clerk glanced at us coldly and stated with finality, "We don't have room, everything is full."

I was exhausted and fed up and ready to argue with him. But my Swedish friend advised, "It's better not to say anything; it's always like this here. Ask him to stamp your ticket, and then we'll be on our way." So he stamped it, important as proof that we had paid for a hotel, even though we had received absolutely nothing for our money, and then we headed to his house, arriving about four in the morning.

This first impression was disheartening. Leaving Cuba a week later, we had problems once again with immigration officials because of the out-of-date information they insisted on using. When we arrived to pick up our exit visas at the state travel office I was informed, "As your trip is via Peru, you need a visa."

I replied, "But neither Peruvians nor Bolivians need a visa to travel between the two countries."

The official was adamant, "No, you're wrong," and he pulled out a fat book published in 1960. In the end, we had no choice but to get the visa the Cuban authorities required. The Peruvian consul commiserated, "Although we have sent them the correct information various times, the Cubans just ignore it. But just so you can leave without problems, we will write a note of clarification." At the end of the letter he added in capital letters, "FOR THE LAST TIME, I WANT TO MAKE CLEAR THAT BOLIVIANS DO NOT NEED A VISA TO ENTER MY COUNTRY!!!" And with this note, the Cubans finally provided us with exit visas.

We encountered similar problems with insensitive bureaucrats not only during this trip, but also when Emilse and I visited Holland a year later after my contract with CEBEMO ended. We were again routed through Cuba, as we used the return portion of the ticket. This time, when we requested the exit visas at the Cuban state travel office, they assured us that everything was fine, but at the airport the agent curtly informed us, "As

Bolivians you need a visa to enter France. Since you don't have one, you can't leave." We tried our best to reason with the agent. We begged him, saying we couldn't miss the plane because we had work responsibilities in Holland, but he would not budge. The next flight was in a week. Back we tramped to the state travel office to complain, and without any apology, they offered us a week in a four-star hotel with free food.

We didn't have much money, and Cuba had two parallel economies: one, based on the U.S. dollar, was for tourists and the Cuban upper middle class, and the other, in the Cuban peso, for the working classes, including low-level professionals and state workers. We stuck to the Cuban peso economy so we could travel a bit, hiring a Cuban taxi driver who took us through Havana and the surrounding area for three days.

In spite of these bureaucratic problems, in general we enjoyed Cuba, because it is a marvelous country. In November, the climate was pleasant in comparison both to Holland, where bone-chilling weather prevails at this time of year and the sun hardly ever shines, and Siglo XX, where we often had to break the ice in the bucket of water so that we could wash our faces in the mornings. The landscape also impressed me. There was a richness of vegetation even in the city, which I noticed even more on the second trip, given that I was arriving from the desert of the altiplano. The sea had a special significance for me, as for all Bolivians, as a result of our loss of the seacoast during the War of the Pacific with Chile during the late nineteenth century. In Holland, I had known the sea, but the waters of the North Atlantic are muddy and cold. The Caribbean is clear, turquoise, and warm, something that most Bolivians only see in the movies. Books were very inexpensive in Cuba, which also gave me great pleasure. The people were very friendly, which was a stark contrast to East Germany. The Germans were not easy to communicate with, and I found them very rigid, whereas the Cubans are Latinos—very open and kind.

The public officials, however, were absurdly slow, similar to their East German counterparts, and seemed incapable of expressing any empathy. For example, in a hotel, if you asked for a glass of water, they somewhat reluctantly brought it half an hour later. The same was true with food. To buy ice cream we stood in a line that stretched for two or three blocks, but the ice cream was delicious, perhaps even more so because of the heat and the wait. I suppose the lack of competition meant that no one felt an urgent need to attend to the public.

A Cuban friend explained that all this was normal, "Sometimes people go to the complaints office. But it's the same there. No one pays any attention to you, and when they do, they are completely indifferent. And after that, who can you complain to?"

The Cuban socialist system is similar to East Germany's, with the difference that in Cuba, they are Fidelistas, everything is Fidel. When you speak to grassroots people, they always say, "Fidel said this, Fidel said that." In Germany there wasn't this *caudillismo,* but rather propaganda was directed at support for the system itself. In both countries, however, many people were desperate to escape to the supposedly free world. They felt trapped, as they couldn't travel freely even to visit their family who lived in other places.

For me, Cuba was not the paradise I had hoped for, although, as in East Germany, almost all basic social problems had been addressed. Nearly everyone had work, housing, health care, and food. But something was missing, certain liberties, including those of movement and expression. I asked myself, "Why don't they give people greater freedom?" I found it sad, because from my perspective the Cuban people had won their independence from the United States, but had not really managed to deepen their revolutionary process. Instead, they had remained a colony and only managed to change their old master for the new one of the Soviet Union.

PART FOUR

Activist in El Alto

Introduction: El Alto

E l Alto—literally "the heights"—sprawls across the altiplano above Bolivia's capital city of La Paz. The twin cities have aptly been described as an indigenous urban center overlooking a colonial city. In 1950, El Alto was a neighborhood of only eleven thousand people, the site of the airport and those few factories that required more space than was available in the narrow canyon that cradles La Paz. But after the 1952 revolution, El Alto expanded steadily for thirty years before it mushroomed in the early 1980s, due first to the El Niño drought of 1982–1983 and then to the dislocation caused by the 1985 New Economic Policy (NEP). When local markets were opened to cheap food imports, peasant producers were unable to compete, and thousands of people flocked to the city, joining miners who had lost their jobs with the closures of the state mines (Arbona 2007).

In 1985 El Alto separated from La Paz, calculating that its independence would improve its access to resources, but was only accorded the legal status of a city in September 1988, with its population approaching half that of La Paz. Fifteen years later, El Alto roughly equaled La Paz in size. As in other low-income cities, 60 percent of its population is under twenty-five years old, and its workforce is mostly nonunionized (Lazar 2008). Many families maintain a strong sense of indigenous identity through the direct ties they maintain with the rural hinterland.

El Alto neighborhoods are characterized by congested streets, unpaved sidewalks, low-rise buildings in varying degrees of completion, and inadequate (or nonexistent) sewer systems. Fifty-four percent of El Alto residents rely on outdoor plumbing for access to water. The limited physical infrastructure proclaims a city that outgrew its municipal government's limited resources and ability to provide basic public services (Arbona 2007).

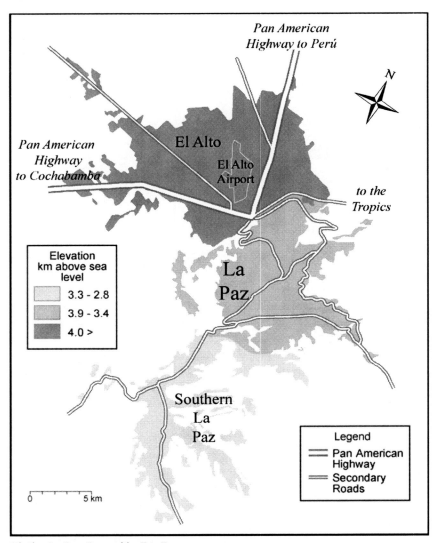

El Alto–La Paz. Prepared by Eric Fox.

Population growth also outpaced job creation, leading to the proliferation of an informal economy that includes activities from mobile merchants marketing DVDs or knock-off watches to street vendors selling ice cream. As in other fast-growing cities, the burgeoning informal sector serves to absorb poorly paid labor, accounting for about 70 percent of the total urban labor force (Farthing 1995).

Although Félix was no longer working as a miner when he returned from Holland, his personal history was still very much wrapped up in the mines. Like most of his *compañeros* (comrades or mates), he identifies himself as a miner to this day, even though he left the mines almost thirty years ago. Settling in El Alto, he found himself surrounded by miners escaping from the remote semi-abandoned mining camps in a desperate scramble for work in the city.

These were the *relocalizados* (relocated), a euphemism coined in 1986 by the neoliberal government in an attempt to minimize the reality of forced dispersal. As miners debated whether to accept government buyout packages, their strength as a union steadily ebbed, exacerbated by political party infighting and the daily struggle to feed their children. Everyone realized that an era had come to an end when some ten thousand recently unemployed miners set out to march on La Paz from Oruro in August 1986, only to be quickly surrounded and demobilized by the military.

In El Alto, as their identity as miners diminished with the passage of time and their inevitable shift to other work, frequently as laborers in construction, they increasingly became aware of how similar their circumstances were to their Aymara migrant neighbors. As a consequence, many ex-miners broadened their political views and overcame the historic rejection of their own indigenous roots that Marxist parties had promulgated.

Gradually, many transformed themselves into neighborhood and local (territorial), rather than work-based (class), organizers. The political culture that has resulted in El Alto's marginal neighborhoods unites elements of Marxist trade unionism with features of the post-1952 campesino unions and the traditional indigenous *ayllus*, all within a context of marked economic insecurity and political frustration (Arbona 2008).

In El Alto, neighborhood organizations have sprouted everywhere to offer a vital site of citizen representation. These organizations, called Juntas Vecinales, or simply *juntas*, together form the Federation of Neighborhood Organizations (Federación de Juntas Vecinales, or FEJUVE). As new settlements stabilize, these organizations play two key roles: they press municipal government to install basic urban services and develop clientelist relationships with political parties to gain access to those services. In 1989 there were 166 Juntas Vecinales in El Alto; by 2006, there were almost 550 (Arbona 2007).

The rise of these residential organizations could have facilitated an expanded leadership role for women, as the home and its management are a woman's traditional sphere. However, while women frequently participate in the neighborhood association programs and actions, the organizations' roots in mining and peasant union structures have virtually ensured that male leadership predominates. Nonetheless, over time, the Juntas Vecinales have achieved more female representation than most popular organizations; in 2004, women held ten of twenty-nine leadership positions, although they were not in central roles (Lazar 2008).

The school associations (*juntas escolares*) are the second-most-important organizational grouping in El Alto and are joined together in a Federation of Parents (Federación de Padres de Familia). The female presence in the school associations is roughly the inverse of that of the neighborhood organizations, with around two-thirds of *junta escolar* members women, while Juntas Vecinales are approximately two-thirds male (Lazar 2008). But while influential, the *juntas escolares* never emerged as a major protagonist, in part because their leadership stemmed from the MIR, which was largely discredited because of the corruption charges leveled at it when it was elected to run the El Alto municipality in 1999 (Arbona 2007).

Chapter 11

Life in El Álto

Three months after the 1985 Presidential Decree 21060, the key element in the New Economic Policy (NEP), was signed, I arrived back in Bolivia. The law embodied a neoliberal structural adjustment program just like those, having economic globalization as their goal, beginning to be applied all over the world. The previous government of Hernán Siles Zuazo (1982–1985) had been boxed into a corner and had no choice but to call elections.

The new president was none other than Víctor Paz Estenssoro, president following the revolution of 1952 until 1956, again between 1960 and 1964, and for a third time, very briefly, in 1964, when he was overthrown by General Barrientos. In 1985, he headed a weak coalition government with the National Democratic Action (Acción Democrática Nacional, or ADN), the party of ex-dictator Hugo Banzer, who drew on his support in the eastern lowlands to recast himself as a democratic politician. Paz Estenssoro's NEP was one of the most extreme structural adjustment programs the world had experienced to that point. For me and thousands of other miners, his decision to shut down the state mines was devastating.

THE NEW ECONOMIC POLICY, DECRETO SUPREMO 21060: ADOPTING NEOLIBERALISM

The 1985 elections marked another crucial turning point in Bolivia. Víctor Paz Estenssoro, at the head of a coalition government, almost immediately signed Presidential Decree 21060, the NEP, which launched Bolivia's neoliberal period by closing state mines, reducing social spending, floating the currency against the U.S. dollar, privatizing state-owned enterprises, opening the country to direct foreign investment, and ending protectionist and import substitution policies. This package formed the basis for the International Monetary Fund's (IMF) structural adjustment programs around the world and is the policy package at the core of modern neoliberal development.

The NEP gave international financial institutions and foreign governments renewed confidence, which was bolstered when it proved remarkably effective in reducing inflation in a matter of weeks, but at an enormous cost to Bolivia's workers. Over twenty thousand miners lost their jobs in one year, with disastrous effects on their families, their communities, and their ability to mobilize politically. Workers and campesinos reacted immediately with a round of strikes and riots, but they failed to slow the NEP's juggernaut, which was muscled through by the government's declaration of a state of siege and backed by fiscal support from the IMF and the World Bank.

While the new policies successfully stabilized the formal economy, miners, factory workers, and campesinos displaced or marginalized by the NEP were forced to eke out a living in the burgeoning informal, contraband, and coca economies, with their income supplemented by remittances from family members who worked abroad. The depth of this economic crisis essentially served to dissipate large-scale resistance and to come close to achieving one of the NEP's explicit goals: destroying the COB.

I returned not to Siglo XX's mines, but to the city of La Paz, with the Archdiocese's orthopedic braces and prosthetics project. It was a terrible time: it felt as if the country was being torn apart, because the state mines, which had accounted for about 75 percent of all exports, were on the verge of fully closing. The miners embarked on a "March for Life," from Siglo XX to La Paz, a trek of over 350 miles, in a vain effort to keep the mines open. The military intervened and blocked the march in Calamarca, about 50 miles south of La Paz. Marchers blamed the union leaders Filemón Escobar, Simón Reyes, and Oscar Salas for capitulating to the government. Shortly after the march was aborted, over twenty-three thousand COMIBOL mine workers lost their jobs.

This alliance of the national oligarchy with multinational capital decimated the Bolivian labor movement, achieving the goal they had sought since the 1952 nationalization of the mines. Their success did not come easy; it required the imprisonment, exile, and murder of leaders and military collaboration in the slaughter of miners, sometimes even in their own homes.

Settling in El Alto

We arrived at our new house in the neighborhood known as Ciudad Satélite—literally Satellite City—one of the oldest settlements in El Alto.

As soon as Valeria and I landed, we both were hit with altitude illness, as El Alto is at 13,300 feet above sea level. We spent a month lower down at my mother-in-law Doña Alicia's house in La Paz's basin at 12,000 feet.

Our daughters were enrolled in school in Llallagua, as Emilse continued working in Siglo XX with her nongovernmental organization (NGO) project and they had to finish their school year there, so I stayed alone in El Alto, traveling seven hours to Llallagua by bus almost every weekend. The girls suffered in Llallagua, as they got sick a lot, and the moment they recovered from one illness, they came down with something else. For them the first year in Bolivia was marked by bouts of diarrhea, hepatitis, and other diseases typical of the place.

The first time I arrived in Llallagua, a young man approached me in the bus terminal and smiled, "How are you, brother?" I didn't recognize him. He laughed, "I'm Wilfredo, your younger brother." I was coming home after six long years, and Willy had grown up. When I reached my mother's house, I burst into tears; I don't know if it was my happiness to be home or a deep sadness because my father was gone.

My mother introduced me to her new husband, whom she had married when she was sixty. Prudencio Mamani was originally from the department of Oruro and of campesino origin, just like my mother. But he was an Uruschipaya, considered one of the most ancient peoples in the Andes. His first wife had died, and he had several grown children. He treated my mother well and was a lot less *machista* [sexist] than my father, who sometimes used to hit my mother when he was drunk.

Prudencio got along well with all of us. Even now, years after he died, his own children still call my mother "Mama," even though she is their stepmother. He had worked in railroad maintenance between Machacamarca and Uncía, but lost his job during the implementation of the structural adjustment program. Because he had no job, the family was preparing to move to Cochabamba. After they left, none of my immediate family remained in Llallagua.

The few remaining miners still lamented the defeat of the March for Life in Calamarca. Everyone realized that everything would be different now that the transnational companies had won an open invitation to exploit the country's resources.

I was really surprised by the impressions that Valeria, then six years old, formed of Bolivia. She thought it was great fun to see children working in the streets and said, "Daddy, why can't I work like those kids?" as if it was something enjoyable. In Europe children don't work, at least not openly.

Reintegrating into Bolivian society was much tougher this second time round, given the changes not only in the country and my family, but also in me as a person after so many years in Holland. I had to start from zero in grasping the new reality. For example, I had no experience living in a poor urban neighborhood. At that point in El Alto, people were demanding municipal autonomy from the city of La Paz. It was not an issue I understood, although I did what I could to help. These kinds of topics were new to me and required different ways of carrying out the struggle. But what was most shocking in El Alto was the incredible self-interest and corruption that drove leaders. The lack of an ideological commitment and of a political party to serve as an instrument of struggle critically limited social movements.

Before I started work with the Archdiocese, I headed to the Congress to find some of my ex-comrades, and they received me nervously, assuming I had shown up to ask for a handout. "Brother, why did you come back to Bolivia?" they whined. "We are not in any position to help you." It shocked me that even though they had won congressional seats, they expressed no commitment to or intention of assisting their grassroots constituency. In my eyes they barely differed from the other representatives, who, once in power, focused on maintaining their privilege rather than fomenting real change.

I saw mining *compañeros* struggling at the margins to find work and a place to live in El Alto. Daily life was incredibly hard, and my knowledge that in Holland a social democratic government adequately provided for its people made it even more painful to witness.

After the girls finished their school year in Llallagua, we moved everyone to El Alto. The Ciudad Satélite neighborhood is a mix of people from mining backgrounds with lower- and middle-income families. We faced discrimination there because we were known as miners, and, in general, city people treat miners as communists and crazies. For Emilse and me the discrimination was palpable. Throughout their schooling, my daughters suffered prejudice because they had an indigenous last name and their family came from the mines.

We experienced this prejudice clearly even from primary-school teachers. During the enrollment period, we visited several schools. When one director found out we had recently arrived from Holland, our daughters were easily accepted. She beamed, "How wonderful that they studied in Holland." When they completed the reading test, she rejoiced, "How well they learned to read in Holland!" without realizing that in Holland they spoke Dutch, and the girls had learned to read in the mines. In another school, when we disclosed to the director that they had studied the previous year in the mines, she responded huffily, "First they have to take a test to check their ability to read." This behavior reflected not only prejudices against their own national school system, but their negative feelings toward miners.

We fought against these biases and conservative ways of thinking. It served us considerably that we had lived and studied abroad. Not only were we better educated, but we also had experienced how things function in other parts of the world.

At times, however, our worldly experience was not enough to deal with the reality of the daily operation of schools in El Alto. School district employees were protected by very powerful unions. The principal of the school where the girls studied in 1987, their first year in La Paz, began to make fun of Valeria because of her last name. I mentioned this at a parents' meeting, and when we discovered that the principal often mistreated other children as well, all the parents were furious. We voted to try to get her fired.

I was fortunate, as I had met René Higueras del Barco, then minister of education, in jail on one occasion, so I decided to go straight to the top. I arranged an interview, and after we exchanged pleasantries, I told him the problem. He looked at me in dismay, "Félix, I would love to help you but my hands are tied. You need to understand that the teachers' union protects the teachers, and there is no way I can order the dismissal of a principal. The district official wouldn't pay attention unless he wanted something from me in return. But I'll see if there is anything I can do."

I reported the results of the meeting, and the parents decided that we would just meet with the principal and express our concerns. Perhaps René made a call as well, who knows? But while the principal stayed on, we did see an improvement in the treatment of both children and parents.

The archbishop turned the project where I was working over to Caritas, a Catholic social assistance agency. The priests had constructed a beautiful, well-equipped workshop for manufacturing prosthetic hands and feet, complete with lathes, drills, and machines to mold plastics and rubber. I assisted a German technician, a specialist, who arrived about when I did with a contract to manage the workshop and train workers. All the people involved were handicapped, mostly people missing a limb.

The German volunteer was disabled too. Because he was in Bolivia for the first time, he suffered enormous culture shock. For example, once at lunchtime, when we had *humintas*, a cornmeal mixture wrapped in a corn sheaf similar to a sweet Mexican tamale, my workmates convinced him to eat the whole thing, including the tough, dry corn husk, which, of course, we throw away. The poor man was miserable, not wanting to reveal that it was disgusting to eat. Later my workmates laughed at his naïveté.

Sometimes they made fun of him in Aymara, but I don't think he suffered too much, because he was liked even by those who teased him.

Because a lack of primary materials was normal, we scraped together recycled bits and pieces, using, for example, cylinder heads from car motors to supply the aluminum for casting prosthetics. I am particularly proud of manufacturing a hand for a workmate from Siglo XX. Like almost everyone we helped, he had lost his hand in a mining accident. He had been an enthusiastic basketball player and worked at the same time in the "block caving" section. He was very grateful, because the prosthetic hand I constructed made his life much easier.

THE GROWTH OF NGOS

Nongovernmental organizations (NGOs) first became active in Bolivia in the 1970s, often funded by the Roman Catholic Church. As young professionals returned from European exile after the dictatorships ended in the early 1980s, they utilized their international contacts to secure funding for new NGOs that explicitly supported education and communications projects. These NGOs often coordinated with labor and peasant movements and served as brokers between the grassroots and the left political parties that had been banned under the dictatorships.

As in other parts of the world, growth was also propelled by increased funding availability during the early 1980s, when NGOs achieved preferential status with many international donor agencies frustrated with corrupt, inefficient, and unresponsive governments. International NGOs particularly favored local NGOs, because they effectively executed short-term projects with results in tune with agency agendas and funding cycles. NGOs mostly provided employment for the educated middle class, and critics often argue that they served their middle-class employees more effectively than they did their supposed beneficiaries (Arellano-Lopez and Petras 1994).

In Bolivia, NGOs assumed increasing responsibility for rural development as the state reduced its social spending in conformance with the NEP. During a period of relative economic stagnation, NGOs were a growth industry, expanding from an estimated one hundred, mostly Church-based organizations in 1980 to over one thousand, increasingly secular organizations by the middle of the 1990s. The lack of precise figures reflects the limited ability of successive governments to coordinate or regulate their activities (Kruse 1994).

To counter the devastating social impact of the NEP, the World Bank introduced a Social Emergency Fund (Fondo Social de Emergencia, or FSE), which supported hundreds of small projects such as school feeding programs and credit groups. Providing thousands of short-term, sub-minimum-wage jobs, many projects were administered by NGOs, often formed specifically to capture the new funding. Other NGOs were initially highly suspicious of the FSE's role as a short-term palliative to garner support for neoliberal policies. But the ready availability of FSE funding was difficult to resist. NGOs were crucial in extending the program's reach to remote communities, supplanting the state's role in the construction of infrastructure and the administration of social investment. Their relative efficacy turned them into a driving force behind the privatization of many government functions.

Some observers maintain that these NGO projects served as a tool to stabilize poverty, destroy the gains made by labor since the 1930s, and facilitate neoliberalism, as the wages paid were insufficient to feed a family and the short-term jobs offered no worker benefits (Arellano-Lopez and Petras 1994). NGOs countered that the funds permitted developing programs in remote areas and building new spaces for resistance, but critics insist that the process co-opted most of them. After four years, when it became apparent that long-term job growth was illusory, the program was renamed the Social Investment Fund (Fondo de Inversión Social, or FIS). Not only did it evolve into a permanent fixture in Bolivia, but the World Bank deemed the program so successful that by the 1990s, it became a standard component of structural adjustment programs implemented throughout Latin America and Africa. The FIS continues to evolve and constitutes an important program in the current Morales administration, although it is now called the National Fund for Productive and Social Investment (Fondo Nacional de Inversión Productiva y Social).

A New Road: Work in FODENPO

During my year with Caritas I began considering what I might do next to sustain my family while still assisting my mining *compañeros*. In the 1960s and 1970s, whenever I participated in union activities my vision was the construction of a political project, often a revolutionary one. Through the passage of the years, the social and political conditions, as well as my consciousness, had shifted. As the miners' movement had been decimated, the challenge was to reconstitute strong social organizations to press for working-class demands, as well as to respond to the immediate needs of the many desperate mining families.

I proposed several development, assistance, and service projects. Working with Emilse, I learned how to write project proposals and obtain financing for them in Holland. Because of my history as a union leader, when I reappeared in La Paz, miners frequently showed up asking for my help.

After the Banzer dictatorship, along with other returned exiles I had begun the paperwork for legal recognition of an NGO called Support for Popular Nutritional Development (Fomento al Desarrollo y Nutrición Popular, or FODENPO) with the intention of assisting low-income people. During the upheaval caused by García Meza's bloody reign, we were unable to get the project off the ground. When I returned the second time, my *compañeros* were mostly still abroad, and none of the principal people involved were in La Paz. I wrote to Raúl Nava, who started the project with me, but had since settled in Sweden, and, with his permission, I began to put meat on the skeletal organization we had created.

I started by addressing the most immediate needs through opening soup kitchens largely directed at miners' children. Three dining rooms opened, one each in El Alto, Cochabamba, and Oruro, with assistance from three Dutch aid organizations. The first small financing arrived in 1988, and although it was focused on assistance, it supported miners in the tremendously complex and difficult period of initial adjustment to new lives. At the same time, working with newly hired technical and administrative staff, we implemented a series of projects, parallel to the dining rooms, for the parents, which created short-term jobs through the Social Emergency Fund (FSE), an assistance program designed as a short-term response to the crisis. Often the projects involved improving the streets of El Alto, by laying stone pavers and constructing sidewalks.

Neither the assistance projects nor the short-term jobs, however, offered any definitive solutions to the crisis the miners faced. Among the FODENPO staff and the beneficiaries as well, we were all conscious that the FSE was offered by the government and international institutions as a palliative to alleviate the worst impacts of neoliberal restructuring. So we researched projects that could offer better long-term options. My experience in Holland showed me the importance of formal technical training, which was almost entirely absent in Bolivia. We had also observed, as we coordinated with ex-miners on the FSE construction projects, that while all the miners insisted they had technical skills, in practice they were rarely competent craftsmen. We learned this the hard way and eventually contracted skilled laborers to assume technical responsibility for each project and teach the miners how to do the work.

These experiences led to the realization that it was easier to train miners' sons in technical skills than the miners themselves. It seemed that the identities of older miners were so strongly shaped that it was almost impossible for them to learn something new, because that implied adopting a different identity. As we aimed to create mid-level technicians—machinists, auto mechanics, electricians, electronics repairmen, and other skilled tradesmen—the trainees needed some basic education in science and mathematics so they could comprehend technical manuals. In other words, we required young men who had graduated from secondary school at least, and most miners had never studied beyond primary school.

Beginning in 1988, I founded a training center in auto mechanics, welding, and auto bodywork, trades that could have greater success in the new labor market. As many of these young people were determined to enter university, with the dream that one day they would emerge as professionals, we successfully convinced some of them that technical training could serve as a trampoline on three levels. First, because of the low quality of teaching in public schools, our technical school students improved both their knowledge and their study skills, which were essential for success in the university. Second, after studying three semesters, the new technicians would be able to find work and supplement their families' incomes. Finally, some of our graduates opened their own workshops and then continued on to advanced study. To back up our assumptions, we conducted a study that culminated in a book called *Technical Training and the Potential Demand for Human Resources in the City of El Alto.*

We trained over one thousand young people with financing from the Dutch NGO Ikon. When they graduated with their certificate in hand, many of them emigrated to Argentina and Brazil to work in far better conditions than most other immigrants. They supplemented their families' income through the remittances they sent home. Demand in the national market didn't expand as we had hoped, and respect for skilled labor and, therefore, wages remained low. In highly developed countries, mid-level technicians earn professional salaries: for example, a plumber in Holland earns as much or more than many other professionals, and his or her skills are highly valued. In Holland I learned that a country that does not treat skilled technicians with respect will be slow to develop.

This project lasted three years, but unfortunately, we were never able to make it self-sustainable, and, as the state didn't offer this type of education, it wasn't feasible to integrate it as a model project into a national technical training system. Over time, the heavily used equipment wore out, and because we couldn't obtain continued private or public support, we had no choice but to close the school after ten years. It was impossible to convince the funders, who mostly had a short-term vision, that an educational project represented a contribution in the long term to social sustainability by training a new generation of skilled labor.

FODENPO as an institution functioned on the basis of soft money and short-term, largely emergency, funding. But the problems Bolivia faced were structural, and the poverty of the miners and their families was not about to disappear, so we had to develop a strategy in the face of declining donations to keep our dining rooms open, as they provided the daily nutritional needs of a destitute sector of the population. With two years of support from Manos Unidas of Spain, we undertook a series of projects in rural areas to produce vegetables, both in open fields and in greenhouses.

We established contracts with communities close to the dining rooms in each city. The project design was simple: for three years FODENPO provided materials and technical support for the construction and management of organic vegetable greenhouses. We split the production evenly between the producing families and the dining rooms. During the three years, the participants learned how to produce vegetables utilizing greenhouses, which are very useful in the altiplano, where nighttime temperatures can drop below freezing throughout the year. After the project ended, the community members continued their greenhouse production, but now they sell their vegetables in local markets.

Meanwhile, the NEP worsened social and economic problems and failed to fulfill promises of rapid economic growth that would alleviate poverty. Political conflicts had repercussions in our activities, because as miners we played a significant part in social movements and were highly trained in social and political topics. In those years, the miners living in El Alto were steadily assuming leadership positions in local organizations, such as the Regional Workers Central (Central Obrera Regional, or COR) and the Federation of Neighborhood Organizations.

Running an NGO in Bolivia is a real challenge, not only in operational terms, but also because of the dirty tricks sometimes played by others, a culture of corruption in public service, and the weakness of too many leaders. These forces all came together during 1991 to contribute to a personal crisis. Three people appeared from Holland and attempted to take possession of FODENPO by mobilizing displaced miners. The first one, Justino Lopes, was a leader of the Oruro ex-miners organization. The other two were Angel Andrade, another exiled Bolivian keen on returning, and his Dutch wife, Marlen van Dongen. The three of them contacted the district attorney in Oruro, Ernesto Aranĺbar, to accuse me publicly of stealing funds from the FODENPO project. The district attorney, based on their declarations and some photocopies of Dutch newspaper articles, which, of course, he couldn't even read, initiated a legal proceeding against me. The couple convinced him that the articles revealed I had received US $700,000 cash from Holland in the name of the ex-miners of Oruro.

The drama started one morning at seven when I was listening to a news program on Radio Fides in La Paz hosted by a Roman Catholic priest, Father Pérez. An Oruro journalist reported that a relocalized miners' assembly had received a report from Angel Andrade and Marlen van Dongen, the latter an official representative of a Dutch NGO, stating that she had personally handed over cash to Félix Muruchi in the name of the miners. This understandably provoked immediate and vociferous protest by the miners. The journalist continued that the Oruro district attorney had issued a warrant for the arrest of Félix Muruchi. I, apparently, was a fugitive from justice, and they feared I might flee the country.

When I heard this I raced to the phone and called Father Pérez at Radio Fides. Curtly I stated, "The so-called fugitive Félix Muruchi is speaking to you about the news report you just gave. It is completely false, because in Oruro FODENPO manages a project with dining rooms for the children of relocalized miners."

Scrambling a bit, the priest invited me to present my point of view. When I explained what was going on, he replied haughtily, "It wasn't me who made the announcement. It was the journalist from Oruro who must have been mistaken. Come tomorrow at the same time so that you can give your side of the story."

To save my name, I had no choice but to initiate legal action against the trio who had slandered me. Even though I broadcast my statement on the radio the next day, it still required some time to regain my prestige. I realized that with NGO projects people could destroy your reputation with one malicious act. I was astonished at how rampant the corruption and self-interest were. Conflicts always arose if there was any money involved.

I contacted the Dutch embassy so that it could verify the formal application process that I had followed to acquire funds for FODENPO. The ambassador called the district attorney in Oruro and informed him, "The actions you are initiating have no basis in fact. The projects that we support through FODENPO have fulfilled all the legal requirements, and a dining room exists in Oruro. Your wisest move would be to call a press conference and issue a retraction. If you don't, I will."

After the district attorney failed to make a public announcement, the ambassador organized a press conference in Oruro, a three-hour drive from La Paz, which the district attorney neglected to attend. The ambassador showed up at the district attorney's office, where he was presented with several documents and was informed that the case had been dropped. "These are photocopies [of newspaper articles] in a language I don't understand," the district attorney explained. "As such, they don't serve as any proof to start a legal process against Félix Muruchi."

The ambassador responded, "The papers are in Dutch, and I know exactly what they say. They say that Bolivian authorities are corrupt."

Because my accusers had no proof, they were arrested in La Paz for slander and defamation of character, and the police discovered that the Dutch woman was a con artist, not an employee in a funding agency. Van

Félix, with one of the authors and the authors' children. Clockwise from lower left: *Félix, Maya Farthing-Kohl, Minka Farthing-Kohl, and Benjamin Kohl, 1991. Photo by L. Farthing.*

Dongen and her husband fled to Holland when they were released on bail. Sometime later, Justino, the third member of the team, did the same. I later found out that the three planned to create distrust among the grassroots so that they could appropriate FODENPO's offices, dining rooms, and other property.

After everything calmed down, I received a call from Dr. Gainzburo Cutipa, my lawyer, telling me that it was urgent that I travel to Oruro, because it appeared problems persisted. When I arrived, the lawyer sent me directly to speak with the district attorney.

He told me, "As you know, the relocalized miners are crazy. Some of them came to my office yesterday demanding that I reinitiate the case. I explained that I had insufficient proof and that the case should be closed. For this reason, I'm going to hand the file over to you, and you should discuss it with your lawyer."

I picked up the documents and returned to Dr. Cutipa. He explained, "The district attorney wants a payment of US $3000 to close the case."

"What? This is ridiculous," I exploded. "I'm not going to give him a penny! Why should I if I haven't done anything wrong?" Not to mention that by that point, my name was completely cleared.

He looked at me incredulously, "Are you serious? You don't have any choice but to pay him off."

Because I didn't want to damage my relationship with my lawyer, I said, "If you want, I can ask the ambassador, and if he authorizes the payment, I will pay it."

Certain I would get the authorization from the wealthy foreigners, he told me, "You better ask him, pal." And so I asked the ambassador, who rejected the idea just as I expected. But by now I had the papers from the district attorney in hand, so he had nothing to use to extract a bribe from me.

Corruption in Bolivia is not only in the public sphere like in the district attorney's office, but also all too common in social organizations. As unemployment is so widespread, NGOs are often converted into sources of patronage through either the hiring of a family member for a public post or the placement of someone in a job through a direct bribe to a government official.

Chapter 12

Politics in El Alto

SOCIAL MOVEMENTS AND OPPOSITIONAL POLITICS

Bolivia's opposition movements in the late 1980s and the 1990s were spearheaded by coca-growing campesinos in the rural lowland area east of Cochabamba known as the Chapare. Most were Quechua speakers drawn from the impoverished valley regions around the city of Cochabamba, joined later by displaced miners, who together actively resisted the imposition of U.S. drug-control policies that targeted the lowest rung of the cocaine production ladder. In the early 1990s, they mobilized frequently in coordination with the remnants of the COB, particularly the militant teachers' unions. Although coca producers were organized in a peasant union structure modeled on workers' unions, as indigenous identity grew in importance, they became increasingly "Indianized."

This indigenous identification has spread steadily across Bolivian society since the mid-1990s, paralleling the resurgence of indigenous surge in identity throughout Latin America (Lucero 2008). As the class-based COB declined as the sole advocate for the poor, other groups redefined the space of opposition. The 1994 Law of Popular Participation (Ley de Participación Popular, or LPP) was critical to this process, as it promoted a decentralization scheme that required citizen participation in planning. Over three-fourths of the municipalities in the country had fewer than five thousand (mostly indigenous) residents. The law allowed them budgetary oversight, thus creating the first legally recognized role for indigenous organizations and new political opportunities for their members, who had almost always been excluded from the highly centralized formal political parties controlled by urban elites. Throughout the country and with varying degrees of success, rural indigenous people confronted local power structures that had blocked their interests for hundreds of years. In the Chapare, the well-organized coca growers easily won municipal elections in 1995 and built on this experience to form their own political party, the Movimiento al Socialismo (MAS), which went on to win four seats in the lower house of Congress in 1997.

An uneasy stalemate between coca growers and the government, which had reigned in the Chapare for more than a decade, unraveled following former dictator Hugo Banzer's ascension to the presidency in 1997. His electoral victory with only 22 percent of the vote required the creation of a multiparty alliance. Much of his support was from people who preferred to remember the economic boom fueled by petroleum-generated dollars in the 1970s rather than the repression of his military government.

Anxious to please the U.S. embassy, Banzer deployed the military to forcibly eradicate coca production in the Chapare. By the end of the 1990s, coca growers scrambled for basic survival in the face of steady and mounting conflicts. Just as the closing of the mines weakened the COB, Banzer's destruction of coca debilitated the coca growers' organization.

The dynamics shifted significantly in 2000, when a powerful movement emerged in Bolivia's third-largest metropolitan area, Cochabamba, where the World Bank had successfully pressured the government to privatize the water supply. The resulting rebellion, which forced the revocation of the contract with foreign firms, was a broad-based effort drawing on neighborhood organizations, unions, students, and indigenous farmers (Olivera 2004).

The victory energized the other social movements that supported it—from the altiplano to the coca-growing lowlands. In the altiplano during the late 1990s, a resurgent indigenous political movement grew under the leadership of an ex-guerrilla and Aymara, Felipe Quispe, known as "El Mallku." Often flamboyant and sometimes erratic, Quispe represented the more radical separatist tendencies of the Aymara Katarista movement that emerged in rural La Paz during the late 1970s.

By late 2000, national oppositional leadership was increasingly driven by urban groups in El Alto, which emerged as the country's militant and radical center. The successful struggle to form the Public University of El Alto (Universidad Pública de El Alto, or UPEA), in which Félix played a role, was also critical in the construction of *alteño* identity and social action, drawing in a new generation of young political activists. The subsequent fight to win autonomy for UPEA took several more years, and its success demonstrated to alteños the value of long-term political mobilization (Lazar 2008).

During the previous decade, municipal politics in El Alto had been dominated by Patriotic Conscience (Conciencia de Patria, or CONDEPA), a populist party renowned for its corruption. Typically, local leaders supported CONDEPA in exchange for a job for at least one relative with the municipality, following the tradition of clientelism so deeply ingrained in Bolivian politics. Addressing neighborhood necessities and demands consequently took a backseat in municipal government policies. CONDEPA party members were called the Condepillos (a play on Condepista, member of the CONDEPA party, and *pillo*, which means "scoundrel" or "thief"). Each year between

1994 and 1999 El Alto's mayor was booted from office for corruption by the city council (Lazar 2008).

When CONDEPA's enormously popular founder, radio personality Carlos Palenque, died unexpectedly in 1997, the party quickly disintegrated. The once-left-wing MIR won municipal elections in December 1999, and its leader, Luis Paredes, continued the clientelist style of CONDEPA, but ran a more competent administration. He had significantly less success in co-opting local community representatives, in part because grassroots groups began to exert greater social control over their leaders (Arbona 2007).

Alteños' ability to control physical access to La Paz permits them to cripple the capital city, just as indigenous rebels had in 1781. The convergence in El Alto of two political identities—miners' and indigenous peoples'—proved crucial in the construction of the most recent challenges to the existing political order. More than once *alteños* have pushed their leadership aside to stage overt rebellions, mobilizing hundreds of thousands of people.

Despite conflicts between leadership, differences in organizational styles, and sometimes wildly varying priorities, Bolivia's disparate movements coalesced in 2003 to oppose a proposed natural gas pipeline designed to export the country's vast natural gas reserves through Chile. The rebellion that resulted was centered in El Alto and ejected President Gonzalo Sánchez de Lozada from office in October 2003 at the cost of almost seventy *alteño* lives. A year and a half later, these same El Alto–led movements forced President Carlos Mesa to resign, contributing to the unprecedented December 2005 election of coca grower Evo Morales as the first indigenous ruler since the Spanish Conquest over 450 years ago.

Bolivia's renewed indigenous movements draw heavily on an oral tradition that stretches back to the Inkan resistance between 1536 and 1572 against Spanish conquerors and the later rebellion led by Tupaj Katari and Bartolina Sisa in 1781. This narrative of resistance, replete with martyrs and heroes, victories and defeats, links current struggles to previous ones, instilling people with a sense of continuity, the inevitability of resistance, and the legitimacy of struggle (Thomson 2002). As Félix's story shows, the psychological power of these narratives in the Bolivian psyche should never be underestimated.

In a country where women and indigenous people did not gain the right to vote until 1952, where democratic transitions have been the exception, and where high rates of rural illiteracy combine with voter manipulation and blatant fraud, the ballot box has yet to prove a reliable means for making demands (Kohl and Farthing 2006). Despite his social movement roots, President Evo Morales faced significant strikes and social protest from both the left and the right during his first term in office.

Politics in El Alto

As the neighborhood organizations promised a new opportunity for political activism in Bolivia's changed circumstances, I joined the one in Ciudad Satélite. In 1997, I ran for president and won almost 100 percent of the votes. According to the regulations, the ruling board of each neighborhood organization, after democratic elections, had to be officially recognized by FEJUVE. We presented the letter formally requesting recognition. But as I hadn't joined CONDEPA, the Federation rejected our request, accusing us of fraud. FEJUVE officials argued it was impossible that we could have won almost every vote. To approve the results, they demanded that I pay for an alcohol-fueled dinner party for five FEJUVE executives. I did, although it infuriated me, because it served to encourage the corruption of everyday life that was so much a part of CONDEPA's and, unfortunately, our country's political culture.

The day after the dinner, Dr. René Alarcón, an important assistant to the mayor, asked me to print five thousand pamphlets promoting Carlos Palenque in exchange for the letter recognizing me as the FEJUVE representative. I was really fed up by then and refused. In response, some FEJUVE representatives with ties to CONDEPA decided that an independent leader could be problematic. They prevented me from taking office with a classic clientelist maneuver: CONDEPA offered bribes and jobs for relatives of committee members willing to sign a letter stating I lacked the support of the neighborhood executive committee. The result was that I was forced to resign from the presidency before I even held the position. Ironically, CONDEPA never paid the promised bribes nor delivered on the promises of employment.

One other time I sought elected office at the invitation of Juan del Granado, who later became the mayor of La Paz, and to whom I had been handcuffed during my arrest under Banzer. In 1993, I presented myself as a candidate for his party Free Bolivia Movement (Movimiento Boliviano Libre, or MBL) to be a deputy representing the City of El Alto. If I won a seat, I would have to share it with four others, each of us serving for one year, a common form of power sharing. We won the seat in El Alto, but the MBL national leadership formed a coalition with the MNR, led by President Gonzalo Sánchez de Lozada (Goni). I withdrew without assuming office, because my experience with the FRI had taught me that these kinds of pacts with traditional parties never favor the people. I knew that Goni's administration would deepen neoliberal policies, which would put me in a compromising position that threatened to destroy the political reputation I had worked so hard all my life to earn.

During the 1990s, daily life became increasingly difficult, as the government failed to provide any real solutions to the crises that plagued the country. Economic and social hardships contributed to tensions that weakened and even broke up families. Even though it remained unclear what movement could represent people's aspirations, I was convinced that, given our long history of struggle, we would find a new form of organization. Educating people and developing increased political awareness were still critical. Actors like the Chapare coca growers, the indigenous peoples of the eastern lowlands, and, a bit later, the campesinos and indigenous people of the altiplano emerged as new focal points of political organization. Although resistance to neoliberal policies was constant, we lacked a mechanism to articulate this nationally and have movements coalesce within an overarching organization.

The COB, which between the 1952 revolution and 1985 fulfilled this role, was but a shadow of its former self, and nothing had emerged to take its place. Nonetheless, many mid-level leaders continued to organize as political activists, and they guided social movements. Other leaders had vacillated in the struggle and succumbed to serving as agents for neoliberal policies, participating, for example, in coalitions with Goni's government.

Development Work and International Experience

During the 1990s, I was granted scholarships for courses and workshops on project administration in Holland, Chile, Ecuador, Israel, and the United States. I also traveled to Europe several times for FODENPO projects. In 1994, I participated for two months in a postgraduate course on project evaluation in Latin America, hosted by the University of Hartford in the U.S. state of Connecticut. In an intensive course with thirty participants, we studied and discussed project management from eight in the morning until seven at night seven days a week. During the course the World Cup was under way in the United States, and, for the first time since 1950, Bolivia was competing. This was a historic moment for us. Bolivia was set to play against Germany in the opening match in Boston, only a few hours by bus from Hartford.

Several of us approached the program director to request the necessary time off. He was blunt, "You didn't come here to see football but to take a course, and that is what you are being paid for. So no, you can't go."

Afterward, we immediately started discussing how much the tickets cost and how we would get there and back. We formed a committee to arrange

Félix ran for office in 1993 as a candidate for the MBL. He is speaking. Juan del Granado, mayor of La Paz, is in the background. From the private collection of Félix Muruchi.

travel and buy tickets. We couldn't hire a bus, however, because none of us had a credit card, something the bus companies couldn't imagine. In the end, we borrowed a credit card from a Salvadoran program participant and paid him back in cash. We had a great time even though Bolivia lost. When we got back we were severely criticized, reflecting a clear cultural gap that no matter how hard we tried, we never overcame. The directors simply could not understand the significance of this event for us.

In 1997, I spent two months in Israel participating in a course on rural schools and agricultural education held at a kibbutz with a group of Latin Americans and Africans. My knowledge of how to build greenhouses and manage protected horticultural systems in dry places like the Bolivian altiplano expanded exponentially, and I applied these lessons to our agricultural development projects. The trip provided me the opportunity to see the conflict between the Palestinians and Israelis with my own eyes. It looked like permanent war. Many days when we went out to conduct practice operations in the countryside, the first thing we were told was where to hide if fighter jets attacked.

Life was horribly tense; it felt as if I were back in Bolivia when the military occupied the mines. We asked our professors to explain the problems between the Israelis and Palestinians. The political studies director argued that, as five thousand years ago the first people living in Jerusalem and its surrounding areas were Israelis, the land therefore belonged to them and they were merely exercising their property rights in the face of Palestinian interlopers. Talking to people in the street, I often heard both Israelis and Palestinians speak of thousands of years ago as if it were yesterday. In Bolivia, by comparison, where the colonization and violent occupation by the Spaniards happened only five hundred years ago, we may still have a long way to go to effectively mobilize our historic memory and fully reclaim our rights.

On Sundays, we visited various important sites in Israel. We went to a Catholic Mass in Jerusalem, and even though it was celebrated in twelve languages, only six believers participated. Another Sunday we went to the River Jordan, particularly significant in Christian beliefs because that is where Jesus was baptized. Several kiosks sold river water for US $5 to US $10 a bottle. As we were soon scheduled to leave the country, several Latinos emptied Coca-Cola bottles so they could fill them with this expensive supposedly holy water. Some of them filled as many as five bottles. In classes the very next day, when we studied the provision of basic services in the city of Jerusalem, the professor disclosed that the water that we drank and showered in every day at our hotel came from the River Jordan. The Latinos looked at each other but didn't say a word.

My daughters finished high school, and both managed to obtain scholarships to study abroad. Valeria completed her international high school degree in Sweden with the help of her godfather, Rolf Ericsson. Sometime later when he was a labor leader in the graphics union, he visited us in Bolivia with a group of Swedish young people. Khantuta won a two-year scholarship for post-high-school studies through the United Nations International Baccalaureate program in Norway. Later, both of them graduated from the Bolivian state university, UMSA (Universidad Mayor de San Andrés), in La Paz. I am very proud that both my daughters have become professionals interested in contributing to Bolivia's social and political development.

I abandoned politics for a long time to concentrate on keeping FODENPO's development projects afloat. However, with the creation of the Public University of El Alto (Universidad Pública de El Alto, or UPEA), my enthusiasm for politics was rekindled.

After El Alto was designated a city in 1988, residents began agitating for a university as a symbol of independence. These demands mushroomed in response to two parallel processes. On the one hand, many young people from El Alto had not been accepted into the UMSA, located in the center of La Paz. On the other, the UMSA, while responsible for public university programs in the department of La Paz, offered only technical degrees at its El Alto campus. So students who sought professional degrees had to travel about an hour to take classes downtown. Residents of El Alto, especially the young, felt as if they were being treated as second-class citizens and protested with increasing vigor.

In 2000, the Banzer administration—he had been elected president in 1997—had no plans to create a university in El Alto. But he had little choice, because the pressure from the social movements kept increasing. That same year, the struggle of the *alteños* culminated in the creation of the UPEA. We hoped that the new university could fulfill more than an educational role and serve as a center for the development and consolidation, at both a technical and political level, of leadership for El Alto.

Banzer took advantage of his political power to make the UPEA completely dependent on his government for the two years he had remaining in his term. The university administration was controlled by people from his political party, which permitted the looting of university funds. Javier Tito Espinoza, a top official in Banzer's ADN party, was named the first rector with the support of the Roman Catholic Church and social organization leaders, although he had no academic qualifications whatsoever. During the year and a half that he ran the university, he stole Bs. $18 million (about US $2.3 million). He finally got caught and currently is in San Pedro prison serving time for corruption.

Back to School

In 2001, thirty years after I left university because of Banzer's coup, I returned to study law at the UPEA. I felt a little like a fish returning to water as I reentered the world of young people filled with aspirations. I could have studied at the UMSA, and if I had, I probably would have had my degree in hand by now, but I must admit the political potential and conflicts in the UPEA attracted me, as did my pride in being from El Alto. In my second year, the law students elected me leader of the Local University Federation (Federación de Universitarios Local, or FUL), a position I held all those years ago in Oruro. In this FUL, my younger brother Willy was also a representative, as he was studying systems engineering. During my one-year term, we created the FUL office in the UPEA and participated actively in the struggles of 2003.

Things started on February 11, 2003, around ten in the morning, when an UPEA student called from downtown La Paz, where he was completing congressional paperwork to guarantee university autonomy. Urgently, he entreated, "Félix, UPEA students need to get down to the Plaza Murillo immediately because Ayacucho College [high school or secondary school] students have occupied the government palace. We UPEA students aren't doing anything."

I raced outside with megaphones to rally the students together, and about fifty people accompanied me to the Plaza Murillo in minibuses. The Plaza was encircled by the army, defending the presidential palace, and they were in turn surrounded by a second ring of police and civilians. I was standing right in front of the government palace when the army began forcing the police and civilians back as several police vehicles roared up with their sirens blaring. Suddenly a policeman fired his gun, by mistake or because he was happy that support had arrived, no one ever figured out. When they heard this, the soldiers, longtime rivals of the police, decided the police were attacking them. Within seconds, soldiers and police alike started to fire. Between the tear gas and the smoke, it was impossible to see anything at all. The police forced those of us without arms out of the Plaza, and we ran like mad, our eyes streaming with tears and faces burning because of the potent and thick gas. Behind us we heard the crackle of gunfire. A block away I ran into some of the university *compañeros*. They were tremendously relieved to see me, and one said, "I thought they had killed you."

In this confrontation, known as Black February, more than twenty people died. People's rage at how government mismanagement had provoked this crisis erupted in a general mutiny that spread throughout the entire country. In El Alto, the multitude, with no planning or control from their leaders, burned the municipal offices, banks, and the offices of lawyers who had defended the corrupt UPEA rector. They also attacked the Coca-Cola and Pepsi factories, as symbols of transnational domination. Although Black February was a general disaster because people died unnecessarily, it highlighted the need to organize at every level. This included the critical task of replacing many of the old and corrupt leaders of FEJUVE.

GONI AND THE GAS WAR

Wealthy mine owner Gonzalo Sánchez de Lozada (Goni), who was raised in the United States, was elected president for the second time in 2002 at the head of a weak coalition government. Widely recognized as a principal architect of the neoliberal policies adopted in 1985, his mid-1990s government spearheaded the privatization of the most profitable state-owned enterprises, as well as devolving greater responsibilities to municipalities, including the important innovation of incorporating local oversight.

In February 2003, at the insistence of the International Monetary Fund (IMF), which was increasingly concerned about the steady rise in Bolivia's public debt, Goni's government moved to institute a flat income tax. Spiraling government insolvency stemmed in no small measure from the cutback in government income occasioned by the 1990s privatizations of Bolivian state hydrocarbons and telecommunications companies that were promoted by international financial institutions (IFIs), including the World Bank and the IMF (Kohl and Farthing 2009). Led by El Alto, the reaction against the income tax was swift and resulted in a bloody clash between the police and military in La Paz's main square, Plaza Murillo.

The next and fatal blow to Goni's legitimacy stemmed from a plan to export natural gas through Chile for eventual consumption in California. One benefit of the 1997 sale of the country's oil and gas industry to multinational firms was new investment in exploration, resulting in the discovery of huge natural gas reserves, making Bolivia, in 2007, the site of the second-largest reserves in Latin America and the fifth in the world. Gas quickly became the symbol of a better future for Bolivia, with social movements and the left wing determined that this newfound wealth underground would benefit the country as a whole rather than international firms and national elites, as has every Bolivian resource since the discovery of silver at Potosí.

After the resounding failure to push through income taxes, the international financial institutions began campaigning for exporting gas reserves through Chile, as it was far cheaper than the proposed alternative through Peru. But this option tapped into the profound and deep-seated resentment toward Chile stemming from Bolivia's loss of its seacoast in the War of the Pacific (1879–1884). In October 2003, broad-based resistance originated in El Alto, but quickly spread throughout the country. After bloody confrontations in the altiplano town of Warisata and in El Alto, President Gonzalo Sánchez de Lozada fled to exile in the United States. Since then, Bolivia has unsuccessfully sought to extradite him and his defense minister, Carlos Sánchez Berzaín, to face charges of murder in unleashing the military on unarmed protesters. In June 2008, the U.S. government granted political asylum to Sánchez Berzaín on the basis of his claim that he was subject to political persecution.

The Gas War

Two thousand three was a historic year in Bolivia. With its mishandling of Black February, Goni's administration forfeited all respect, and its ability to ensure order deteriorated. The events of February marked the beginning of almost constant demonstrations against government policies until October, when we *alteños* led protests that culminated in Goni's resignation and expulsion from the country. Our rebellion against the corruption embedded in *alteño* neighborhood organizations was vital to our success.

In October the people united in what we called the Gas War. This grew out of a cycle of protests that exploded when the government decided to build a pipeline through Chile. Even worse, we were to sell our gas at discount prices to the United States at a time when there was a shortage of gas and food throughout the country. Many El Alto leaders, because of opportunism and nepotism, didn't respect grassroots demands to carry on the struggle. In response, the grassroots created parallel and independent organizations to seize neighborhood power and spread the movement through the entire city of El Alto.

I was a member of the mobilization commission in Ciudad Satélite, and other neighborhoods initiated similar actions. These commissions provided the political direction to FEJUVE during the crisis. People in Ciudad Satélite, which is lower-middle-class but sees itself as upper-middle-class, were generally reluctant to participate, but considerable pressure was brought to bear from the surrounding neighborhoods. Some Ciudad Satélite residents had organized a barricade to "defend" the neighborhood from the surrounding, much poorer areas. But this barricade was soon confused with the others set up around other neighborhoods to keep out the army. We also organized a group, mostly ex-miners from Siglo XX, to march together in the huge demonstrations in El Alto.

The spirit in these marches was incredible: tens of thousands of people full of energy and optimism that we could transform our country. Many shouted, "It's now or never." I remember one day on Sagarnaga Street, just above La Paz's main cathedral in the Plaza San Francisco, we spotted paramilitaries on the roof of a building, who had begun to shoot at the crowd. Moments later the demonstrators torched the large wooden entrance doors, and it gave us great satisfaction to see those killers fleeing from the smoking building. The air was filled with energy, passion, political commitment, and determination, and I was hopeful that this time we would win. Throughout the long days of demonstrations, even though by now I was well into my fifties, I never felt tired or worn out.

During the confrontations between the soldiers and unarmed civilians, people were killed in El Alto. One morning I passed by the office of FEJUVE, where I ran into the top leader, Mauricio Cori, sobbing, "I haven't slept for two nights. I never thought this would happen to me. Why was I elected? It seems like it was only so someone could push me around. I really can't lead."

I tried to calm him down, "Look, I know this is hard for you. But you have to be brave and rise to the occasion. We are all depending on you."

He kept weeping, "They've already killed a lot of people. What am I going to do?"

To me the answer was obvious. "It's simple," I told him. "Get all the dead bodies brought to this office so we can arrange a public wake. We'll hold a huge, daylong memorial event to canonize our dead and publicly mourn them. Our grieving will draw the attention of the national and international press to the repressive policies of Goni's government and demonstrate that the government has committed an act of mass murder against the Aymara people."

He looked at me dubiously, "What if the families aren't willing to bring those killed here?"

I responded, "Well, then, we'll use the coffins that have been donated and present them to the public in a symbolic act." And that's exactly what we did. The next day a peaceful march of nearly half a million Bolivians wound its way from El Alto to the Plaza San Francisco in the center of La Paz. Combined with marches of support throughout the country, nearly a million people took to the streets out of a population of nine million. On October 17, Goni resigned and fled to exile in the United States. Ever since then, we have demanded his extradition to Bolivia to stand trial for the murders of civilians in El Alto.

Following established constitutional procedures, Vice President Carlos Mesa assumed Bolivia's presidency. In an effort to respect participatory democracy, Mesa came up the hill to El Alto to pacify the highly mobilized movement with promises to fulfill the October agenda. This coalesced around three demands: a referendum on hydrocarbon renationalization, a trial to hold Goni and other leaders in his government accountable, and, finally, a Constituent Assembly to write a more appropriate founding document for a country made up of indigenous people and workers. At that point, we gave Mesa the benefit of the doubt and entrusted the resolution of our demands to the hands of the elected leaders.

In the following weeks, UPEA students pressed for a law decreeing university autonomy. It was finally granted in November 2003, only weeks after Mesa assumed office. In the following months, other social movements demanded government action on long-standing problems. Most important was the call for the renationalization of La Paz and El Alto's water company, Aguas del Illimani, which had been sold to a French firm that, given its imperative for profit, was unable to address the need for water in poor neighborhoods.

In 2004, I returned to Chiloé in southern Chile, for the first time since I was a prisoner there in 1976, with my family and Juan Arbona, a Puerto Rican friend. I didn't find it easy, because Puerto Quellón had changed beyond recognition. The explosion in transnational fishing operations transformed the sleepy town into a small city with large supermarkets everywhere. I only saw a few people I knew: a working-class family who now ran a small supermarket. They told me that many of the people I had known had died or moved away. I felt disoriented and found it hard to identify the places where I had known people. But what hadn't changed was the police station, and as I looked at it I physically recoiled from the memories of the era of repression under Pinochet. My daughter wanted to take a picture of me in front of the station, but I just couldn't face it.

President Carlos Mesa proved incapable of fulfilling the October agenda, and he resigned from office in June 2005 after massive protests filled the streets for almost three weeks. I wrote several letters to Mesa demanding the nationalization of Aguas del Illimani, and I marched with friends, family, and students from the UPEA almost every day, sometimes in the 16 de Julio neighborhood in El Alto, and on other occasions, in the city of La Paz itself. Once again, following constitutional procedures, the president of the Supreme Court, Eduardo Beltze Rodríguez, assumed the interim presidency. His only responsibility was to call elections within 180 days. These elections resulted in the historic ascension of Evo Morales to the presidency in January 2006.

Pachakuti: *Overturning the Traditional Order*

This overturning of Bolivia's traditional order has its origins in our history. In the Chaco War against Paraguay in the early 1930s, miners, indigenous people, and young students and intellectuals were thrown together, generating a movement that culminated in the 1952 revolution led by the MNR. The promise of this revolution was betrayed by the MNR itself, a party that was finally and definitively defeated in 2005. Most of the other traditional parties born after the revolution failed to incorporate the demands of the majority, whether marginal urban dwellers, workers, or indigenous groups. In 2005, a phenomenon similar to the 1952 revolution occurred, in which the impoverished urban classes united with the middle class and the indigenous population, this time to elect Evo Morales.

Evo's victory was propelled by the social movements. The success of the MAS is in no small measure due to its not being a political party, but this is also its limitation, as it lacks a coherent ideology and party discipline to move a revolutionary process forward.

INDIGENOUS IDENTITY

Indigenous identity is fluid in modern Bolivia and has long been a social rather than a racial category. In remote areas, indigenous people still change out of their indigenous clothing when they go to market towns, because they know they will be treated better if they are less Indian, demonstrating the importance of dress, rather than skin color or racial characteristics, in determining ethnicity (Zorn 1997).

Particularly after the 1952 revolution, with its explicit modernizing project, those seeking upward mobility escaped impoverished rural areas for the cities, adopting Western-style clothing and speaking Spanish. Being light-skinned and urban was considered modern and desirable; being dark and rural was viewed as ignorant, dirty, and backward. These feelings remain just below the surface for many Bolivians, indigenous and nonindigenous alike. So intense was the racism against indigenous culture and characteristics that people would go to great lengths to deny their indigenous roots.

This was nowhere more true than in the mines. While almost all miners are of indigenous heritage, for many, like Félix, whose first language is Quechua, the process of becoming a proletarian—as defined by left-wing political thinking, with its origins in Europe—involved rejecting one's indigenous roots. After 1952, the communist left considered indigenous people as petit bourgeois because they owned small parcels of land, while the miners were the proletariat and therefore the vanguard of the working class. This confluence of left-wing politics, internalized racism against indigenous people, and the MNR modernizing project served to deepen the distance of miners from their rural indigenous cousins.

But indigenous resistance to domination and racism has surged repeatedly throughout Bolivian history (Thomson 2002), and when a strictly class-based analysis failed to address poverty and discrimination, indigenous pride resurfaced in the 1970s among highland Aymara. Drawing on the ideas of Aymara intellectual Fausto Reinaga, a small group began to spread these ideas throughout the country, leading to the emergence of the national campesino union (CSUTCB) in 1979 as an important national social movement.

In the 2001 census, 68 percent of the population over fifteen years old self-identified as a member of at least one indigenous group (INE 2001). Only 35 percent of the population remains in rural areas, and 62 percent of the urban population also self-identify as members of one (or more) ethnic group. In some urban areas, different indigenous groups have begun to blend together: in Cochabamba, while some neighborhoods can be almost entirely Quechua- or Aymara-speaking, in others, people speak both languages. Despite the accelerated rural-to-urban migration Bolivia has experienced since the early 1980s, the historic process of transition from campesino (literally, rural person) to urban *cholo* (and eventually mestizo) has been transformed into one where indigenous identities remain strong even in urban areas.

Félix's story reveals his shift from an almost exclusively class-oriented understanding of the world to one more shaped by a growing recognition of the importance of his ethnic identity. His process differs markedly from the stories told in earlier autobiographies of Bolivian miners such as Domitila Chungara and Moema Viezzer's *Let Me Speak* and Juan Rojas and June Nash's *I Spent My Life in the Mines*. Félix's change from "indigenous" campesino to "miner" when his family migrated to the mines and his subsequent experience as a student and a young man in the mines can be seen as a process of self-colonization, a process that he, like Bolivia as a whole, has begun to question (Nash 2009).

This process has been under way during the past fifteen years throughout the Americas, from the Zapatista movement in southern Mexico to indigenous uprisings in Ecuador to growing Mapuche resistance in Chile. With it come changes in analysis, locus of political action from workplace to community, and forms of decision-making and problem-solving (Lucero 2008).

Reflections on an Activist's Life

In 1945, a year before I was born, Bolivia abolished bonded labor, but indigenous peoples didn't have the right to freely walk in city plazas or vote in elections. By January 2006, after decades of political struggle, we had won not only the vote but also had propelled one of our own into office. While this was a great victory, we still need to achieve equality among Bolivians and create a fair justice system. We obtained the right to own land with the Agrarian Reform of 1953, but we still don't possess territorial rights. We have the universal right to education, but we still lack adequate primary and secondary schools, as well as equal access to postsecondary education. We won the right to organize, but we don't control productive processes, because we still suffer under a neoliberal economic system that privileges national elites and transnational corporations. We have regained greater control over natural resources, but international asymmetry continues as multinational capital gains more from the exploitation of our resource wealth than do the Bolivian people. We have gained the ability to communicate in certain forums, but we lack access to the mainstream media, which shape the ideology of our people. Women have gained greater opportunities, but machismo still dominates daily life. We have an indigenous president, but racism is still rampant, as shown by the attacks on indigenous people in Sucre on May 24, 2008, which have gone unpunished.

Despite these challenges, as I look back over my life, I feel that I was able to contribute a grain of sand to the historic processes of change in my country. I am proud that I have lived as an activist, an agent, who along with thousands of other Bolivians, many of whom sacrificed far more than I, achieved some measure of social and economic justice. There is still much to do, however, and these tasks remain essential missions for this and for future generations. We will not achieve national liberation until we completely eradicate poverty, whether the poor are indigenous or *q'haras* (whites). As history tells us, we will only achieve this through strong and broadly participatory social movements that respect the will of the majority and the rights of the minorities.

Bibliographic Sources and Information on Bolivia

E arly on we decided that we wanted to provide a streamlined, accessible story that used Félix's life to frame recent Bolivian history. At the same time, we recognized the need to provide further information for a nonspecialized English audience requiring more background. The chapter introductions and text boxes provide the context and avoid including notes that would break up the flow of the story. We hope this brief bibliographic note that focuses on the literature in English will motivate interested readers to learn more about the country, and, at the same time, we are confident that university students or researchers interested in specific topics can easily generate detailed bibliographies.

Two general histories of Bolivia provide a rapid introduction to the country. Klein (2003), although primarily an economic history, remains the standard English history text on Bolivia. Undergraduate and high school students may find Morales's (2010) book a more engaging read. For those who want to delve deeper into colonial history, Larson (1988) and Thomson (2002) provide fascinating studies. Much of the Republic and the roots of the 1952 revolution are explored in detail by Laura Gotkowitz (2007). Her work complements Silvia Rivera's (1987) seminal description of indigenous resistance.

James Dunkerley's (1984) masterful work offers the most comprehensive study of Bolivian politics from the 1952 revolution to the country's return to civilian government in 1982. And the volume edited by Grindle and Domingo (2003) provides an interesting assessment of the Bolivian revolution fifty years on. Our book (Kohl and Farthing 2006) offers a thorough synthesis of the neoliberal period (1985 to 2005).

Nash (1993) is perhaps the most widely read ethnography of life in the mines. While we used an excerpt of Gall's (1966) more journalistic account of Siglo XX to give a feel of the place and time, his detailed history of the mines (1974a and 1974b) fills in far more detail. Chungara's autobiography

(1978) is a classic testimonial that documents the life of a leader of the Housewives Committee of Siglo XX, as well as the hunger strike that brought down the government of Hugo Banzer in 1978. Crabtree et al. (1987) provide an insightful analysis that shows how global economic processes affected the demand for primary materials such as Bolivian tin and therefore the country's miners. The role of Bolivia's left-wing parties is detailed by POR activist Guillermo Lora (1977), Alexander and Parker (2005), and John (2009).

The 2000 water war in Cochabamba, which transformed Bolivia from the poster child for structural adjustment to the inspiration of the antiglobalization movement, has generated a spate of recent books. Olivera (2004) describes the water war; his account is complemented in that volume by analytical essays by Alvaro García Linera, who entered office as Evo Morales' vice president in 2006, and Raquel Gutiérrez-Aguilar. Crabtree (2005) provides a concise summary of social movement struggles up to Morales's election, and Shultz and Draper (2008) provide more detailed information. For a discussion of Morales's first term in office, see *Latin American Perspectives* (vol. 38, no. 3 [2010] and vol. 38, no. 4 [2010]—both special issues on Bolivia).

The story about political struggle in El Alto that Félix tells is very much recounted from the viewpoint of the miners rather than the thousands of campesinos who have migrated there from the countryside. For a broader view of social movements and struggles in El Alto, we recommend four sources: Gill (2000), Arbona (2007, 2008), and Lazar (2008).

While this story focuses on the highlands, for a more complete understanding of the country, it is important to consider books written about the eastern lowland regions, such as Postero (2007) and Gustafson (2009), which make an important contribution to understanding more pieces of Bolivia's complex society.

Glossary

Aguayo (Aymara), *Awayu* (Quechua): Term for a traditional Andean women's mantle and carrying cloth, used on the back to transport everything from potatoes to babies.

Altiplano: High plateau in the Andean mountain range. Most of it is higher than 12,000 feet above sea level.

Ayllu: Pre-Columbian nested moiety structure, a form of social organization that reflects a combination of both kinship and territorial ties that persists in some parts of the Andes. *Ayllu* membership generally includes a service requirement with rotating leadership, participatory decision-making, and mechanisms to ensure a relatively equitable distribution of resources.

Ayni: Rural Andean reciprocity that involves a labor or product exchange between *ayllu* members. It is frequently used in planting, harvesting, and house construction.

Bastón de mando: Wood-and-silver scepter used to indicate authority and the passing of authority from one leader to the next.

Caciques: The native lords who traditionally exercised authority in communities. The Spaniards adapted this system to ensure their control.

Campesino: "Country person," or peasant. This term for rural indigenous people was introduced after the 1952 revolution because *indio* was widely used as a derogatory term. *Campesino* reflected the modernist aspirations of the 1952 revolutionary project.

Cargos: Literally, "loads," but refers to community-obligated leadership service among highland indigenous groups.

Ch'alla (noun) and *ch'allar* (verb): A ritual blessing that typically involves sprinkling alcohol, usually wrapping the object or person to be blessed in confetti and streamers. In many places the *ch'alla* has been adopted by urban mestizos as part of everyday life. For example, people may pour a few drops of beer or alcohol on the ground to honor the Pachamama before taking a drink.

Charqui: Dried meat, most commonly llama. This Andean technique has led to the diffusion of beef jerky in the English-speaking world.

Chicha: Fermented corn beer, usually made in valley regions such as Cochabamba and Chuquisaca in large earthenware pots. In rural areas, a white flag hanging outside a house means that *chicha* is for sale.

Chicote: Small whip often carried by a community authority to indicate his status.

Chola: Urban-indigenous woman. It has a wide range of meanings—from affectionate and positive to derogatory—depending on the tone and context.

Cholita: Diminutive of *chola*.

Chuño: Dehydrated potatoes, an Andean staple, made by leaving potatoes outside to freeze at night during the coldest part of the winter. As the sun warms them during the day, the ice crystals thaw and the potatoes are trampled, which squeezes out the water. The process is repeated for up to two weeks. Once dried, they can be stored for up to seven years, but must be rehydrated by soaking before cooking.

Compadre: Literally, "co-parent." It refers to a system of *compadrazgo*, or fictive kin, that involves reciprocal (although often asymmetrical) obligations between a child's family and the *compadres*.

Compañero/a: Translates as male comrade and female comrade or male partner and female partner. It is used widely by the left in Latin America to refer to a partner in a political struggle.

Criollos: Spanish immigrants and their descendants, who make up approximately 5 percent of Bolivia's population.

Encomienda: Labor and land tenure system introduced by the Spanish crown to reward loyal subjects, who were given a certain number of native inhabitants and the land where they lived, with the provision that the new Spanish owner would provide instruction in the Spanish language and Roman Catholicism and pay tribute.

Fiestas: Community festivals that follow the agricultural and religious cycle and can last several days, especially in rural areas.

Gringos: A term developed during the Mexican Revolution that generally refers to people from the United States but nowadays can be any North American or European. Depending on how it is used, it can be either derogatory or affectionate.

Haciendas: Large agricultural estates set up by the Spaniards to supply food to the mines.

Indios: Origin of the term "Indian" for peoples in the Americas originated with Christopher Columbus, who mistakenly believed that he had landed in the country of India in 1492. The term was quickly adopted to apply to all aboriginal cultural groups found in the Americas. It has been used as a derogatory term in Bolivia, implying "primitive" or "stupid."

Inkuña (or *tari*): Aymara term for a traditional Andean cloth used by women to carry coca or other valuables, and in rituals, where it serves as an altar.

Mate de coca: Coca tea. This widely available herbal infusion is routinely consumed for its health-giving qualities, which range from calming an upset stomach to ameliorating the effects of altitude sickness.

Mestizos: People with both Spanish and indigenous heritage. In Bolivia, the term often includes urbanized indigenous people who have adopted Western dress, customs, and language, and in some cases turn their backs on their indigenous heritage.

Minifundio: Small landholding that results from the intergenerational fragmentation of land through inheritance among multiple heirs.

Mink'a: A form of collective work in the Andes. It often refers to work done for community infrastructure projects like building schools or roads.

Mita: "Regular turn," a public service obligation instituted by the Inka Empire that required subjects to provide labor on a regular basis. The system was adapted by the Spanish conquerors to require labor service from communities in the mines during the colonial period. Often each community had to send one of every seven men per year to work in the mines.

Pachamama: Mother Earth, a major deity in the Andes. She presides over fertility, planting, and harvesting. The ritual offering of the *ch'alla* is offered to the Pachamama.

Palliris: Women and children who work the tailings of a mine searching for overlooked mineral. They are usually the poorest of all miners.

Pijchear (verb): To chew coca. Coca is taken one leaf at a time, and the stem is removed from the leaf before it is carefully inserted in the cheek, often with lime to release the alkaloid stimulants.

Pongueaje: The personal service Indian tenant farmers on haciendas were required to perform for landowners in addition to the crop share they were obligated to pay. *Mitanaje* was the same type of service obligation required of women. Both *pongueaje* and *mitanaje* were abolished by President Villarroel in 1945.

Rutusqa: First ritual haircutting in an Andean community, usually performed when a child is two years old. Relatives, *compadres,* and friends come to celebrate the haircutting, often bearing gifts of money that they attach to the child's clothing.

Tantawaya: "Bread baby" in Quechua and Aymara. A figure made in the shape of a human from bread dough during Todos Santos. The figures are placed on the altars that honor the family's dead.

T'inku: Literally, "encounter," but commonly refers to ritual battles between different *ayllus.* While largely ceremonial, *t'inkus* may lead to loss of life. *T'inku* is still practiced in the north of Potosí in the towns of Sacaca (February) and Macha (May). Theories of its purpose suggest that it may serve to reduce intracommunity tensions, allow young men to demonstrate their prowess to young women (although women participate in the *t'inku* on occasion), and/or contribute to a good harvest through the offering of blood to the Pachamama.

Tío: God of the mine who, if treated with adequate respect and plentiful offerings, is supposed to guarantee miners' safety and success while working underground.

Bibliography

Alexander, Robert J., with Eldon M. Parker. 2005. *A History of Organized Labor in Bolivia.* Westport, Conn.: Praeger.

Anderson, Jon Lee. 1997. *Che Guevara: A Revolutionary Life.* New York: Grove Press.

Arbona, Juan. 2007. "Neo-liberal Ruptures: Local Political Entities and Neighbourhood Networks in El Alto, Bolivia." *Geoforum* 38:127–137.

———. 2008. "Histories and Memories in the Organisation and Struggles of the Santiago II Neighbourhood of El Alto, Bolivia." *Bulletin of Latin American Research* 27:24–42.

Arrellano-Lopez, Sonia, and James Petras. 1994. "Non-Governmental Organizations and Poverty Alleviation in Bolivia." *Development and Change* 25 (3):555–568.

Baird, Robert P. 2010. "The U.S. Paid Money to Support Hugo Banzer's 1971 Coup in Bolivia." Digital Emunction. http://www.digitalemunction.com/2010/05/30/exclusive-the-u-s-paid-money-to-support-hugo-banzers-1971-coup-in-bolivia/ (accessed July 13, 2010).

Brenner, Phillip, ed. 2008. *A Contemporary Cuba Reader: Reinventing the Revolution.* Lanham, Md.: Rowman and Littlefield Publishers.

Chungara, Domitila. 1978. *Let Me Speak!* New York: Monthly Review Press.

CIA (Central Intelligence Agency). 2007. "Bolivia." *The World Factbook.* http://www.umsl.edu/services/govdocs/wofact2007/geos/bl.html (accessed December 19, 2009).

Crabtree, John. 2005. *Patterns of Protest: Politics and Social Movements in Bolivia.* London: Latin America Bureau.

Crabtree, John, Gavan Duff, and Jenny Pearce. 1987. *The Great Tin Crash: Bolivia and the World Tin Market.* London: Latin American Bureau.

Dinges, John. 2004. *The Condor Years: How Pinochet and His Allies Brought Terrorism to Three Continents.* New York: New Press.

Dunkerley, James. 1984. *Rebellion in the Veins: Political Struggle in Bolivia, 1952–82*. London: Verso.

Farthing, Linda. 1995. "Bolivia: The New Underground." In *Free Trade and Economic Restructuring in Latin America*, ed. Fred Rosen and Deidre McFadyen, pp. 141–150. New York: Monthly Review Press.

———. 2009. "Bolivia's Dilemma: Development Confronts the Legacy of Extraction." *NACLA Report on the Americas* 042 (5):25–29.

Gall, Norman. 1966. "Slow Death in the Mines." *New Leader* (New York), June 6. http://www.normangall.com/bolivia_art1.htm (accessed June 14, 2010).

———. 1974a. "Bolivia: The Price of Tin. Part I: Patiño Mines and Enterprises." American Universities Field Staff, West Coast South America Series, vol. 21, nos. 1 and 2. http://www.normangall.com/bolivia_art2.htm (accessed June 15, 2010).

———. 1974b. "Bolivia: The Price of Tin. Part II: The Crisis of Nationalization." American Universities Field Staff, West Coast South America Series, vol. 21, nos. 1 and 2. http://www.normangall.com/bolivia_art3.htm (accessed June 15, 2010).

Gill, Lesley. 1997. "Creating Citizens, Making Men: The Military and Masculinity in Bolivia." *Cultural Anthropology* 12, no. 4 (November 1997):527–550.

———. 2000. *Teetering on the Rim: Global Restructuring, Daily Life, and the Armed Retreat of the Bolivian State*. New York: Columbia University Press.

Gotkowitz, Laura. 2007. *A Revolution for Our Rights: Indigenous Struggles for Land and Justice in Bolivia, 1880–1952*. Durham, N.C.: Duke University Press.

Grindle, Merilee, and Pilar Domingo, eds. 2003. *Proclaiming Revolution: Bolivia in Comparative Perspective*. London: Institute for Latin American Studies.

Gustafson, Bret. 2009. *New Languages of the State: Indigenous Resurgence and the Politics of Knowledge in Bolivia*. Durham, N.C.: Duke University Press.

Hite, Katherine. 2000. *When the Romance Ended: Leaders of the Chilean Left, 1968–1998*. New York: Columbia University Press.

Human Development Reports (HDR). 2009. "Human Development Report 2009." New York: United Nations Development Programme. http://hdrstats.undp.org/en/indicators/161.html (accessed December 11, 2009).

Hylton, Forrest, and Sinclair Thomson. 2007. *Revolutionary Horizons: Past and Present in Bolivian Politics*. New York: Verso.

Instituto Nacional de Estadística (INE). 2001. Censo 2001. La Paz.

John, S. Sándor. 2009. *Bolivia's Radical Tradition: Permanent Revolution in the Andes.* Tucson: University of Arizona Press.

Klein, Herbert S. 2003. *A Concise History of Bolivia.* Cambridge, UK, and New York: Cambridge University Press.

Kohl, Benjamin. 2010. "Bolivia under Morales: A Work in Progress." *Latin American Perspectives* 38 (3): 107–122.

Kohl, Benjamin, and Linda Farthing. 2006. *Impasse in Bolivia: Neoliberal Hegemony and Popular Resistance.* London: Zed.

———. 2009. "'Less than Fully Satisfactory Development Outcomes': International Financial Institutions and Social Unrest in Bolivia." *Latin American Perspectives* 36 (3):59–78.

Kolata, Alan L. 1993. *The Tiwanaku: Portrait of an Andean Civilization.* Cambridge, UK: Blackwell Publishers.

Kruse, Thomas A. 1994. "The Politics of Structural Adjustment and the NGOs: A Look at the Bolivian Case." Master's in regional planning thesis project, Cornell University.

Larson, Brooke. 1988. *Colonialism and Agrarian Transformation in Bolivia: Cochabamba, 1550–1900.* Princeton, N.J.: Princeton University Press.

———. 2004. *Trials of Nation Making: Liberalism, Race, and Ethnicity in the Andes, 1810–1910.* Cambridge: Cambridge University Press.

Latin American Perspectives. 2010. "Bolivia under Morales." *Latin American Perspectives* 38, nos. 3 and 4.

Lazar, Sian. 2008. *El Alto, Rebel City: Self and Citizenship in Andean Bolivia.* Durham, N.C.: Duke University Press.

Linger, Eloise. 2007. "Cuba's Ascent from Economic Ruin and Political Isolation: Has Latin America Begun to Roar?" Paper presented at the annual meeting of the American Sociological Association, New York, New York, August 11.

Lora, Guillermo. 1977. *A History of Bolivia's Labour Movement: 1848–1971.* Cambridge: Cambridge University Press.

Lucero, José Antonio. 2008. *Struggles of Voice: The Politics of Indigenous Representation in the Andes.* Pittsburgh: University of Pittsburgh Press.

Luykx, Aurolyn. 1999. *The Citizen Factory: Schooling and Cultural Production in Bolivia.* Albany: State University of New York Press.

Malloy, James, and Eduardo Gamarra. 1988. *Revolution and Reaction: Bolivia, 1964–1985.* New Brunswick, N.J.: Transaction Books.

Mann, Charles. 2005. *1491: New Revelations of the Americas before Columbus.* New York: Knopf.

Morales, Waltraud. 2010. *A Brief History of Bolivia.* 2nd ed. New York: Checkmark Books.

Murra, John V. 1980. *The Economic Organization of the Inka State*. Research in Economic Anthropology, Supplement 1. Greenwich, Conn.: JAI Press.

Muruchi Poma, Germán. 2007. *Evo Morales. Die Biografie*. Leipzig: Militzke Verlag.

Nash, June. 1993. *We Eat the Mines and the Mines Eat Us: Dependency and Exploitation in Bolivian Tin Mines*. 2nd ed. New York: Columbia University Press.

————. 2009. Personal communication, manuscript review: *From the Mines to the Streets*.

————, ed. 1992. *I Spent My Life in the Mines: The Story of Juan Rojas, Bolivian Tin Miner*. New York: Columbia University Press.

Núñez, Rafael, and Eve Sweetser. 2006. "With the Future behind Them: Convergent Evidence from Aymara Language and Gesture in the Crosslinguistic Comparison of Spatial Construals of Time." *Cognitive Science* 30:410–450.

Olivera, Oscar. 2004. *Cochabamba! Water War in Bolivia*. Boston: South End Press.

Orta, Andrew. 2004. *Catechizing Culture: Missionaries, Aymara and the "New Evangelization."* New York: Columbia University Press.

Pica-Ciamarra, U. 2009. "Livestock-Poverty Linkages in Latin America." *Livestock Research for Rural Development* 21, article #11. http://www.lrrd.org/lrrd21/1/pica21011.htm (accessed December 19, 2009).

Platt, Tristan. 1982. "The Role of the Andean *Ayllu* in the Reproduction of the Petty Commodity Régime in Northern Potosí (Bolivia)." In *Ecology and Exchange in the Andes*, ed. D. Lehman, pp. 27–69. Cambridge: Cambridge University Press.

————. 1987. "The Andean Experience of Bolivian Liberalism, 1825–1900: Roots of Rebellion in 19th-Century Chayanta (Potosí)." In *Resistance, Rebellion, and Consciousness in the Andean Peasant World: 18th to 20th Centuries*, ed. S. Stern, pp. 34–94. Madison: University of Wisconsin Press.

Poma, Muruchi. 2008. *Evo Morales: De Cocalero a Presidente de Bolivia*. Barcelona: Flor del Viento.

Postero, Nancy Grey. 2007. *Now We Are Citizens: Indigenous Politics in Postmulticultural Bolivia*. Palo Alto, Calif.: Stanford University Press.

Rance, Susanna. 1991. "The Hand That Feeds Us." *NACLA Report on the Americas* 25, no. 1 (July):34–45.

Renfrew, Colin, and Paul Bahn. 2008. *Archaeology: Theories, Methods, and Practice*. 5th ed. London and New York: Thames & Hudson.

Rivera, Silvia Cusicanqui. 1987. *Oppressed But Not Defeated: Peasant*

Struggles among the Aymara and Qhechwa in Bolivia, 1900–1980. Geneva: United Nations Research Institute for Social Development.

Roniger, Luis, and James N. Green, eds. 2007. *Exile and the Politics of Exclusion in Latin America.* Special issue of *Latin American Perspectives* 34, no. 4.

Shultz, Jim, and Melissa Draper. 2008. *Dignity and Defiance: Stories from Bolivia's Challenge to Globalization.* Berkeley: University of California Press.

Stobart, Henry. 2006. *Music and the Poetics of Production in the Bolivian Andes.* Aldershot, UK: Ashgate.

Thomson, Sinclair. 2002. *We Alone Shall Rule: Native Andean Politics in the Age of Insurgency.* Madison: University of Wisconsin Press.

U.S. Department of State. 2003. *Bolivia.* Country Reports on Human Rights Practices. Washington, D.C.: Bureau of Democracy, Human Rights, and Labor.

Weisbrot, Mark, and Luis Sandoval. 2006. *Bolivia's Challenges.* Washington, D.C.: Center for Economic Policy Research.

———. 2008. *The Distribution of Bolivia's Most Important Natural Resources and Autonomy Conflicts.* Washington, D.C.: Center for Economic Policy Research.

Zorn, Elayne. 1997. "Marketing Diversity: Global Transformations in Cloth and Identity in Highland Peru and Bolivia." PhD dissertation, Cornell University.

———. 2004. *Weaving a Future: Tourism, Cloth, and Culture on an Andean Island.* Iowa City: University of Iowa Press.

Index

Page numbers in *italics* refer to images.

CPSIA information can be obtained at www.ICGtesting.com
Printed in the USA
BVOW02s1822031013

332567BV00002B/5/P